F

Daniel Goleman, a former science journalist for the *New York Times*, is the author of thirteen books and lectures frequently to professional groups and business audiences and on college campuses. He co-founded the Collaborative for Academic, Social and Emotional Learning at the Yale University Child Studies Center (now at the University of Illinois at Chicago). He lives in Massachusetts.

Also by Daniel Goleman

Leadership: The Power of Emotional Intelligence

The Brain and Emotional Intelligence

Ecoliterate

Ecological Intelligence

Social Intelligence

Primal Leadership

Destructive Emotions

Working with Emotional Intelligence

Healing Emotions

Emotional Intelligence

The Creative Spirit

Vital Lies, Simple Truths

The Meditative Mind

FOCUS

The Hidden Driver of Excellence

Daniel Goleman

BLOOMSBURY
LONDON • NEW DELHI • NEW YORK • SYDNEY

First published in Great Britain 2013
First published in India 2013
This edition published 2014

Image on p.84 supplied by Clipart.com
Designed by William Ruoto

This edition published with permission from
Bloomsbury Publishing Plc, 50 Bedford Square, London, WC1B 3DP

Bloomsbury Publishing is a trademark of Bloomsbury Plc

Bloomsbury Publishing, London, New Delhi, New York and Sydney

A CIP catalogue record for this book is available from the British Library

For sale in the Indian subcontinent only

ISBN 978 9 3840 5298 0

10 9 8 7 6 5 4 3 2 1

Bloomsbury Publishing India
Vishrut Building, DDA Complex, Building No. 3
Ground Floor, Pocket C – 6 & 7, Vasant Kunj
New Delhi 110070
www.bloomsbury.com

Printed and bound in India by Replika Press Pvt Ltd

For the well-being of generations to come

CONTENTS

Part IV: The Bigger Context

Part V: Smart Practice

Part VI: The Well-Focused Leader

Part VII: The Big Picture

1

THE SUBTLE FACULTY

To watch John Berger, house detective, track the shoppers wandering the first floor of a department store on Manhattan's Upper East Side is to witness attention in action. In a nondescript black suit, white shirt, and red tie, walkie-talkie in hand, John moves perpetually, his focus always riveted on one or another shopper. Call him the eyes of the store.

It's a daunting challenge. There are more than fifty shoppers on his floor at any one time, drifting from one jewelry counter to the next, perusing the Valentino scarves, sorting through the Prada pouches. As they browse the goods, John browses them.

John waltzes among the shoppers, a study in Brownian motion. For a few seconds he stands behind a purse counter, his eyes glued to a prospect, then flits to a vantage point by the door, only to glide to a corner where a perch allows him a circumspect look at a potentially suspicious trio.

While customers see only the merchandise, oblivious to John's watchful eye, he scrutinizes them all.

There's a saying in India, "When a pickpocket meets a saint, all he sees are the pockets." In any crowd what John would see are the pickpockets. His gaze roams like a spotlight. I can imagine his face seeming to screw up into a giant ocular orb reminiscent of the one-eyed Cyclops. John is focus embodied.

What does he scan for? "It's a way their eyes move, or a motion in their body" that tips him off to the intention to pilfer, John tells me. Or those shoppers bunched together, or the one furtively glancing around. "I've been doing this so long I just know the signs."

As John zeroes in on one shopper among the fifty, he manages to ignore the other forty-nine, and everything else—a feat of concentration amid a sea of distraction.

Such panoramic awareness, alternating with his constant vigilance for a telling but rare signal, demands several varieties of attention—sustained attention, alerting, orienting, and managing all that—each based in a distinctly unique web of brain circuitry, and each an essential mental tool.[1]

John's sustained scan for a rare event represents one of the first facets of attention to be studied scientifically. Analysis of what helped us stay vigilant started during World War II, spurred on by the military's need to have radar operators who could stay at peak alert for hours—and by the finding that they missed more signals toward the end of their watch, as attention lagged.

At the height of the Cold War, I remember visiting a researcher who had been commissioned by the Pentagon to study vigilance levels during sleep deprivation lasting three to five days—about how long it estimated the military officers deep in some bunker would need to stay awake during World War III. Fortunately his experiment never had to be tested against hard reality, although his encouraging finding was that even after three or more sleepless nights people could pay keen attention if their motivation was high enough (but if they didn't care, they would nod off immediately).

In very recent years the science of attention has blossomed far beyond vigilance. That science tells us these skills determine how well we perform any task. If they are stunted, we do poorly; if muscular, we can excel. Our very nimbleness in life depends on this subtle faculty. While the link between attention and excellence remains hidden most of the time, it ripples through almost everything we seek to accomplish.

This supple tool embeds within countless mental operations. A short list of some basics includes comprehension, memory, learning, sensing how we feel and why, reading emotions in other people, and interacting smoothly. Surfacing this invisible factor in effectiveness lets us better see the benefits of improving this mental faculty, and better understand just how to do that.

Through an optical illusion of the mind we typically register the end products of attention—our ideas good and bad, a telling wink or inviting smile, the whiff of morning coffee—without noticing the beam of awareness itself.

Though it matters enormously for how we navigate life, attention in all its varieties represents a little-noticed and underrated mental asset. My goal here is to spotlight this elusive and underappreciated mental faculty in the mind's operations and its role in living a fulfilling life.

Our journey begins with exploring some basics of attention; John's vigilant alertness marks just one of these. Cognitive science studies a wide array, including concentration, selective attention, and open awareness, as well as how the mind deploys attention inwardly to oversee mental operations.

Vital abilities build on such basic mechanics of our mental life. For one, there's self-awareness, which fosters self-management. Then there's empathy, the basis for skill in relationship. These are fundamentals of emotional intelligence. As we'll see, weakness here can sabotage a life or career, while strengths increase fulfillment and success.

Beyond these domains, systems science takes us to wider bands of focus as we regard the world around us, tuning us to the complex systems that define and constrain our world.[2] Such an outer focus confronts a hidden challenge in attuning to these vital systems: our brain was not designed for that task, and so we flounder. Yet systems awareness helps us grasp the workings of an organization, an economy, or the global processes that support life on this planet.

All that can be boiled down to a threesome: inner, other, and outer focus. A well-lived life demands we be nimble in each. The good news on attention comes from neuroscience labs and school classrooms, where the findings point to ways we can strengthen this vital muscle of the mind. Attention works much like a muscle—use it poorly and it can wither; work it well and it grows. We'll see how smart practice can further develop and refine the muscle of our attention, even rehab focus-starved brains.

For leaders to get results they need all three kinds of focus. Inner focus attunes us to our intuitions, guiding values, and better decisions. Other focus smooths our connections to the people in our lives. And outer focus lets us navigate in the larger world. A leader tuned out of his internal world will be rudderless; one blind to the world of others will be clueless; those indifferent to the larger systems within which they operate will be blindsided.

And it's not just leaders who benefit from a balance in this triple focus. All of us live in daunting environments, rife with the tensions and competing goals and lures of modern life. Each of the three varieties of attention can help us find a balance where we can be both happy and productive.

Attention, from the Latin *attendere*, to reach toward, connects us with the world, shaping and defining our experience. "Attention," cognitive neuroscientists Michael Posner and Mary Rothbart write, provides the mechanisms "that underlie our awareness of the world and the voluntary regulation of our thoughts and feelings."[3]

Anne Treisman, a dean of this research area, notes that how we deploy our attention determines what we see.[4] Or as Yoda says, "Your focus is your reality."

THE ENDANGERED HUMAN MOMENT

The little girl's head came only up to her mother's waist as she hugged her mom and held on fiercely as they rode a ferry to a vacation island. The mother, though, didn't respond to her, or even seem to notice: she was absorbed in her iPad all the while.

There was a reprise a few minutes later, as I was getting into a shared taxi van with nine sorority sisters who that night were journeying to a weekend getaway. Within a minute of taking their seats in the dark van, dim lights flicked on as every one of the sisters checked an iPhone or tablet. Desultory conversations sputtered along while they texted or scrolled through Facebook. But mostly there was silence.

The indifference of that mother and the silence among the sisters are symptoms of how technology captures our attention and disrupts our connections. In 2006 the word *pizzled* entered our lexicon; a combination of *puzzled* and *pissed*, it captured the feeling people had when the person they were with whipped out a BlackBerry and started talking to someone else. Back then people felt hurt and indignant in such moments. Today it's the norm.

Teens, the vanguard of our future, are the epicenter. In the early years of this decade their monthly text message count soared to 3,417, double the number just a few years earlier. Meanwhile their time on the phone dropped.[5] The average American teen gets and sends more than a hundred texts a day, about ten every waking hour. I've seen a kid texting while he rode his bike.

A friend reports, "I visited some cousins in New Jersey recently and their kids had every electronic gadget known to man. All I ever saw were the tops of their heads. They were constantly checking their iPhones for who had texted them, what had updated on Facebook, or they were lost in some video game. They're totally unaware of what's happening around them and clueless about how to interact with someone for any length of time."

Today's children are growing up in a new reality, one where they are attuning more to machines and less to people than has ever been true in human history. That's troubling for several reasons. For one, the social and emotional circuitry of a child's brain learns from contact and conversation with everyone it encounters over the course of a day. These interactions mold brain circuitry; the fewer hours spent with people—and the more spent staring at a digitized screen—portends deficits.

Digital engagement comes at a cost in face time with real people—the medium where we learn to "read" nonverbals. The new crop of natives in this digital world may be adroit at the keyboard, but they can be all thumbs when it comes to reading behavior face-to-face, in real time—particularly in sensing the dismay of others when they stop to read a text in the middle of talking with them.[6]

A college student observes the loneliness and isolation that go along with living in a virtual world of tweets, status updates, and "posting pictures of my dinner." He notes that his classmates are losing their ability for conversation, let alone the soul-searching discussions that can enrich the college years. And, he says, "no birthday, concert, hangout session, or party can be enjoyed without taking the time to distance yourself from what you are doing" to make sure that those in your digital world know instantly how much fun you are having.

Then there are the basics of attention, the cognitive muscle that lets us follow a story, see a task through to the end, learn, or create. In some ways, as we'll see, the endless hours young people spend staring at electronic gadgets may help them acquire specific cognitive skills. But there are concerns and questions about how those same hours may lead to deficits in core mental skills.

An eighth-grade teacher tells me that for many years she has had successive classes of students read the same book, Edith Hamilton's *Mythology.* Her students have loved it—until five years or so ago. "I started to see kids not so excited—even high-achieving groups could not get engaged with it," she told me. "They say the reading is too hard; the sentences are too complicated; it takes a long time to read a page."

She wonders if perhaps her students' ability to read has been somehow compromised by the short, choppy messages they get in texts. One student confessed he'd spent two thousand hours in the last year playing video games. She adds, "It's hard to teach comma rules when you are competing with World of WarCraft."

At the extremes, Taiwan, Korea, and other Asian countries see Internet addiction—to gaming, social media, virtual realities—among youth as a national health crisis, isolating the young. Around 8 percent of American gamers between ages eight and eighteen seem to meet psychiatry's diagnostic criteria for addiction; brain studies reveal changes in their neural reward system while they game that are akin to those found in alcoholics and drug abusers.[7] Occasional horror stories tell of addicted gamers who sleep all day and game all night, rarely stop to eat or clean themselves, and even get violent when family members try to stop them.

Rapport demands joint attention—mutual focus. Our need to make an effort to have such human moments has never been greater, given the ocean of distractions we all navigate daily.

THE IMPOVERISHMENT OF ATTENTION

Then there are the costs of attention decline among adults. In Mexico, an advertising rep for a large radio network complains, "A few years ago you could make a five-minute video for your presentation at an ad agency. Today you have to keep it to a minute and a half. If you don't grab them by then, everyone starts checking for messages."

A college professor who teaches film tells me he's reading a biography of one of his heroes, the legendary French director François Truffaut. But, he finds, "I can't read more than two pages at a stretch. I get this overwhelming urge to go online and see if I have a new email. I think I'm losing my ability to sustain concentration on anything serious."

The inability to resist checking email or Facebook rather than focus on the person talking to us leads to what the sociologist Erving Goffman, a masterly observer of social interaction, called an "away," a gesture that tells another person "I'm not interested" in what's going on here and now.

At the third All Things D(igital) conference back in 2005, conference hosts unplugged the Wi-Fi in the main ballroom because of the glow from laptop screens, indicating that those in the audience were not glued to the action onstage. They were away, in a state, as one participant put it, of "continuous partial attention," a mental blurriness induced by an overload of information inputs from the speakers, the other people in the room, and what they were doing on their laptops.[8] To battle such partial focus today, some Silicon Valley workplaces have banned laptops, mobile phones, and other digital tools during meetings.

After not checking her mobile for a while, a publishing executive confesses she gets "a jangly feeling. You miss that hit you get when there's a text. You know it's not right to check your phone when you're with someone, but it's addictive." So she and her husband have a pact: "When we get home from work we put our phones in a drawer. If it's in front of me I get anxious; I've just got to check it. But now we try to be more present for each other. We talk."

Our focus continually fights distractions, both inner and outer. The question is, What are our distractors costing us? An executive at a financial firm tells me, "When I notice that my mind has been somewhere else during a meeting, I wonder what opportunities I've been missing right here."

Patients are telling a physician I know that they are "self-medicating" with drugs for attention deficit disorder or narcolepsy to keep up with their work. A lawyer tells him, "If I didn't take this, I couldn't read contracts." Once patients needed a diagnosis for such prescriptions; now for many those medications have become routine performance enhancers. Growing numbers of teenagers are faking symptoms of attention deficit to get prescriptions for stimulants, a chemical route to attentiveness.

And Tony Schwartz, a consultant who coaches leaders on how to best manage their energy, tells me, "We get people to become more aware of how they use attention—which is *always* poorly. Attention is now the number-one issue on the minds of our clients."

The onslaught of incoming data leads to sloppy shortcuts, like triaging email by heading, skipping much of voice mails, skimming messages and memos. It's not just that we've developed habits of attention that make us less effective, but that the weight of messages leaves us too little time simply to reflect on what they really mean.

All of this was foreseen way back in 1977 by the Nobel-winning economist Herbert Simon. Writing about the coming information-rich world, he warned that what information consumes is "the attention of its recipients. Hence a wealth of information creates a poverty of attention."[9]

PART I

THE ANATOMY OF ATTENTION

2

BASICS

As a teenager I got into the habit of listening to the string quartets of Béla Bartók—which I found slightly cacophonous but still enjoyed—while doing my homework. Somehow tuning out those discordant tones helped me focus on, say, the chemical equation for ammonium hydroxide.

Years later, when I found myself writing articles on deadline for the *New York Times*, I remembered that early drill in ignoring Bartók. At the *Times* I labored away in the midst of the science desk, which in those years occupied a classroom-sized cavern into which were crammed desks for the dozen or so science journalists and a half dozen editors.

There was always a Bartók-ish hum of cacophony. Nearby there might be three or four people chatting; you'd overhear the near end of a phone conversation—or several—as reporters interviewed sources; editors shouted across the room to ask when an article would be ready for them. There were rarely, if ever, the sounds of silence.

And yet we science writers, myself among them, would reliably deliver our ready-to-edit copy right on time, day after day. No one ever pleaded, *Everyone please be quiet*, so we could concentrate. We all just redoubled our focus, tuning out the roar.

That focus in the midst of a din indicates selective attention, the neural capacity to beam in on just one target while ignoring a staggering sea of incoming stimuli, each one a potential focus in itself. This is what William James, a founder of modern psychology, meant when he defined attention as "the sudden taking possession by the mind, in clear and vivid form, of one of what seems several simultaneously possible objects or trains of thought."[1]

There are two main varieties of distractions: sensory and emotional. The sensory distractors are easy: as you read these words you're tuning out of the blank margins surrounding this text. Or notice for a moment the feeling of your tongue against your upper palate—just one of an endless wave of incoming stimuli your brain weeds out from the continuous wash of background sounds, shapes and colors, tastes, smells, sensations, and on and on.

More daunting is the second variety of lures: emotionally loaded signals. While you might find it easy to concentrate on answering your email in the hubbub of your local coffee shop, if you should overhear someone mention your name (potent emotional bait, that) it's almost impossible to tune out the voice that carries it—your attention reflexively alerts to hear what's being said about you. Forget that email.

The biggest challenge for even the most focused, though, comes from the emotional turmoil of our lives, like a recent blowup in a close relationship that keeps intruding into your thoughts. Such thoughts barge in for a good reason: to get us to think through what to do about what's upsetting us. The dividing line between fruitless rumination and productive reflection lies in whether or not we come up with some tentative solution or insight and then can let those distressing thoughts go—or if, on the other hand, we just keep obsessing over the same loop of worry.

The more our focus gets disrupted, the worse we do. For instance, a test of how much college athletes are prone to having their concentration disrupted by anxiety correlates significantly with how well or poorly they will perform in the upcoming season.[2]

The ability to stay steady on one target and ignore everything else operates in the brain's prefrontal regions. Specialized circuitry in this area boosts the strength of incoming signals we want to concentrate on (*that email*) and dampens down those we choose to ignore (*those people chattering away at the next table*).

Since focus demands we tune out our emotional distractions, our neural wiring for selective attention includes that for inhibiting emotion. That means those who focus best are relatively immune to emotional turbulence, more able to stay unflappable in a crisis and to keep on an even keel despite life's emotional waves.[3]

Failure to drop one focus and move on to others can, for example, leave the mind lost in repeating loops of chronic anxiety. At clinical extremes it means being lost in helplessness, hopelessness, and self-pity in depression; or panic and catastrophizing in anxiety disorders; or countless repetitions of ritualistic thoughts or acts (*touch the door fifty times before leaving*) in obsessive-compulsive disorder. The power to disengage our attention from one thing and move it to another is essential for well-being.

The stronger our selective attention, the more powerfully we can stay absorbed in what we've chosen to do: get swept away by a moving scene in a film or find a powerful poetry passage exhilarating. Strong focus lets people lose themselves in YouTube or their homework to the point of being oblivious to whatever tumult might be nearby—or their parents calling them to come eat dinner.

You can spot the focused folks at a party: they are able to immerse themselves in a conversation, their eyes locked on the other person as they stay fully absorbed in their words—despite that speaker next to them blaring the Beastie Boys. The unfocused, in contrast, are in continual play, their eyes gravitating to whatever might grab them, their attention adrift.

Richard Davidson, a neuroscientist at the University of Wisconsin, names focus as one of a handful of essential life abilities, each based in a separate neural system, that guide us through the turbulence of our inner lives, our relationships, and whatever challenges life brings.[4]

During sharp focus, Davidson finds, key circuitry in the prefrontal cortex gets into a synchronized state with the object of that beam of awareness, a state he calls "phase-locking."[5] If people are focused on pressing a button each time they hear a certain tone, the electrical signals in their prefrontal area fire precisely in synch with the target sound.

The better your focus, the stronger your neural lock in. But if instead of concentration there's a jumble of thoughts, synchrony vanishes.[6] Just such a drop in synchrony marks people with attention deficit disorder.[7]

We learn best with focused attention. As we focus on what we are learning, the brain maps that information on what we already know, making new neural connections. If you and a small toddler share attention toward something as you name it, the toddler learns that name; if her focus wanders as you say it, she won't.

When our mind wanders off, our brain activates a host of brain circuits that chatter about things that have nothing to do with what we're trying to learn. Lacking focus, we store no crisp memory of what we're learning.

ZONING OUT

Time for a quick quiz:

1. What's that technical term for brain wave synchrony with a sound you hear?
2. What are the two main varieties of distraction?

3. What aspect of attention predicts how well college athletes perform?

If you can answer these off the top of your head, you've been sustaining focused attention while you read—the answers were in the last few pages of this book (and can be found at the bottom of this page).*

If you can't recall the answers, you may have been zoning out from time to time while you read. And you're not alone.

A reader's mind typically wanders anywhere from 20 to 40 percent of the time while perusing a text. The cost for students, not surprisingly, is that the more wandering, the worse their comprehension.[8]

Even when our minds are not wandering, if the text turns to gibberish—like *We must make some circus for the money*, instead of *We must make some money for the circus*—about 30 percent of the time readers continue reading along for a significant stretch (an average of seventeen words) before catching it.

As we read a book, a blog, or any narrative, our mind constructs a mental model that lets us make sense of what we are reading and connects it to the universe of such models we already hold that bear on the same topic. This expanding web of understanding lies at the heart of learning. The more we zone out while building that web, and the sooner the lapse after we begin reading, the more holes.

When we read a book, our brain constructs a network of pathways that embodies that set of ideas and experiences. Contrast that deep comprehension with the interruptions and distractions that typify the ever-seductive Internet. The bombardment of texts, videos, images, and miscellaneous of messages we get online seems the enemy of the more full understanding that comes from what Nicholas Carr calls "deep reading," which requires sustained con-

*Answers: 1. phase-locking; 2. sensory and emotional; 3. how well the athletes can concentrate and ignore distractions.

centration and immersion in a topic rather than hopscotching from one to another, nabbing disconnected factoids.[9]

As education migrates onto Web-based formats, the danger looms that the multimedia mass of distractions we call the Internet will hamper learning. Way back in the 1950s the philosopher Martin Heidegger warned against a looming "tide of technological revolution" that might "so captivate, bewitch, dazzle, and beguile man that calculative thinking may someday come to be . . . the only way of thinking."[10] That would come at the loss of "meditative thinking," a mode of reflection he saw as the essence of our humanity.

I hear Heidegger's warning in terms of the erosion of an ability at the core of reflection, the capacity to sustain attention to an ongoing narrative. Deep thinking demands sustaining a focused mind. The more distracted we are, the more shallow our reflections; likewise, the shorter our reflections, the more trivial they are likely to be. Heidegger, were he alive today, would be horrified if asked to tweet.

HAS ATTENTION SHRUNK?

There's a swing band from Shanghai playing lounge music in a crowded Swiss convention hall, with hundreds of people milling about. In the midst of the manic throng, standing stock-still at a small circular bar table, Clay Shirky has zoned in to his laptop and is typing furiously.

I met Clay, a New York University–based social media maven, some years back, but rarely have the chance to see him in the flesh. For several minutes I'm standing about three feet away from Clay, off to his right, watching him—positioned in his peripheral vision, if he had any attention bandwidth to spare. But Clay takes no notice until I speak his name. Then, startled, he looks up and we start chatting.

Attention is a limited capacity: Clay's rapt concentration fills that full bore until he shifts to me.

"Seven plus or minus two" chunks of information has been taken as the upper limit of the beam of attention since the 1950s, when George Miller proposed what he called this "magical number" in one of psychology's most influential papers.[11]

More recently, though, some cognitive scientists have argued that four chunks is the upper limit.[12] That caught the public's limited attention (for a brief moment, anyway), as the new meme spread that this mental capacity had shrunk from seven to four bits of information. "Mind's Limit Found: 4 Bits of Information," one science news site proclaimed.[13]

Some took the presumed downsizing of what we can hold in mind as an indictment of the distractedness of everyday life in the twenty-first century, decrying the shrinking of this crucial mental ability. But they misinterpret the data.

"Working memory hasn't shrunk," said Justin Halberda, a cognitive scientist at Johns Hopkins University. "It's not the case that TV has made our working memory smaller"—that in the 1950s we all had an upper limit of seven plus or minus two bits of information, and now we have only four.

"The mind tries to make the most of its limited resources," Halberda explained. "So we use memory strategies that help"—say, combining different elements, like 4, 1, and 5, into a single chunk, such as the area code 415. "When we perform a memory task, the result might be seven plus or minus two bits. But that breaks down into a fixed limit of four, plus three or four more that memory strategies add. So both four and seven are right, depending on how you measure it."

Then there's what many people think of as "splitting" attention in multitasking, which cognitive science tells us is a fiction, too. Rather than having a stretchable balloon of attention to deploy in tandem, we have a narrow, fixed pipeline to allot. Instead of splitting it, we actually switch rapidly. Continual switching saps attention from full, concentrated engagement.

"The most precious resource in a computer system is no longer its processor, memory, disk or network, but rather human attention," a research group at Carnegie Mellon University notes.[14] The solution they propose to this human bottleneck hinges on minimizing distractions: Project Aura proposes to do away with bothersome systems glitches so we don't waste time in hassles.

The goal of a hassle-free computing system is laudable. This solution, however, may not get us that far: it's not a technological fix we need but a cognitive one. The source of distractions is not so much in the technology we use as in the frontal assault on our focusing ability from the mounting tide of distractions.

Which gets me back to Clay Shirky, particularly his research on social media.[15] While none of us can focus on everything at once, all of us together create a collective bandwidth for attention that we each can access as needed. Witness Wikipedia.

As Shirky proclaims in his book *Here Comes Everybody*, attention can be seen as a capacity distributed among many people, as can memory or any cognitive expertise. "What's trending now" indexes how we are allotting our collective attention. While some argue that our tech-facilitated learning and memory dumb us down, there's also a case to be made that they create a mental prosthesis that expands the power of individual attention.

Our social capital—and range of attention—increases as we up the number of social ties through which we gain crucial information, like tacit knowledge of "how things work here," whether in an organization or a new neighborhood. Casual acquaintances can be extra sets of eyes and ears on the world, key sources of the guidance we need to operate in complex social and information ecosystems. Most of us have a handful of strong ties—close, trusted friends—

but we can have hundreds of so-called weak ties (for example, our Facebook "friends"). Weak ties have high value as multipliers of our attention capacity, and as a source of tips for good shopping deals, job possibilities, and dating partners.[16]

When we coordinate what we see and what we know, our efforts in tandem multiply our cognitive wealth. While at any given moment our quota for working memory remains small, the total of data we can pull through that narrow width becomes huge. This collective intelligence, the sum total of what everyone in a distributed group can contribute, promises maximal focus, the summation of what multiple eyes can notice.

A research center at the Massachusetts Institute of Technology on collective intelligence sees this emerging capacity as abetted by the sharing of attention on the Internet. The classic example: millions of websites cast their spotlight within narrow niches—and a Web search selects and directs our focus so we can harvest all that cognitive work efficiently.[17]

The MIT group's basic question: "How can we connect people and computers so that collectively we act with more intelligence than any one person or group?"

Or, as the Japanese say, "All of us are smarter than any one of us."

DO YOU LOVE WHAT YOU DO?

The big question: When you get up in the morning, are you happy about getting to work, school, or whatever it is that occupies your day?

Research by Harvard's Howard Gardner, Stanford's William Damon, and Claremont's Mihaly Csikszentmihalyi zeroed in on what they call "good work," a potent mix of what people are excellent at, what engages them, and their ethics—what they believe matters.[18] Those are more likely to be high-absorption callings: people love what they are doing. Full absorption in what we do feels good, and pleasure is the emotional marker for flow.

People are in flow relatively rarely in daily life.[19] Sampling people's moods at random reveals that most of the time people are either stressed or bored, with only occasional periods of flow; only about 20 percent of people have flow moments at least once a day. Around 15 percent of people never enter a flow state during a typical day.

One key to more flow in life comes when we align what we do with what we enjoy, as is the case with those fortunate folks whose jobs give them great pleasure. High achievers in any field—the lucky ones, anyway—have hit on this combination.

Apart from a career change, there are several doorways to flow. One may open when we tackle a task that challenges our abilities to the maximum—a "just-manageable" demand on our skills. Another entryway can come via doing what we are passionate about; motivation sometimes drives us into flow. But either way the final common pathway is full focus: these are each ways to ratchet up attention. No matter how you get there, a keen focus jump-starts flow.

This optimal brain state for getting work done well is marked by greater neural harmony—a rich, well-timed interconnection among diverse brain areas.[20] In this state, ideally, the circuits needed for the task at hand are highly active while those irrelevant are quiescent, with the brain precisely attuned to the demands of the moment. When our brains are in this zone we are more likely to perform at our personal best whatever our pursuit.

Workplace surveys, though, find large numbers of people are in a very different brain state: they daydream, waste hours cruising the Web or YouTube, and do the bare minimum required. Their attention scatters. Such disengagement and indifference are rampant, especially among repetitive, undemanding jobs. To get the disengaged workers any nearer the focused range demands upping their motivation and enthusiasm, evoking a sense of purpose, and adding a dollop of pressure.

On the other hand, another large group are stuck in the state neurobiologists call "frazzle," where constant stress overloads their nervous system with floods of cortisol and adrenaline. Their attention fixates on their worries, not their job. This emotional exhaustion can lead to burnout.

Full focus gives us a potential doorway into flow. But when we choose to focus on one thing and ignore the rest, we surface a constant tension—usually invisible—between a great neural divide, where the top of the brain tussles with the bottom.

3

ATTENTION TOP AND BOTTOM

I turned my attention to the study of some arithmetical questions, apparently without much success," wrote the nineteenth-century French mathematician Henri Poincaré. "Disgusted with my failure, I went to spend a few days at the seaside."[1]

There, as he walked on a bluff above the ocean one morning, the insight suddenly came to him "that the arithmetical transformations of indeterminate ternary quadratic forms were identical with those of non-Euclidian geometry."

The specifics of that proof do not matter here (fortunately so: I could not begin to understand the math myself). What's intriguing about this illumination is *how* it came to Poincaré: with "brevity, suddenness, and immediate certainty." He was taken by surprise.

The lore of creativity is rife with such accounts. Carl Gauss, an eighteenth- and nineteenth-century mathematician, worked on proving a theorem for four years, with no solution. Then, one day, the answer came to him "as a sudden flash of light." Yet he could not name the thread of thought that connected his years of hard work with that flash of insight.

Why the puzzle? Our brain has two semi-independent, largely separate mental systems. One has massive computing power and operates constantly, purring away in quiet to solve our problems, surprising us with a sudden solution to complex pondering. Since it operates beyond the horizon of conscious awareness we are blind to its workings. This system presents the fruit of its vast labors to us as though out of nowhere, and in a multitude of forms, from guiding the syntax of a sentence to constructing complex full-blown mathematical proofs.

This back-of-the-mind attention typically comes to the center of focus when the unexpected happens. You're talking on your cell phone while driving (the driving part is back-of-the-mind) and suddenly a horn honk makes you realize the light has changed to green.

Much of this system's neural wiring lies in the lower part of our brain, in subcortical circuitry, though its efforts break into awareness by notifying our neocortex, the brain's topmost layers, from below. Through their pondering, Poincaré and Gauss reaped breakthroughs from the brain's lower layers.

"Bottom-up" has become the phrase of choice in cognitive science for such workings of this lower-brain neural machinery.[2] By the same token, "top-down" refers to mental activity, mainly within the neocortex, that can monitor and impose its goals on the subcortical machinery. It's as though there were two minds at work.

The bottom-up mind is:

- faster in brain time, which operates in milliseconds
- involuntary and automatic: always on
- intuitive, operating through networks of association
- impulsive, driven by emotions
- executor of our habitual routines and guide for our actions
- manager for our mental models of the world

By contrast, the top-down mind is:

- slower

- voluntary
- effortful
- the seat of self-control, which can (sometimes) overpower automatic routines and mute emotionally driven impulses
- able to learn new models, make new plans, and take charge of our automatic repertoire—to an extent

Voluntary attention, willpower, and intentional choice are top-down; reflexive attention, impulsc, and rote habit are bottom-up (as is the attention captured by a stylish outfit or a nifty ad). When we choose to tune in to the beauty of a sunset, concentrate on what we're reading, or have a deep talk with someone, it's a top-down shift. Our mind's eye plays out a continual dance between stimulus-driven attention capture and voluntarily directed focus.

The bottom-up system multitasks, scanning a profusion of inputs in parallel, including features of our surroundings that have not yet come into full focus; it analyzes what's in our perceptual field before letting us know what it selects as relevant for us. Our top-down mind takes more time to deliberate on what it gets presented with, taking things one at a time and applying more thoughtful analysis.

Through what amounts to an optical illusion of the mind, we take what's within our awareness to equal the whole of the mind's operations. But in fact the vast majority of mental operations occur in the mind's backstage, amid the purr of bottom-up systems.

Much (some say all) of what the top-down mind believes it has chosen to focus on, think about, and do is actually plans dictated bottom-up. If this were a movie, psychologist Daniel Kahneman wryly notes, the top-down mind would be a "supporting character who believes herself to be the hero."[3]

Dating back millions of years in evolution, the reflexive, quick-acting bottom-up circuitry favors short-term thinking, impulse, and speedy decisions. The top-down circuits at the front and top of the brain are a later addition, their full maturation dating back mere hundreds of thousands of years.

Top-down wiring adds talents like self-awareness and reflection, deliberation, and planning to our mind's repertoire. Intentional, top-down focus offers the mind a lever to manage our brain. As we shift our attention from one task, plan, sensation or the like to another, the related brain circuitry lights up. Bring to mind a happy memory of dancing and the neurons for joy and movement spring to life. Recall the funeral of a loved one and the circuitry for sadness activates. Mentally rehearse a golf stroke and the axons and dendrites that orchestrate those moves wire together a bit more strongly.

The human brain counts among evolution's good-enough, but not perfect, designs.[4] The brain's more ancient bottom-up systems apparently worked well for basic survival during most of human prehistory—but their design makes for some troubles today. In much of life the older system holds sway, usually to our advantage but sometimes to our detriment: overspending, addictions, and recklessly speeding drivers all count as signs of this system out of whack.

The survival demands of early evolution packed our brains with preset bottom-up programs for procreation and child-rearing, for what's pleasurable and what's disgusting, for running from a threat or toward food, and the like. Fast-forward to today's very different world: we so often need to navigate life top-down despite the constant undertow of bottom-up whims and drives.

A surprising factor constantly tips the balance toward bottom-up: the brain economizes on energy. Cognitive efforts like learning to use your latest tech upgrade demand active attention, at an energy cost. But the more we run through a once-novel routine, the more it morphs into rote habit and gets taken over by bottom-up circuitry, particularly neural networks in the basal ganglia, a golf-ball-sized mass nestled at the brain's bottom, just above the spinal cord. The more we practice a routine, the more the basal ganglia take it over from other parts of the brain.

The bottom/top systems distribute mental tasks between them so we can make minimal effort and get optimal results. As familiarity makes a routine easier, it gets passed off from the top to the bottom. The way we experience this neural transfer is that we need pay less attention—and finally none—as it becomes automatic.

The peak of automaticity can be seen when expertise pays off in effortless attention to high demand, whether a master-level chess match, a NASCAR race, or rendering an oil painting. If we haven't practiced enough, all of these will take deliberate focus. But if we have mastered the requisite skills to a level that meets the demand, they will take no extra cognitive effort—freeing our attention for the extras seen only among those at top levels.

As world-class champions attest, at the topmost levels, where your opponents have practiced about as many thousands of hours as you have, any competition becomes a mental game: your mind state determines how well you can focus, and so how well you can do. The more you can relax and trust in bottom-up moves, the more you free your mind to be nimble.

Take, for example, star football quarterbacks who have what sports analysts call "great ability to see the field": they can read the other team's defensive formations to sense the opponent's intentions to move, and once the play starts instantly adjust to those movements, gaining a priceless second or two to pick out an open receiver for a pass. Such "seeing" requires enormous practice, so that what at first requires much attention—*dodge that rusher*—occurs on automatic.

From a mental computation perspective, spotting a receiver while under the pressure of several 250-pound bodies hurtling toward you from various angles is no small feat: the quarterback has to keep in mind the pass routes of several potential receivers at the same time he processes and responds to the moves of all eleven opposing players—a challenge best managed by well-practiced bottom-up circuits (and one that would be overwhelming if he had to consciously think through each move).

RECIPE FOR A SCREWUP

Lolo Jones was winning the women's 100-meter hurdles race, on her way to a gold medal at the 2008 Beijing Olympics. In the lead, she was clearing the hurdles with an effortless rhythm—until something went wrong.

At first it was very subtle: she had a sense that the hurdles were coming at her too fast. With that, Jones had the thought *Make sure you don't get sloppy in your technique. . . . Make sure your legs are snapping out.*

With those thoughts, she overtried, tightening up a bit too much—and hit the ninth hurdle of ten. Jones finished seventh, not first, and collapsed on the track in tears.[5]

Looking back as she was about to try again at the 2012 London Olympics (where she eventually finished fourth in the 100-meter race), Jones could recall that earlier moment of defeat with crystal clarity. And if you asked neuroscientists, they could diagnose the error with equal certainty: when she began to think about the details of her technique, instead of just leaving the job to the motor circuits that had practiced these moves to mastery, Jones had shifted from relying on her bottom-up system to interference from the top.

Brain studies find that having a champion athlete start pondering technique during a performance offers a sure recipe for a screwup. When top soccer players raced a ball around and through a line of traffic cones—and had to notice which side of their foot was controlling the ball—they made more errors.[6] The same happened when baseball players tried to track whether their bat was moving up or down during a swing for a pitched ball.

The motor cortex, which in a well-seasoned athlete has these moves deeply etched in its circuits from thousands of hours of practice, operates best when left alone. When the prefrontal cortex activates and we start thinking about how we're doing, how to do what we're doing—or, worse, what *not* to do—the brain gives over some control to circuits that know how to think and worry, but not how to deliver the move itself. Whether in the hundred meters, soccer, or baseball, it's a universal recipe for tripping up.

That's why, as Rick Aberman, who directs peak performance for the Minnesota Twins baseball team, tells me, "When the coach reviews plays from a game and only focuses on what *not* to do next time, it's a recipe for players to choke."

It's not just in sports. Making love comes to mind as another activity where getting too analytic and self-critical gets in the way. A journal article on the "ironic effects of trying to relax under stress" suggests still another.[7]

Relaxation and making love go best when we just let them happen—not try to force them. The parasympathetic nervous system, which kicks in during these activities, ordinarily acts independently of our brain's executive, which thinks about them.

Edgar Allan Poe dubbed the unfortunate mental tendency to bring up some sensitive topic you resolved not to mention "the imp of the perverse." An article fittingly called "How to Think, Say, or Do Precisely the Worst Thing for Any Occasion," by Harvard psychologist Daniel Wegner, explains the cognitive mechanism that animates that imp.[8]

Flubs, Wegner has found, escalate to the degree we are distracted, stressed, or otherwise mentally burdened. In those circumstances a cognitive control system that ordinarily monitors errors we might make (like *don't mention that topic*) can inadvertently act as a mental prime, increasing the likelihood of that very mistake (like *mentioning that topic*).

When Wegner has had experimental volunteers try *not* to think of a particular word, when they then are pressured to respond quickly to a word association task, ironically they often offer up that same forbidden word.

Overloading attention shrinks mental control. It's in the moments we feel most stressed that we forget the names of people we know well, not to mention their birthdays, our anniversaries, and other socially crucial data.[9]

Another example: obesity. Researchers find that the prevalence of obesity in the United States over the last thirty years tracks the explosion of computers and tech gadgets in people's lives—and suspect this is no accidental correlation. Life immersed in digital distractions creates a near-constant cognitive overload. And that overload wears out self-control.

Forget that resolve to diet. Lost in the digital world we mindlessly reach for the Pringles.

THE BOTTOM-UP SKEW

A survey of psychologists asked them if there might be "one nagging thing" that they did not understand about themselves.[10]

One said that for two decades he had studied how gloomy weather makes one's whole life look bleak, unless you become aware of how the gloom worsens your mood—but that even though he understood all that, gloomy skies still made him feel bad.

Another was puzzled by his compulsion to write papers that

show how some research is badly misguided, and how he continues to do so even though none of the relevant researchers has paid much attention.

And a third said that though he had studied "male sexual overperception bias"—the misinterpretation of a woman's friendliness as romantic interest—he still succumbs to the bias.

The bottom-up circuitry learns voraciously—and quietly—taking in lessons continually as we go through the day. Such implicit learning need never enter our awareness, though it acts as a rudder in life nonetheless, for better or for worse.

The automatic system works well most of the time: we know what's going on and what to do and can meander through the demands of the day well enough while we think about other things. But this system has weaknesses, too: our emotions and our motives create skews and biases in our attention that we typically don't notice, and don't notice that we don't notice.

Take social anxiety. In general, anxious people fixate on anything even vaguely threatening; those with social anxiety compulsively spot the least sign of rejection, such as a fleeting expression of disgust on someone's face—a reflection of their habitual assumption that they will be social flops. Most of this emotional transaction goes on out of awareness, leading people to avoid situations where they might get anxious.

An ingenious method for remedying this bottom-up skew is so subtle that people have no idea that their attention patterns are being rewired (just as they had no idea that wiring was going on as they acquired it in the first place). Called "cognitive bias modification," or CBM, this invisible therapy has those suffering from severe social anxiety look at photos of an audience while they are asked to track when flashing patterns of lights appear and press a button as quickly as they can.[11]

Flashes never appear in the area of the pictures that are threatening, like frowning faces. Though this intervention stays beneath their awareness, over the course of several sessions the bottom-up circuitry learns to direct attention to nonthreatening cues. Though people haven't a clue about the subtle repatterning of attention, their anxiety in social situations dials down.[12]

That's a benign use of this circuitry. Then there's advertising. The old-school tactics for getting attention in a crowded marketplace—what's new, improved, surprising—still work. But a mini-industry of brain studies in the service of marketing has led to tactics based on manipulating our unconscious mind. One such study found, for example, that if you show people luxury items or just have them think about luxury goods, they become more self-centered in their decisions.[13]

One of the most active areas of research on unconscious choice centers on what gets us to reach for some product when we shop. Marketers want to know how to mobilize our bottom-up brain.

Marketing research finds, for instance, that when people are shown a drink along with happy faces that flit across a screen too rapidly to be registered consciously—but nonetheless are noticed by the bottom-up systems—they drink more than when those fleeting images are angry faces.

A review of such research concludes that people are "massively unaware" of these subtle marketing forces, even as they shape how we shop.[14] Bottom-up awareness makes us suckers for subconscious primes.

Life today seems ruled to a troubling degree by impulse; a flood of ads drives us, bottom-up, to desire a sea of goods and spend today without regard to how we will pay tomorrow. The reign of impulse for many goes beyond overspending and overborrowing to overeating and other addictive habits, from bingeing on Twizzlers to spending countless hours staring at one or another variety of digital screen.

NEURAL HIJACKS

Walk into someone's office, and what's the first thing you notice? That's a clue to what's driving your bottom-up focus in that moment. If you're set on a financial goal, you might immediately take in an earnings graph on the computer screen. If you have arachnophobia, you'll fixate on that dusty web in the corner of the window.

These are subconscious choices in attention. Such attention capture occurs when the amygdala circuitry, the brain's sentinel for emotional meaning, spots something it finds significant; an oversize insect, wrathful look, or cute toddler gives you an idea of the brain's settings for such instinctual interest.[15] This midbrain fixture of the bottom-up system reacts far more quickly in neural time than does the top-down prefrontal area; it sends signals upward to activate higher cortical pathways that alert the (relatively) sluggish executive centers to wake up and pay attention.

Our brain's attention mechanisms evolved over hundreds of thousands of years to survive in a fang-and-claw jungle where threats approached our ancestors within a specific visual range and set of rates—somewhere around the lunge of a snake and the speed of a leaping tiger. Those of our ancestors whose amygdala was quick enough to help us dodge that snake and evade that tiger passed on their neural design to us.

Snakes and spiders, two animals that the human brain seems primed to notice with alarm, capture attention even when their images are flashed so fast we have no conscious awareness of having seen them. The bottom-up circuits spot them more quickly than neutral objects, and send an alarm (flash those images by an expert on snakes or spiders and she will still have attention capture—but no alarm signal).[16]

The brain finds it impossible to ignore emotional faces, particularly furious ones.[17] Angry faces have super-salience: scan a crowd and someone with an angry face will pop out. The bottom brain will even spot a cartoon with V-shaped eyebrows (like the kids in *South Park*) more quickly than it takes in a happy face.

We are wired to pay reflexive attention to "super-normal stimuli," whether for safety, nutrition, or sex—like a cat that can't help chasing a fake mouse on a string. In today's world, ads that play on those same pre-wired inclinations tug at us bottom-up, too, getting our reflexive attention. Just tie sex or prestige to a product to activate these same circuits to prime us to buy for reasons we don't even notice.

Our particular proclivities make us all the more vulnerable. That's why alcoholics are riveted by vodka ads, randy folks by the sexy people in a spot for a vacation getaway.

This is bottom-up preselected attention; such capture from below is automatic, an involuntary choice. We're most prone to emotions driving focus this way when our minds are wandering, when we are distracted, or when we're overwhelmed by information—or all three.

Then there are emotions gone wild. I was writing this very section yesterday, sitting at my desktop, when out of the blue I had a crippling attack of lower back pain. Maybe not out of nowhere: it had been building quietly since morning. But then as I sat at my desk it suddenly ripped through my body, from my lower spine straight up to the pain centers in my brain.

When I tried to stand, the bolt of pain was so severe I crumpled back into my chair. What's worse, my mind started racing about the worst that might happen: *I'll be crippled by this for life, I'll have to get regular steroid injections* . . . and that train of thought brought my panicked mind to recall that a fungus in a poorly run drug-compounding facility had led to the death from meningitis of twenty-seven patients who had gotten just those very injections.

As it happens, I had just deleted a block of text on a related point, which I intended to move to about here in this book. But with my attention in the grip of pain and worry, I completely forgot about it—and so it has vanished into a black hole.

Such emotional hijacks are triggered by the amygdala, the brain's radar for threat, which constantly scans our surroundings for dangers. When these circuits spot a threat (or what we interpret as one—they are often mistaken), a superhighway of neuronal circuitry running upward to the prefrontal areas sends a barrage of signals that let the lower brain drive the upper: our attention narrows, glued to what's upsetting us; our memory reshuffles, making it easier to recall anything relevant to the threat at hand; our body goes into overdrive as a flood of stress hormones prepares our limbs to fight or run. We fixate on what's so disturbing and forget the rest.

The stronger the emotion, the greater our fixation. Hijacks are the superglue of attention. But the question is, How long does our focus stay captured? That depends, it turns out, on the power of the left prefrontal area to calm the aroused amygdala (there are two amygdalae, one in each brain hemisphere).

That amygdala-prefrontal neuronal superhighway has branches to the left and right prefrontal sides. When we are hijacked the amygdala circuitry captures the right side and takes over. But the left side can send signals downward that calm the hijack.

Emotional resilience comes down to how quickly we recover from upsets. People who are highly resilient—who bounce back right away—can have as much as thirty times more activation in the left prefrontal area than those who are less resilient.[18] The good news: as we'll see in part 5, we can increase the strength of the amygdala-calming left prefrontal circuitry.

LIFE ON AUTOMATIC

My friend and I are rapt in conversation in a busy restaurant, toward the end of our lunch. He's immersed in his narrative, telling me about a particularly intense moment he's had recently.

He's been so lost in telling me about it that he's not done with his food. My plate was cleared a while ago.

At that point the server comes to our table and asks him, "Are you enjoying your lunch?"

He barely notices her, mutters a dismissive, "No, not yet," and continues on with his story without missing a beat.

My friend's reply, of course, was not to what the server actually said, but rather to what waiters *usually* say at that point in a meal: "Have you finished?"

That small mistake typifies the downside of a life lived bottom-up, on automatic: we miss the moment as it actually comes to us, reacting instead to a fixed template of assumptions about what's going on. And we miss the humor of the moment:

Waiter: "Are you enjoying your lunch?"

Customer: "No, not yet."

Back in the day when there were often long lines in many offices as people waited to use a copier, Harvard psychologist Ellen Langer had people go to the head of the line and simply say, "I've got to make some copies."

Of course, everyone else in line was there to make copies, too. Yet more often than not, the person at the head of the line would let Langer's confederate go ahead. That, says Langer, exemplifies mindlessness, attention on automatic. An active attention, by contrast, might lead the person at the front of the line to question whether there really was some privileged urgent need for those copies.

Active engagement of attention signifies top-down activity, an antidote to going through the day with a zombie-like automaticity. We can talk back to commercials, stay alert to what's happening around us, question automatic routines or improve them. This focused, often goal-oriented attention, inhibits mindless mental habits.[19]

So while emotions can drive our attention, with active effort we can also manage emotions top-down. Then the prefrontal areas take charge of the amygdala, tuning down its potency. An angry face, or even that cute baby, can fail to capture our attention when the circuits for top-down control of attention take over the brain's choices of what to ignore.

4

THE VALUE OF A MIND ADRIFT

Let's step back for a moment, and think again about thinking. In what I've written so far there is an implicit bias: that focused, goal-driven attention has more value than open, spontaneous awareness. But the easy assumption that attention need be in the service of solving problems or achieving goals downplays the fruitfulness of the mind's tendency to drift whenever left to its own devices.

Every variety of attention has its uses. The very fact that about half of our thoughts are daydreams suggests there may well be some advantages to a mind that can entertain the fanciful.[1] We might revise our own thinking about a "wandering mind," by considering that rather than wandering *away* from what counts, we may well be wandering *toward* something of value.[2]

Brain research on mind wandering faces a unique paradox: top-down intent does not yield a fruitful bottom-up routine. It's impossible to instruct someone to have a spontaneous thought—that is, to make the person's mind wander.[3] If you want to capture wandering thoughts in the wild, you've got to take them whenever they happen to pop up. One preferred research strategy: while people are having their brains scanned, ask them at random moments what they are experiencing. This yields a messy mix of the contents of the mind, including a great deal of wandering.

The inner tug to drift away from effortful focus is so strong that cognitive scientists see a wandering mind as the brain's "default" mode—where it goes when it's not working away on some mental task. The circuitry for this default network, a series of brain imaging studies has found, centers on the medial, or middle, zone of the prefrontal cortex.

More recent brain scans revealed a surprise: during mind wandering *two* major brain areas seem to be active, not just the medial strip that had long been associated with a drifting mind.[4] The other—the executive system of the prefrontal cortex—had been thought crucial for keeping us focused on tasks. Yet the scans seem to show both areas activated as the mind meandered.

That's a bit of a puzzle. After all, mind wandering by its very nature takes focus from the business at hand and hampers our performance, particularly on cognitively demanding matters. Researchers tentatively solve that puzzle by suggesting that the reason mind wandering hurts performance may be its borrowing the executive system for other matters.

This gets us back to what the mind wanders *toward*: more often than not, our current personal concerns and unresolved business—stuff we've got to figure out (more on this in the next chapter). While mind wandering may hurt our immediate focus on some task at hand, some portion of the time it operates in the service of solving problems that matter for our lives.

In addition, a mind adrift lets our creative juices flow. While our minds wander we become better at anything that depends on a flash of insight, from coming up with imaginative wordplay to inventions and original thinking. In fact, people who are extremely adept at mental tasks that demand cognitive control and a roaring working memory—like solving complex math problems—can struggle with creative insights if they have trouble switching off their fully concentrated focus.[5]

Among other positive functions of mind wandering are generating scenarios for the future, self-reflection, navigating a complex social world, incubation of creative ideas, flexibility in focus, pondering what we're learning, organizing our memories, just mulling life—and giving our circuitry for more intensive focusing a refreshing break.[6]

A moment's reflection leads me to add two more: reminding me of things I have to do so they don't get lost in the mind's shuffle, and entertaining me. I'm sure you can suggest some other useful features, if you let your mind drift awhile.

THE ARCHITECTURE OF SERENDIPITY

A Persian fairy tale tells of the Three Princes of Serendip, who "were always making discoveries, by accident and sagacity, of things they were not in quest of."[7] Creativity in the wild operates much like that.

"New ideas won't appear if you don't have permission within yourself," Salesforce CEO Marc Benioff tells me. "When I was a VP at Oracle, I took off to Hawaii for a month just to relax, and when I did that it opened up my career to new ideas, perspectives, and directions."

In that open space Benioff realized the potential uses for cloud computing that led him to quit Oracle, start Salesforce in a rented apartment, and evangelize for what was then a radical concept. Salesforce was a pioneer in what is now a multibillion-dollar industry.

By contrast, a scientist too determined to confirm his hypothesis risks ignoring findings that don't fit his expectations—dismissing them as noise or error, not a doorway to new discoveries—and so misses what might become more fruitful theories. And the naysayer in the brainstorming session, the guy who always shoots down any new idea, throttles innovative insight in its infancy.

Open awareness creates a mental platform for creative breakthroughs and unexpected insights. In open awareness we have no devil's advocate, no cynicism or judgment—just utter receptivity to whatever floats into the mind.

But once we've hit upon a great creative insight, we need to capture the prize by switching to a keen focus on how to apply it. Serendipity comes with openness to possibility, then homing in on putting it to use.

Life's creative challenges rarely come in the form of well-formulated puzzles. Instead we often have to recognize the very need to find a creative solution in the first place. Chance, as Louis Pasteur put it, favors a prepared mind. Daydreaming incubates creative discovery.

A classic model of the stages of creativity roughly translates to three modes of focus: orienting, where we search out and immerse ourselves in all kinds of inputs; selective attention on the specific creative challenge; and open awareness, where we associate freely to let the solution emerge—then home in on the solution.

The brain systems involved in mind wandering have been found active just before people hit upon a creative insight—and, intriguingly, are unusually active in those with attention deficit disorder, or ADD. Adults with ADD, relative to those without, also show higher levels of original creative thinking and more actual creative achievements.[8] The entrepreneur Richard Branson, founder of the corporate empire built on Virgin Air and other companies, has offered himself as a poster boy for success with ADD.

The Centers for Disease Control and Prevention says almost 10 percent of children have the disorder in a form mixed with hyperactivity. In adults, the hyperactivity fades, leaving ADD;

around 4 percent of adults seem to have the problem.[9] When challenged by a creative task, for example, finding novel uses for a brick, those with ADD do better, despite their zoning out—or perhaps because of it.

We all might learn something here. In an experiment where volunteers were challenged with the novel-uses task, those whose minds had been wandering—compared with those whose attention had been fully concentrated—came up with 40 percent more original answers. And when people who had creative accomplishments like a novel, patent, or art show to their credit were tested for screening out irrelevant information to focus on a task, their minds wandered more frequently than did others'—indicating an open awareness that may have served them well in their creative work.[10]

In our less frenetic creative moments, just before an insight the brain typically rests in a relaxed, open focus, marked by an alpha rhythm. This signals a state of daydreamy reverie. Since the brain stores different kinds of information in wide-reaching circuitry, a freely roaming awareness ups the odds of serendipitous associations and novel combinations.

Rappers immersed in "freestyling," where they improvise lyrics in the moment, show heightened activity in the mind-wandering circuitry, among other parts of the brain—allowing fresh connections between far-ranging neural networks.[11] In this spacious mental ecology we are more likely to have novel associations, the *aha* sense that marks a creative insight—or a good rhyme.

In a complex world where almost everyone has access to the same information, new value arises from the original synthesis, from putting ideas together in novel ways, and from smart questions that open up untapped potential. Creative insights entail joining elements in a useful, fresh way.

Imagine for a moment biting into a crisp apple: the patina of colors on its skin, the sounds of the crunch as you bite into it, the wash of tastes, smells, and textures. Take a moment to experience that virtual apple.

As that imagined moment came to life in your mind your brain almost certainly generated a gamma spike. Such gamma spikes are familiar to cognitive neuroscientists; they occur routinely during mental operations like the virtual apple bite—and just before creative insights.

It would be making too much of this to see gamma waves as some secret of creativity. But the *site* of the gamma spike during a creative insight seems telling: an area associated with dreams, metaphors, the logic of art, myth, and poetry. These operate in the language of the unconscious, a realm where anything is possible. Freud's method of free association, where you speak whatever comes into your mind without censoring, opens one door to this open-awareness mode.

Our mind holds endless ideas, memories, and potential associations waiting to be made. But the likelihood of the right idea connecting with the right memory within the right context—and all that coming into the spotlight of attention—diminishes drastically when we are either hyperfocused or too gripped by an overload of distractions to notice the insight.

Then there's what's stored in other people's brains. For about a year the astronomers Arno Penzias and Robert Wilson searched the universe with powerful new equipment, much stronger than any that had yet been used for scanning the vastness of the skies. They were overwhelmed by a sea of fresh data, and tried to simplify their work by ignoring some meaningless static they assumed was due to faulty equipment.

One day a chance encounter with a nuclear physicist gave them an insight (and eventually, a Nobel Prize). The insight led them to realize that what they had been interpreting as "noise" was actually a faint signal from the continued reverberations of the big bang.

THE CREATIVE COCOON

"The intuitive mind is a sacred gift and the rational mind is a faithful servant," Albert Einstein once said. "We have created a society that honors the servant and has forgotten the gift."[12]

For many of us it's a luxury just to get some uninterrupted private moments during the day when we can lean back and reflect. Yet those count as some of the most valuable moments in our day, especially when it comes to creativity.

But there's something more required if those associations are to bear fruit in a viable innovation: the right atmosphere. We need free time where we can sustain an open awareness.

The nonstop onslaught of email, texts, bills to pay—life's "full catastrophe"—throws us into a brain state antithetical to the open focus where serendipitous discoveries thrive. In the tumult of our daily distractions and to-do lists, innovation dead-ends; in open times it flourishes. That's why the annals of discovery are rife with tales of a brilliant insight during a walk or a bath, on a long ride or vacation. Open time lets the creative spirit flourish; tight schedules kill it.

Take the late Peter Schweitzer, a founder of the field of evaluating cryptography, encrypted codes that look like nonsense to the unschooled eye but protect the secrecy of everything from government records to your credit card.[13] Schweitzer's specialty: breaking codes in a friendly test of encryption that tells you if some adversary like a rogue hacker can crack your system and steal your secrets.

This daunting challenge requires you to generate a large array of novel potential solutions to an extraordinarily complicated problem, and then test each one by working it through a methodical number of steps.

Schweitzer's laboratory for this intense task was not some sound-insulated, windowless office. Typically he'd mull an encrypted code while on a long walk or simply soaking up some sun, eyes closed. "It looked like someone taking a nap, but he was doing higher math in his head," as a colleague put it. "He'd lie around sunbathing, and meanwhile his mind would be going a zillion miles an hour."

The import of such cocoons in time and space emerged from a Harvard Business School study of the inner work lives of 238 members of creative project teams tasked with innovative challenges from solving complex information technology problems to inventing kitchen gadgets.[14] Progress in such work demands a steady stream of small creative insights.

Good days for insights had nothing to do with stunning breakthroughs or grand victories. The key turned out to be having small wins—minor innovations and troubling problems solved—on concrete steps toward a larger goal. Creative insights flowed best when people had clear goals but also freedom in how they reached them. And, most crucial, they had protected time—enough to really think freely. A creative cocoon.

5

FINDING BALANCE

"The faculty of voluntarily bringing back a wandering attention, over and over again, is the very root of judgment, character, and will," observed the founder of American psychology, William James.

But, as we've seen, if you ask people, "Are you thinking about something other than what you're currently doing?" the odds are fifty-fifty their minds will be wandering.[1]

Those odds change greatly depending on what that current activity happens to be. A random survey of thousands of people found focus in the here-and-now understandably was highest by far while they were making love (apparently even among those people who answered that badly timed inquiry from a phone app). A more distant second was exercising, followed by talking with someone, and then playing. In contrast, mind wandering was most frequent while they were working (employers take note), using a home computer, or commuting.

On average, people's moods were generally skewed to the unpleasant while their minds wandered; even thoughts that had seemingly neutral content were shaded with a negative emotional tone. Mind wandering itself seemed to be a cause of unhappiness some or much of the time.

Where do our thoughts wander when we're not thinking of anything in particular? Most often, they are all about me. The "me,"

William James proposed, weaves together our sense of self by telling our story—fitting random bits of life into a cohesive narrative. This it's-all-about-me story line fabricates a feeling of permanence behind our ever-shifting moment-to-moment experience.

"Me" reflects the activity of the default zone, that generator of the restless mind, lost in a meandering stream of thought that has little or nothing to do with the present situation and everything to do with, well, me. This mental habit takes over whenever we give the mind a rest from some focused activity.

Creative associations aside, mind wandering tends to center on our self and our preoccupations: *all the many things I have to do today; the wrong thing I said to that person; what I should have said instead.* While the mind sometimes wanders to pleasant thoughts or fantasy, it more often seems to gravitate to rumination and worry.

The medial prefrontal cortex fires away as our self-talk and ruminations generate a background of low-level anxiety. But during full concentration a nearby area, the lateral prefrontal cortex, inhibits this medial area. Our selective attention *de*selects these circuits for emotional preoccupations, the most powerful type of distraction. Responding to what's going on, or active focus of any kind, shuts off the "me," while passive focus returns us to this comfy mire of rumination.[2]

It's not the chatter of people around us that is the most powerful distractor, but rather the chatter of our own minds. Utter concentration demands these inner voices be stilled. Start to subtract sevens successively from 100 and, if you keep your focus on the task, your chatter zone goes quiet.

THE LAWYER AND THE RAISIN

As a litigator, the lawyer had fueled his career by mobilizing a seething anger at the injustices done his clients. Energized by outrage, he was relentless in pursuing his cases, making his arguments with a fiery force, staying up long into the night researching and preparing. Often he'd lie awake much of the night fuming as he reviewed his clients' predicament over and over and plotted legal strategy.

Then, on a vacation, he met a woman who taught meditation and asked her for instruction. To his surprise, she started by handing him a few raisins. She then led him through the steps in eating one of the raisins slowly and with full focus, savoring the richness of every moment in that process: the sensations as he lifted it into his mouth and chewed, the burst of flavors as he bit into it, the sounds of eating. He immersed himself in the fullness of his senses.

Then, as she instructed him, he brought that same full in-the-moment focus to the natural flow of his breath, letting go of any and all thoughts that floated through his mind. With her guidance he continued that meditation on his breath for the next fifteen minutes.

As he did so, the voices in his mind went quiet. "It was like flipping a switch into a Zen-like state," he said. He liked it so much that he has made it a daily habit: "After I'm done, I feel really calm—I like that a lot."

When we turn such full attention to our senses, the brain quiets its default chatter. Brain scans during mindfulness—the form of meditation the lawyer was trying—reveal it quiets the brain circuits for me-focused mental chatter.[3]

That in itself can be an immense relief. "To the extent absorption means dropping this mind-wandering state and getting a total focus on an activity, we're likely to be deactivating the default circuits," neuroscientist Richard Davidson says. "You can't ruminate about yourself while you're absorbed in a challenging task."

"This is one reason people love dangerous sports like mountain climbing, a situation where you have to be totally focused," Davidson adds. Powerful focus brings a sense of peace, and with it, joy. "But when you come down the mountain, the self-referencing network brings your worries and cares right back."

In Aldous Huxley's utopian novel *Island*, trained parrots fly over to people at random and chirp, "Here and now, boys, here and now!" That reminder helps the denizens of this idyllic island pop their daydreams and refocus on what's happening in this very place and moment.

A parrot seems an apt choice as messenger: animals live only in the here-and-now.[4] A cat hopping into a lap to be stroked, a dog eagerly waiting for you at the door, a horse cocking its head to read your intentions as you approach: all share the same focus on the present.

This capacity to think in ways that are independent of an immediate stimulus—about what's happened and what *might* happen in all its possibilities—sets the human mind apart from that of almost every other animal. While many spiritual traditions, like Huxley's parrots, see mind wandering as a source of woe, evolutionary psychologists see this as a great cognitive leap. Both views have some truth.

In Huxley's vision the eternal now harbors everything we need for fulfillment. Yet the human ability to think about things not happening in that eternal present represents a prerequisite for all the achievements of our species that required planning, imagination, or logistic skill. And that's just about everything that's a uniquely human accomplishment.

Mulling things *not* going on here and now—"situation-independent thought" as cognitive scientists call it—demands we decouple the contents of our mind from what our senses perceive at the moment. So far as we know, no other species can make this radical shift from an external focus to an inward one with anything near the power of the human mind, or nearly so often.

The more our mind wanders, the less we can register what's going on right now, right here. Take comprehending what we're reading. When volunteers had their gaze monitored while they read the entirety of Jane Austen's *Sense and Sensibility*, erratic eye movements signaled that a great deal of mindless reading went on.[5] Wandering eyes indicate a breakdown in the connection between understanding and visual contact with the text, as the mind meanders elsewhere (there might have been far less meandering if the volunteers had been free to choose what they read—say *Blink* or *Fifty Shades of Grey*, depending on their taste).

Using tools such as fluctuations in eye gaze or "random experience sampling" (in other words, just asking someone what's happening) while people are having their brains scanned, neuroscientists observe that major neural dynamic: while the mind wanders, our sensory systems shut down, and, conversely, while we focus on the here and now, the neural circuits for mind wandering go dim.

At the neural level mind wandering and perceptual awareness tend to inhibit each other: internal focus on our train of thought tunes out the senses, while being rapt in the beauty of a sunset quiets the mind.[6] This tune-out can be total, as when we get utterly lost in what we're doing.

Our usual neural settings allow a bit of wandering while we engage the world—or just enough engagement while we are adrift, as when we daydream while we drive. Of course, such partial tuning out bears risks: one study of a thousand drivers injured in accidents found that about half said their mind was wandering just before the accident; the more intense the disruptive thoughts, the more likely it was that the driver caused the accident.[7]

Situations that do not demand constant task-focus—particularly boring or routine ones—free the mind to wander. As the mind drifts off and the default network activates more strongly, our neural circuits for task-focus go quiet—another variety of neural decoupling akin to that between the senses and daydreaming. Since daydreaming competes for neural energy with task-focus and sensory perception, there's small wonder that as we daydream we make more errors in anything that requires us to pay focused attention.

THE WANDERING MIND

"Whenever you notice your mind wandering," a fundamental instruction in meditation advises, "bring your mind back to its point of focus." The operative phrase here is *whenever you notice*. As our mind drifts off, we almost never notice the moment it launches into some other orbit on its own. A meander away from the focus of meditation can last seconds, minutes, or the entire session before we notice, if we do at all.

That simple challenge is so hard because the very brain circuits we need to catch our mind as it wanders are recruited into the neural web that sets the mind adrift in the first place.[8] What are they doing? Apparently, managing the random bits that fill a wandering mind into a detailed train of thought, like *How do I pay my bills?* Such thoughts require cooperation between the mind's drifting circuitry and the organizational talents of the executive circuits.[9]

Catching a wandering mind in the act is elusive; more often than not when we are lost in thought we fail to realize that our mind has wandered in the first place. Noticing that our mind has wandered marks a shift in brain activity; the greater this meta-awareness, the weaker the mind wandering becomes.[10] Brain imaging reveals that at the moment we catch our mind adrift that act of meta-awareness lessens the activity of the executive and medial circuits, but it does not completely suppress them.[11]

Modern life values sitting in school or an office, focusing on one thing at a time—an attentional stance that may not always have paid off in early human history. Survival in the wild, some neuroscientists argue, may have depended at crucial moments on a rapidly shifting attention and swift action, without hesitating to think what to do. What we now diagnose as an attentional deficit may reflect a natural variation in focusing styles that had advantages in evolution—and so continues to be dispersed in our gene pool.

When facing a focus-demanding mental task like tough math problems, as we've seen, those with ADD show both more mind wandering and increased activity in the medial circuitry.[12] But when conditions are right, those with ADD can have keen focus, fully absorbed in the activity at hand. Such conditions might arise more often in an art studio, basketball court, or stock exchange floor—just not in the classroom.

AN EVEN KEEL

On 12/12/12, the very day a quirk in the Mayan calendar supposedly foretold as the end of the world (according to clearly unfounded rumors), my wife and I happened to take one of our granddaughters to the Museum of Modern Art. A budding artist, she was keen to see the offerings of that famous New York City museum.

Among the first displays to greet us on entering the first gallery at MoMA were two industrial-sized vacuum cleaners, spotless white three-wheeled cylinders with neat pin-striping. They were stacked one atop the other encased in Plexiglas cubes, the neon lights beneath each making them gleam. Our granddaughter was not impressed; she was eager to see Van Gogh's *Starry Night* in a gallery several floors above.

Just the night before, the main curator at MoMA had convened an evening on the theme of "attention and distraction." The focusing of attention holds the key to museum displays: the frames around the art announce where we should look. Those glass cubes and neon lights directed our attention *here*, toward the sparkling vacuum cleaners, and away from *there*—whatever else was in the gallery.

That point came home to me as we left. Near an out-of-the-way wall in the museum's cavernous lobby I noticed some chairs stacked haphazardly, waiting to be placed for some special event. Lurking near them in the shadows, I could barely discern what appeared to be a vacuum cleaner. No one paid it the least attention.

But our attention need not be at the mercy of how the world around us gets framed; we can choose to observe the vacuum cleaner in the shadow as much as the one in the spotlight. An even keel in attention reflects a mental mode where we simply notice whatever comes into awareness without getting caught up or swept away by any particular thing. Everything flows through.

This openness can be seen in everyday moments when, for instance, you find yourself waiting a turn behind a customer who is taking endless time, and instead of focusing on resentment or on how this will make you late, you simply let yourself enjoy the store's background music.

Emotional reactivity flips us into a different mode of attention, one where our world contracts into fixation on what's upsetting us. Those who have difficulty sustaining open awareness typically get caught up by irritating details like that person in front of them in the security line at the airport who took forever to get carry-on ready for the scanner—and will still be fuming about it while waiting for their plane at the gate. But there are no emotional hijacks in open awareness—just the richness of the moment.

One brain measure for such open attention assesses how well people can track an occasional number embedded in a stream of letters: S, K, O, E, 4, R, T, 2, H, P . . .

Many people, it turns out, fix their attention on the first number, 4, and miss seeing the second, 2. Their attention blinks. Those with strong open focus, though, register the second number, too.

People who are able to rest their attention in this open mode notice more about their surroundings. Even in the bustle of an airport they can maintain awareness of what's going on, rather than getting lost in one detail or another. In brain tests, those who score highest on open awareness register a greater amount of detail flashing by in a moment's time than do most people. Their attention does not blink.[13]

This enriching of attention applies, too, to our interior life—in the open mode we take in far more of our feelings, sensations, thoughts, and memories than we do when, say, we're focused on marching through our to-do list or rushing to back-to-back meetings.

"The capacity to remain with your attention open in a panoramic awareness," says Davidson, "lets you attend with equanimity, without getting caught in a bottom-up capture that ensnares the mind in judging and reactivity, whether negative or positive."

It also decreases mind wandering. The goal, he adds, is to be better able to engage in mind wandering when you want to, and not otherwise.

RESTORING ATTENTION

On vacation at a tropical resort with his family, magazine editor William Falk bemoans, he found himself sitting staring at his work while his daughter waited for him to go to the beach.

"Not so long ago," Falk reflects, "I would have found it unthinkable to work while on vacation; I recall glorious two-week sojourns where I had no contact with bosses, employees, even friends. But that was before I traveled with a smartphone, an iPad, and a laptop, and learned to like living in a constant stream of information and connection."[14]

Consider the cognitive effort demanded by our new normal information overload—the explosion of news streams, emails, phone calls, tweets, blogs, chats, reflections about opinions about opinions that we expose our cognitive processors to daily.

That neural buzz adds tension to the demands of getting something done. Selecting one sharp focus requires inhibiting a multitude of others. The mind has to fight off the pull of everything else, sorting out what's important from what's irrelevant. That takes cognitive effort.

Tightly focused attention gets fatigued—much like an overworked muscle—when we push to the point of cognitive exhaustion. The signs of mental fatigue, such as a drop in effectiveness and a rise in distractedness and irritability, signify that the mental effort needed to sustain focus has depleted the glucose that feeds neural energy.

The antidote to attention fatigue is the same as for the physical kind: take a rest. But what rests a mental muscle?

Try switching from the effort of top-down control to more passive bottom-up activities, taking a relaxing break in a restful setting. The most restful surroundings are in nature, argues Stephen Kaplan at the University of Michigan, who proposes what he calls "attention restoration theory."[15]

Such restoration occurs when we switch from effortful attention, where the mind needs to suppress distractions, to letting go and allowing our attention to be captured by whatever presents itself. But only certain kinds of bottom-up focus act to restore energy for focused attention. Surfing the Web, playing video games, or answering email does not.

We do well to unplug regularly; quiet time restores our focus and composure. But that disengagement is just the first step. What we do next matters, too. Taking a walk down a city street, Kaplan points out, still puts demands on attention—we've got to navigate through crowds, dodge cars, and ignore honking horns and the hum of street noise.

In contrast, a walk through a park or in the woods puts little such demand on attention. We can restore by spending time in nature—even a few minutes strolling in a park or any setting rich in fascinations like the muted reds of clouds at sunset or a butterfly's flutter. This triggers bottom-up attention "modestly," as Kaplan's group put it, allowing circuits for top-down efforts to replenish their energy, restoring attentiveness and memory, and improving cognition.[16]

A walk through an arboretum led to better focus on return to concentrated tasks than a stroll though downtown.[17] Even sitting by a mural of a nature scene—particularly one with water in it—is better than the corner coffee shop.[18]

But I wonder. These moments seem fine for switching off intense concentration, but open the way for the still-busy wandering mind-set of the default circuitry. There's another step we can take in switching off the busy mind: full focus on something relaxing.

The key is an immersive experience, one where attention can be total but largely passive. This starts to happen when we gently arouse the sensory systems, which quiet down those for effortful focus. Anything we can get enjoyably lost in will do it. Remember, in that survey of people's moods the single most focusing activity in anyone's day, and the most pleasant, is lovemaking.

Total, positive absorption shuts off the inner voice, that running dialogue with ourselves that goes on even during our quiet moments. That's a main effect of virtually every contemplative practice that keeps your mind focused on a neutral target, like your breath or a mantra.

Traditional advice for ideal settings for a "retreat" seems to include all the ingredients needed for cognitive restoration. Monasteries designed for meditation are typically in restful, quiet natural environments.

Not that we need go to such extremes. For William Falk, the remedy was simple: he stopped his work and went to play with his daughter in the waves. "Tumbling and hooting in the pounding surf with my daughter, I was fully present in the moment. Fully alive."

PART II

SELF-AWARENESS

6

THE INNER RUDDER

Football, basketball, debate, you name it—the big rival to my high school in the Central Valley of California was in the next town down Highway 99. Over the years I've gotten friendly with a student from that other school.

During high school he wasn't much interested in studies—in fact, he almost flunked out. Growing up on a ranch on the outskirts of town he spent a lot of time alone, reading science fiction and tinkering with hot rods, his passion. The week before he was to graduate, a car sped past from behind as he was making a left turn into his driveway, smashing his small sports car to bits. He almost died.

After recuperating, my friend went to the local community college, where he discovered a calling that riveted his attention and mobilized his creative talents: filmmaking. After transferring to a film school he made a movie for his student project that caught the eye of a Hollywood director, who hired him as an assistant. The director asked my friend to work on a pet project, a small-budget film.

That, in turn, led to my friend getting a studio to back him as director and producer of another small film based on his own script—a movie that the studio almost killed before its release, yet which did surprisingly better than anyone expected.

But the arbitrary cuts, edits, and other changes the studio bosses made before releasing that movie were a bitter lesson for my friend, who valued creative control of his work as paramount. When he went on to make a movie based on another script of his own, a big Hollywood studio offered him a standard deal whereby the studio financed the project and held the power to change the film before its release. He refused the deal—his artistic integrity was more important.

Instead my friend "bought" creative control by going off on his own and putting every penny of his profits from the first film into this second project. When he was almost done, his money ran out. He went looking for loans, but bank after bank turned him down. Only a last-minute loan from the tenth bank he implored saved the project.

The film was *Star Wars*.

George Lucas's insistence on keeping creative control despite the financial struggle that it entailed for him signifies enormous integrity—and, as the world knows, it also turned out to be a lucrative business decision. But this decision wasn't motivated by the pursuit of money; back then ancillary rights meant selling movie posters and T-shirts, a trivial source of revenue. At the time, everyone who knew the film industry warned George against going out on his own.

Such a decision requires immense confidence in one's own guiding values. What allows people to have such a strong inner compass, a North Star that steers them through life according to the dictates of their deepest values and purposes?

Self-awareness, particularly accuracy in decoding the internal cues of our body's murmurs, holds the key. Our subtle physiological reactions reflect the sum total of our experience relevant to the decision at hand.

The decision rules derived from our life experiences reside in subcortical neural networks that gather, store, and apply algorithms from every event in our lives—creating our inner rudder.[1]

The brain harbors our deepest sense of purpose and meaning in these subcortical regions—areas connected poorly to the verbal areas of the neocortex, but richly to the gut. We know our values by first getting a visceral sense of what feels right and what does not, then articulating those feelings for ourselves.

Self-awareness, then, represents an essential focus, one that attunes us to the subtle murmurs within that can help guide our way through life. And, as we shall see, this inner radar holds the key to managing what we do—and just as important, what we *don't* do. This internal control mechanism makes all the difference between a life well lived and one that falters.

SHE'S HAPPY AND SHE KNOWS IT

The scientific test for self-awareness in animals is, in theory, simple: put a mark on their face, show them a mirror, and observe whether their actions indicate they realize that the face with the mark over there reflects their own.

Actually doing such a test for self-awareness in elephants is not so simple. For starters, you need to build an elephant-proof mirror. Try an eight-foot-by-eight-foot acrylic reflecting surface glued to plywood supported by steel framing, and bolted to the concrete wall of an elephant enclosure.

That's what researchers did at the Bronx Zoo, where Happy, a thirty-four-year-old Asian elephant, lives with her two hulking friends, Maxine and Patty. The researchers let the elephants get used to the mirrors for a few days. Then they put a large white X on the head of one or another of the elephants to see if she would realize she had a mark there—an indication of self-recognition.

There's a further complication when it comes to testing elephants. They "groom" themselves by taking mud baths and spraying dust all over themselves with their trunks. That adds a fair amount of debris to their skin, upping the odds that what we humans think of as a prominent mark might be trivial—just more of the usual detritus—to an elephant. And, indeed, Maxine and Patty paid no attention to their X.

But the day Happy got the big white X on her head she went over to the mirror and spent ten seconds looking at herself, then walked off—rather like humans when we glance in the mirror before going out to start our day. She then repeatedly felt around the X with the sensitive tip of her trunk, signifying self-awareness.

Only a highly select few in the animal kingdom have passed this test, including some varieties of apes and chimps, and dolphins (in an aquatic adaptation of the test). These species, like elephants, are among the handful of animals whose brains harbor a class of neurons some neuroscientists believe are uniquely essential for self-awareness. Named for their discoverer, Constantin von Economo (and called VENs for short), these spindle-shaped neurons can be double the size of most brain cells and have fewer branches—though much longer ones—connecting to other cells.[2]

Their size and spindle-like shape give VENs a unique advantage over other neurons: the signals they send travel faster and farther. And their main locations in areas that connect the executive brain to the emotional centers position them as personal radar. These areas light up when we see our reflection in the mirror. Neuroscientists see them as part of the brain's circuitry for our sense of self at every level: of "this is me," of "how I feel now," and of our personal identity.

THE BRAIN'S MAP OF THE BODY

After being diagnosed with the liver cancer that was to take his life a few years later, Steve Jobs gave a heartfelt talk to a graduating class at Stanford University. His advice: "Don't let the voice of others' opinions drown out your inner voice. And most important, have the courage to follow your heart and intuition. They somehow already know what you truly want to become."[3]

But how do you hear "your inner voice," what your heart and intuition somehow already know? You need to depend on your body's signals.

You may have seen the rather bizarre image of a body as mapped by the somatosensory cortex, which tracks the sensations registered by various areas of our skin: this critter has a tiny head but huge lips and tongue, teeny arms but giant fingers—all reflecting the relative sensitivity of nerves in various body parts.

Similar monitoring of our internal organs is done by the insula, tucked behind the frontal lobes of the brain. The insula maps our body's insides via circuitry linking to our gut, heart, liver, lungs, genitals—every organ has its specific spot. This lets the insula act as a control center for organ functions, sending signals to the heart to slow its beat, the lungs to take a deeper breath.

Attention turned inward toward any part of the body amps up the insula's sensitivity to the particular area we're checking on. Tune in to your heartbeat and the insula activates more neurons in that circuitry. How well people can sense their heartbeat, in fact, has become a standard way to measure their self-awareness. The better people are at this, the bigger their insula.[4]

The insula attunes us to more than our organs; our very sense of how we are feeling depends on it.[5] People who are oblivious to their own emotions (and also—tellingly, as we'll see—to how other people feel) have sluggish insula activity compared with the high activation found in people highly attuned to their inner emotional life. At the tuned-out extreme are those with alexithymia, who just don't know what they feel, and can't imagine what someone else might be feeling.[6]

Our "gut feelings" are messages from the insula and other bottom-up circuits that simplify life decisions for us by guiding our attention toward smarter options. The better we are at reading these messages, the better our intuition.

Take that tug you might sometimes feel when you suspect you're forgetting something important just as you're leaving on a big trip. A marathon runner tells me of a time she was on her way to a race four hundred miles away. She felt that tug—and ignored it. But as she continued on down the freeway, it kept coming back. Then she realized what was tugging at her: she had forgotten her shoes!

A stop at a mall that was just about to close saved the day. But her new shoes were a different brand from the ones she normally wore. As she told me, "I have never been more sore!"

Somatic marker is neuroscientist Antonio Damasio's term for the sensations in our body that tell us when a choice feels wrong or right.[7] This bottom-up circuitry telegraphs its conclusions through our gut feelings, often long before the top-down circuits come to a more reasoned conclusion.

The ventromedial prefrontal area, a key part of this circuitry, guides our decision making when we face life's most complex decisions, like who to marry or whether to buy a house. Such choices can't be made by a cold, rational analysis. Instead we do better to simulate what it would feel like to choose A versus B. This brain area operates as that inner rudder.

There are two major streams of self-awareness: "me," which builds narratives about our past and future; and "I," which brings us into the immediate present. The "me," as we've seen, links together what we experience across time. The "I," in stark contrast, exists only in the raw experience of our immediate moment.

The "I," our most intimate sense of our self, reflects the piecemeal sum of our sensory impressions—particularly our body states. "I" builds from our brain's system for mapping the body via the insula.[8]

Such internal signals are our inner guides, helping us at many levels, from living a life in keeping with our guiding values to remembering our running shoes.

As a veteran performer at Cirque du Soleil told me, for their grueling routines Cirque performers strive for what she called "perfect practice," where the laws of physical motion and rules of biomechanics come together with timing, angles, and speed, so you get "more perfect more of the time—you're never perfect all of the time."

And how do the performers know when they're nearing perfection? "It's the feeling. You know it in your joints before you know it in your head."

7

SEEING OURSELVES AS OTHERS SEE US

"We have a 'No jerks allowed' rule, but our chief tech officer is one," an executive at a California tech incubator tells me. "He executes very well, but he's a huge bully, freezes people out who he doesn't like, plays favorites.

"He's got zero self-awareness," she adds. "He just does not realize when he's being a bully. If you point out to him he's just done it again, he shifts the blame, gets angry, or thinks you're the problem."

The company's CEO later told me, "We worked with him for another three months or so, and then finally had to let him go. He couldn't change—he was a bully, and didn't even see it."

All too often when we "lose it" and fall back on a less desirable way of acting, we're oblivious to what we do. And if no one tells us, we stay that way.

One surefire test for self-awareness is a "360-degree" evaluation, where you're asked to rate yourself on a range of specific behaviors or traits. Those self-ratings are checked against evaluations by a dozen or so people whom you have asked to rate you on the same scale. You pick them because they know you well and you respect their judgment—and their ratings are anonymous, so they can feel free to be frank. The gap between how you see yourself and how the others rate you offers one of the best evaluations you can get anywhere of your own self-awareness.

There's an intriguing relationship between self-awareness and power: There are relatively few gaps between one's own and others' ratings among lower-level employees. But the higher someone's position in an organization, the bigger the gap.[1] Self-awareness seems to diminish with promotions up the organization's ladder.

One theory: That gap widens because as people rise in power within an organization the circle shrinks of others willing or courageous enough to speak to them honestly about their quirks. Then there are those who simply deny their deficits, or can't see them in the first place.

Whatever the reason, tuned-out leaders see themselves as being far more effective than do those they are guiding. A lack of self-awareness leaves you clueless. Think *The Office*.

A 360-degree evaluation applies the power of seeing ourselves through the eyes of others, which offers another pathway to self-awareness. Robert Burns, the Scottish poet, praised this pathway in verse:

> *Oh that the gods*
> *The gift would gi'e us*
> *To see ourselves*
> *As others see us.*

A more sardonic view was offered by W. H. Auden, who observed that, so "I may love myself," we each create a positive self-image in our minds by selective forgetting of what's unflattering to us and recalling what's admirable about us. And, he added, we do something similar with the image we try to create "in the minds of others in order that they may love me."

And philosopher George Santayana took this full circle, by noting that what other people think of us would matter little—except that once we know it, it "so deeply tinges what we think of ourselves." Social philosophers have called this mirroring effect the "looking glass self," how we imagine others see us.

Our sense of self, in this view, dawns in our social interactions; others are our mirrors, reflecting us back to ourselves. The idea has been summed up as "I am what I think you think I am."

THROUGH OTHERS' EYES—AND EARS

Life affords us little chance to see how others really see us. That may be why the course Bill George teaches at Harvard Business School, called Authentic Leadership Development, is among the most popular, overenrolled every time it is offered (the same goes with a similar course at Stanford's business school).

As George told me, "We don't know who we are until we hear ourselves speaking the story of our lives to someone we trust." To expedite that heightening of self-awareness, George has created what he calls "True North Groups," with "True North" referring to finding one's inner compass and core values. His course gives students the chance to be in such a group.

A precept of the groups: self-knowledge begins with self-revelation.

These groups (which anyone can form) are as open and intimate as—or even more so than—twelve-step meetings or therapy groups, according to George, providing "a safe place where members can discuss personal issues they do not feel they can raise elsewhere—often not even with their closest family members."[2]

It's not just seeing ourselves as others see us. There's also hearing ourselves as others hear us. We don't.

The journal *Surgery* reports a study where surgeons' tone of voice was evaluated, based on ten-second snippets recorded during sessions with their patients.[3] Half the surgeons whose voices were rated had been sued for malpractice; half had not. The voices of those who had been sued were far more often rated as domineering and uncaring.

Surgeons spend more time than most other physicians explaining technical details to their patients, as well as disclosing the worst risks of surgery. It's a difficult conversation, one that can put patients into a state of high anxiety and a heightened vigilance to emotional cues.

When it comes to the patient listening to the surgeon explain the technical details—and the frightening potential risks—the brain's radar for danger goes into high alert, searching for cues and clues to how safe all this really might be. That heightened sensitivity may be one reason the empathy or concern—or rather, the lack of either—conveyed in a surgeon's tone of voice tends to predict whether he will be sued if something goes wrong.

The acoustics of our skull case render our voice as it sounds to us very different from what others hear. But our tone of voice matters immensely to the impact of what we say: research has found that when people receive negative performance feedback in a warm, supportive tone of voice, they leave feeling positive—despite the negative feedback. But when they get positive performance reviews in a cold and distant tone of voice, they end up feeling bad despite the good news.[4]

One remedy proposed in the *Surgery* article: give surgeons an audio replay of their voice as they talked to patients, so they can hear how they sound and get coaching on ways to make their voice communicate empathy and caring—to hear themselves as others hear them.

GROUPTHINK: SHARED BLIND SPOTS

In the wake of the economic meltdown of investment vehicles based on subprime derivatives, a financial type whose job had been creating those very derivative instruments was interviewed. He explained how in his job he would routinely take huge lots of subprime mortgages and divide them into three tranches: the best of the worst, the not-as-good, and the worst of the worst. Then he would take each of the tranches and again divide it into thirds—and create derivatives for investments based on each.

He was asked, "Who would want to buy these?"

His reply: "Idiots."

Of course, seemingly very smart people did invest in those derivatives, ignoring signals that they were not worth the risk, and emphasizing whatever might support their decision. When this tendency to ignore evidence to the contrary spreads into a shared self-deception, it becomes groupthink. The unstated need to protect a treasured opinion (by discounting crucial disconfirming data) drives shared blind spots that lead to bad decisions.

President George W. Bush's inner circle and their decision to invade Iraq based on imaginary "weapons of mass destruction" offers a classic example. So do the circles of financial players who fostered the mortgage derivatives meltdown. Both instances of catastrophic groupthink entailed insulated groups of decision-makers who failed to ask the right questions or ignored disconfirming data in a self-affirming downward spiral.

Cognition is distributed among members of a group or network: some people are specialists in one area, while others have complementary strengths of expertise. When information flows most freely among the group and into it, the best decisions will be made. But groupthink begins with the unstated assumption *We know everything we need to.*

A firm that manages investments for very wealthy people gave Daniel Kahneman a treasure trove: eight years of investment results for twenty-five of its financial advisers. Analyzing the data, Kahneman found that there were no relationships between any given adviser's results from year to year—in other words, none of the advisers was consistently any better than the others at managing the clients' money. The results were no better than chance.

Yet everyone behaved as though there were a special skill involved—and the top performers each year got big bonuses. His results in hand, Kahneman had dinner with the top brass at the firm and informed them that they were "rewarding luck as if it were skill."

That should have been shocking news. But the executives calmly went on with their dinner and, Kahneman says, "I have no doubt that the implications were quickly swept under the rug and that life in the firm went on just as before."[5]

The illusion of skill, deeply embedded in the culture of that industry, was under attack. But "facts that challenge such basic assumptions—and thereby threaten people's livelihood and self-esteem—are simply not absorbed," he adds.

Back in the 1960s, as the civil rights movement was boiling in the South, I joined a picket line at a local grocery store in my California hometown that did not then hire African-Americans. But it was not until years later, when I heard about the work of John Ogbu, a Nigerian anthropologist then at the University of California, Berkeley—who came to my nearby town to study what he called its "caste system"—that I realized there *was* one, a kind of de facto segregation.[6] My high school was all-white, with a sprinkling of Asians and Hispanics; another high school was mostly black, with some Hispanics; the third was a mix. I had just never thought about it.

When it came to the grocery store, I could readily see *their* part in discrimination—but I was blind to the larger pattern I was enmeshed within, the overall social ladder inherent in where people lived, and so where they went to school (in those days). Inequity in a society fades into the background, something we habituate to rather than orient toward. It takes effort to shift it back into our collective focus.

Such self-deception seems a universal twist of attention. For instance, when drivers rated their abilities behind the wheel, about three-quarters thought they were better than average. Strangely, those who had been in an auto accident were *more* likely to rate themselves as better drivers than did those whose driving record was accident-free.

Even stranger: In general, most people rate themselves as being less likely than others to overrate their abilities. These inflated self-ratings reflect the "better-than-average" effect, which has been found for just about any positive trait, from competence and creativity to friendliness and honesty.

I read Kahneman's account in his fascinating book *Thinking Fast and Slow* while on a Boston-to-London flight. As the plane landed I chatted with the fellow across the aisle, who had been eyeing the cover. He told me he planned to read the book—and happened to mention that he invested the assets of wealthy individuals.

As our plane taxied down the long runway and found its way to our gate at Heathrow, I summarized the main points for him, including this tale about the financial firm—adding that it seemed to imply his industry rewarded luck as though it were skill.

"I guess," he replied with a shrug, "I don't have to read the book now."

When Kahneman had reported his results to the money managers themselves, they responded with a similar indifference. As he says of such disconcerting data, "The mind does not digest them."

It takes meta-cognition—in this case, awareness of our lack of awareness—to bring to light what the group has buried in a grave of indifference or suppression. Clarity begins with realizing what we do not notice—and don't notice that we don't notice.

Smart risks are based on wide and voracious data-gathering checked against a gut sense; dumb decisions are built from too narrow a base of inputs. Candid feedback from those you trust and respect creates a source of self-awareness, one that can help guard against skewed information inputs or questionable assumptions. Another antidote to groupthink: expand your circle of connection beyond your comfort zone and inoculate against in-group isolation by building an ample circle of no-BS confidants who keep you honest.

A smart diversification goes beyond gender and ethnic group balance to include a wide range of ages, clients, or customers, and any others who might offer a fresh perspective.

"Early on in our operation, our servers failed," an executive at a cloud computing company says. "Our competitors were monitoring us, and soon we got a flood of calls from reporters asking what was going on. We didn't answer the calls, because we didn't know what to say.

"Then one employee, a former journalist, came up with a creative solution: a website called 'Trust Cloud' where we were completely open about what was happening with our server—what the problem was, how we were trying to fix it, everything."

That was a foreign idea to most executives there; they had come from tech companies where heightened secrecy was routine. The unquestioned assumption that they should keep the problem to themselves was a potential seed of groupthink.

"But once we became transparent," the executive says, "the problem went away. Our customers were reassured they could know what was happening, and reporters stopped calling."

"Sunlight," as Supreme Court justice Felix Frankfurter once said, "is the best disinfectant."

8

A RECIPE FOR SELF-CONTROL

When my sons were just two or so and would get upset, I sometimes used distraction to calm them down: *Look at that birdie*, or an all-service, enthusiastic *What's that?* with my gaze or finger directing their focus toward something or other.

Attention regulates emotion. This little ploy uses selective attention to quiet the agitated amygdala. So long as a toddler stays tuned to some interesting object of focus, the distress calms; the moment that thing loses its fascination, the distress, if still held on to by networks in the amygdala, comes roaring back.[1] The trick, of course, lies in keeping the baby intrigued long enough for the amygdala to calm.

As infants learn to use this attention maneuver for themselves, they acquire one of their first emotional self-regulation skills—one that has vast importance for their destiny in life: how to manage the unruly amygdala. Such a ploy takes executive attention, a capacity that starts to flower in the third year of life when a toddler can show "effortful control"—focusing at will, ignoring distractions, and inhibiting impulse.

Parents might notice this landmark when a toddler makes the intentional choice to say "no" to a temptation, like waiting for dessert until after she's taken some more bites of what's on her plate. That, too, depends on executive attention, which blossoms into willpower and self-discipline—as in managing our disturbing feelings and ignoring whims so we can stay focused on a goal.

By age eight most children master greater degrees of executive attention. This mental tool manages the operation of other brain networks for cognitive skills like learning to read and do math, and academics in general (we'll look into this more in part 5).

Our mind deploys self-awareness to keep everything we do on track: meta-cognition—thinking about thinking—lets us know how our mental operations are going and adjust them as needed; meta-emotion does the same with regulating the flow of feeling and impulse. In the mind's design, self-awareness is built into regulating our own emotions, as well as sensing what others feel. Neuroscientists see self-control through the lens of the brain zones underlying executive function, which manages mental skills like self-awareness and self-regulation, critical for navigating our lives.[2]

Executive attention holds the key to self-management. This power to direct our focus onto one thing and ignore others lets us bring to mind our waistline when we spot those quarts of Cheesecake Brownie ice cream in the freezer. This small choice point harbors the core of willpower, the essence of self-regulation.

The brain is the last organ of the body to mature anatomically, continuing to grow and shape itself into our twenties—and the networks for attention are like an organ that develops in parallel with the brain.

As every parent of more than one child knows, from day one each baby differs: one is more alert, or calmer, or more active than another. Such differences in temperament reflect the maturation and genetics of various brain networks.[3]

How much of our talent for attention comes from our genes? It depends. Different attention systems, it turns out, have different degrees of heritability.[4] The strongest heritability is for executive control.

Even so, building this vital skill depends to a large extent on what we learn in life. Epigenetics, the science of how our environment affects our genes, tells us that inheriting a set of genes is not in itself enough for them to matter. Genes have what amounts to a biochemical on/off switch; if they are never turned on we may as well not have them. The "on" switch comes in many forms, including what we eat, the dance of chemical reactions within the body, and what we learn.

WILLPOWER IS DESTINY

Decades of research results show the singular importance of willpower in determining the course of life. One of the first of these was a small project in the 1960s in which kids from deprived homes were given special attention in a preschool program that helped them cultivate self-control, among other life skills.[5] That project had hoped to boost their IQ, but it failed at that. Still, years later, when those preschoolers were compared with similar kids who had not participated in the program, over the course of life they had lower rates of teen pregnancies, school dropouts, delinquency, and even days missed from work.[6] The findings were a major argument for what has become the Head Start preschool programs, now found everywhere in the United States.

And then there was the "marshmallow test," a legendary study done by psychologist Walter Mischel at Stanford University in the 1970s. Mischel invited four-year-olds one by one into a "game room" at the Bing Nursery School on the Stanford campus. In the room the child was shown a tray with marshmallows or other treats and told to pick one she would like.

Then came the hard part. The experimenter told the child, "You can have your treat now, if you want. But if you don't eat it until I come back from running an errand, you can have two then."

The room was sanitized of distractions: no toys, no books, not even a picture. Self-control was a major feat for a four-year-old under such dire conditions. About a third grabbed the marshmallow on the spot, while another third or so waited the endless fifteen minutes until they were rewarded with two (the other third fell somewhere in the middle). Most significant: the ones who resisted the lure of the sweet had higher scores on measures of executive control, particularly the reallocation of attention.

How we focus holds the key to willpower, says Mischel. His hundreds of hours of observation of little kids fighting off temptation reveal "the strategic allocation of attention," as he puts it, to be the crucial skill. The kids who waited out the full fifteen minutes did it by distracting themselves with tactics like pretend play, singing songs, or covering their eyes. If a kid just stared at the marshmallow, he was a goner (or more precisely, the marshmallow was).

At least three sub-varieties of attention, all aspects of the executive, are at play when we pit self-restraint against instant gratification. The first is the ability to voluntarily disengage our focus from an object of desire that powerfully grabs our attention. The second, resisting distraction, lets us keep our focus elsewhere—say, on fantasy play—rather than gravitating back to that juicy whatever. And the third allows us to keep our focus on a goal in the future, like the two marshmallows later. All that adds up to willpower.

Well and good for children who show self-control in a contrived situation like the marshmallow test. But what about resisting the temptations of real life? Enter the children of Dunedin, New Zealand.

Dunedin has a populace of just over one hundred thousand

souls and houses one of that country's largest universities. This combination made the town ripe for what may be the most significant study yet in the annals of science on the ingredients of life success.

In a dauntingly ambitious project, 1,037 children—all the babies born over a period of twelve months—were studied intensively in childhood and then tracked down decades later by a team assembled from several countries. The team represented many disciplines, each with its own perspective on that key marker for self-awareness, self-control.[7]

These kids underwent an impressive battery of tests over their school years, such as assessing their tolerance for frustration and their restlessness, on the one hand, and powers of concentration and persistence on the other.[8]

After a two-decade lull all but 4 percent of the kids were tracked down (a feat far easier in a stable country like New Zealand than, say, in the hypermobile United States). By then young adults, they were assessed for:

- *Health.* Physicals and lab tests looked at their cardiovascular, metabolic, psychiatric, respiratory, even dental and inflammatory conditions.
- *Wealth.* Whether they had savings, were single and raising a child, owned a home, had credit problems, had investments, or had retirement funds.
- *Crime.* All court records in Australia and New Zealand were searched to see if they had been convicted of a crime.

The better their self-control in childhood, the better the Dunedin kids were doing in their thirties. They had sounder health, were more successful financially, and were law-abiding citizens.

The worse their childhood impulse management, the less they made, the shakier their health, and the more likely it was that they had a criminal record.

The big shock: statistical analysis found that a child's level of self-control is every bit as powerful a predictor of her adult financial success and health (and criminal record, for that matter) as are social class, wealth of family of origin, or IQ. Willpower emerged as a completely independent force in life success—in fact, for financial success, self-control in childhood proved a *stronger* predictor than either IQ or social class of the family of origin.

The same goes for school success. In an experiment where American eighth graders were offered a dollar now or two dollars in a week, this simple gauge of self-control turned out to correlate with their grade point average better than did their IQ. High self-control predicts not just better grades, but also a good emotional adjustment, better interpersonal skills, a sense of security, and adaptability.[9]

Bottom line: kids can have the most economically privileged childhood, yet if they don't master how to delay gratification in pursuit of their goals those early advantages may wash out in the course of life. In the United States, for example, only two in five children of parents in the top 20 percent of wealth end up in that privileged status; about 6 percent drift down to the bottom 20 percent in income.[10] Conscientiousness seems as powerful a boost in the long run as fancy schools, SAT tutors, and pricey educational summer camps. Don't underestimate the value of practicing the guitar or keeping that promise to feed the guinea pig and clean its cage.

Another bottom line: Anything we can do to increase children's capacity for cognitive control will help them throughout life. Even Cookie Monster can learn to do better.

COOKIE MONSTER LEARNS TO NIBBLE

The day I dropped by Sesame Workshop, headquarters for the TV neighborhood of Bert and Ernie, Big Bird, Cookie Monster, and the rest of the gang beloved in the 120-plus nations where Sesame Street airs, there was a meeting of the core staff with cognitive and brain scientists.

Sesame Street's DNA wraps entertainment around the science of learning. "At the core of every clip on *Sesame Street* is a curriculum goal," said Michael Levine, executive director of the Joan Ganz Cooney Center at the show's workshop. "Everything we show is pretested for its educational value."

A network of academic experts reviews show content, while the real experts—preschoolers themselves—ensure that the target audience will understand the message. And shows with a particular focus, like a math concept, are tested again for their educational impact on what the preschoolers actually learned.

That day's meeting with scientists had cognitive essentials as a theme. "We need top researchers sitting with top writers in developing the shows," said Levine. "But we need to get it right: listen to the scientists, but then play with it—have some fun."

Take a lesson in impulse control, the secret sauce in a segment about the Cookie Connoisseur Club. Alan, the owner of Hooper's Store on Sesame Street, baked cookies to be sampled by the club—but no one had planned for Cookie Monster to join. When Cookie arrives by surprise on the scene he, of course, wants to eat all the cookies.

Alan explains to Cookie that if you want to be a member of the club, you need to control your impulse to gobble up all the cookies. Instead, you learn to savor the experience. First you pick up the cookie and look for imperfections, then smell it, and finally nibble a bit. But Cookie, impulse embodied, can only gobble the cookie down.

To get the self-regulation strategies right in this segment, says Rosemarie Truglio, senior vice president for education and research, they consulted with none other than Walter Mischel, the mastermind behind the marshmallow test.

Mischel proposed teaching Cookie cognitive control strategies like "Think of the cookie as something else" and reminding himself of that something. So Cookie sees the cookie is round and looks like a yo-yo, and dutifully repeats to himself over and over that the cookie is a yo-yo. But then he gobbles anyway.

To help Cookie take just a nibble—a major triumph of willpower—Mischel suggested a different impulse-delay strategy. Alan tells Cookie, "I know this is hard for you, but what's more important: this cookie now, or getting into the club where you'll get all kinds of cookies?" That did the trick.

A mind too easily distracted by the least hint of a cookie will not have the staying power to understand fractions, let alone calculus. Parts of the *Sesame Street* curriculum highlight such elements of executive control, which creates a mental platform prerequisite for tackling the "STEM" topics: science, technology, engineering, and math.

"Teachers in early grades tell us, I need kids to come to me ready to sit down, focus, manage their emotions, listen to directions, collaborate, and make friends," Truglio explained. "Then I can teach them letters and numbers."

"Cultivating a sense for math and early literacy skills," Levine told me, requires self-control, based on changes in executive function during the preschool years. The inhibitory controls related to executive functioning correlate closely with both early math and reading ability. "Teaching these self-regulation skills," he added, "may actually rewire parts of the brain for kids in whom they have been underdeveloped."

THE POWER TO CHOOSE

Like this piece of art? People around the world say depictions of scenes like this are among their very favorite: an idyllic view from a high vantage point, looking toward water, a meadow, maybe some animals. Perhaps this universal preference dates back to the long epoch in human prehistory when our species roamed the savannas, or huddled in caves tucked into a hillside for protection and warmth.

If from here you manage to stay with what I've written and not look back at that peaceful scene, though you may feel a mental pull to peek, you create in your own brain a tussle between focus and distraction. That tension occurs anytime we try to stay concentrated on one thing and ignore the lure of another. It means there's a neural conflict going on, an arousal level tug-of-war in top-down versus bottom-up circuitry.

And by the way, remember, don't look over there at that art—stay right here with what I'm telling you about what's going on in your brain. This inner conflict duplicates the battle a kid fights when her mind wants to wander away from her math homework, to check for texts from her BFF.[11]

Test high school students for their natural talent in math and you'll find a spread: some kids are pretty terrible, many are merely not so good, and 10 percent or so show great potential. Take that top 10 percent and track them as they go through a tough math class for a year; most will get top grades. But contrary to predictions, a portion of these high-potential students will fare poorly.

Now give each of the math students a device that buzzes at random times through the day and asks them to rate their mood at that moment. If they happen to be working on math, those who did well will report being in a positive mood far more often than being in an anxious one. But those who do poorly will report the reverse: about five times more anxious episodes than pleasant episodes.[12]

That ratio holds a secret of why those with great potential for learning can sometimes end up floundering. Attention, cognitive science tells us, has a limited capacity: working memory creates a bottleneck that lets us hold just so much in mind at any given moment (as we saw in chapter 1). As our worries intrude on the limited capacity of our attention, these irrelevant thoughts shrink the bandwidth left for, say, math.

The ability to notice that we are getting anxious and to take steps to renew our focus rests on self-awareness. Such metacognition lets us keep our mind in the state best suited for the task at hand, whether algebraic equations, following a recipe, or haute couture. Whatever our best talents may be, self-awareness will help us display them at their peak.

Of the many nuances and varieties of attention, two matter greatly for self-awareness. Selective attention lets us focus on one target and ignore everything else. Open attention lets us take in information widely in the world around us and the world within us, and pick up subtle cues we'd otherwise miss.

Extremes in either of these kinds of attention—being too focused outwardly or too open to what's going on around us—can, as Richard Davidson puts it, "make it impossible to be self-aware."[13] Executive function includes attention to attention itself, or more generally, awareness of our mental states; this lets us monitor our focus and keep it on track.

Executive function (as cognitive control is sometimes called) can be taught (as we've just seen, and will explore in more detail in part 5). Teaching executive skills to preschoolers makes them more ready for their school years than does a high IQ or having already learned to read.[14] As the *Sesame Street* team knows, teachers want students with good executive function, as signified by self-discipline, attention control, and the ability to resist temptations. Such executive functions predict good math and reading scores throughout school, apart from—and more than—a child's IQ.[15]

Of course it's not just for kids. This power to direct our focus onto one thing and ignore others lies at the core of willpower.

A BAG OF BONES

In fifth-century India, monks were encouraged to contemplate the "thirty-two body parts," a list of unappealing corners of human biology: dung, bile, phlegm, pus, blood, fat, snot, and so on. This focus on distasteful aspects was meant to build detachment from one's own body, as well as to help celibate monks disavow lust—in other words, to boost willpower.

Fast-forward sixteen hundred years and contrast that ascetic effort with its extreme opposite. As I was told by a social worker who rescues teen sex workers in Los Angeles: "It's unbelievable how impulsive some kids can be. They live on the streets, but if they got a thousand dollars, they'd spend it all on the most expensive iPhone, instead of getting a roof over their heads to find the security they need."

His program helps HIV-infected youngsters get government funds; takes them off the streets; and gives them free medical care, a stipend for an apartment and food, even a gym membership. "I actually saw friends of some of these kids," he tells me, "go out to become HIV-positive so they could get the benefits."

That same contrast between high cognitive control and its utter lack was discovered in a more innocent vein years ago in that Stanford test of gratification delay in four-year-olds tempted by a marshmallow. When fifty-seven of those Stanford preschoolers were tracked down forty years later, "high delayers" who resisted the marshmallow at age four were still able to delay gratification, but the "low delayers" were still poor at stifling impulse.

Then their brains were scanned while they resisted temptation. High delayers activated circuits in their prefrontal cortex key to controlling thoughts and actions—including the right inferior frontal gyrus, which says no to impulse. But low delayers activated their ventral striatum, a circuit in the brain's reward system that springs to life when we yield to life's temptations and guilty pleasures, like a drug or a luscious dessert.[16]

In the Dunedin study, the teen years mattered especially for cognitive control. As adolescents those lower in self-control were the ones most likely to take up smoking, to become an unplanned teen parent, or to drop out of school—all snares that close doors to later opportunities and trap them in lifestyles that accelerate that path to lower-income jobs, poorer health, and, in some cases, criminal careers.

So does this mean that kids with hyperactivity or attention

deficit disorder are doomed to problems? Not at all—as for kids overall, there was a gradient of bad-to-good outcomes among those with ADHD. Even for this group relatively greater self-control predicted a better life outcome, despite their attention problems while in school.

It's not just four-year-olds and teens. The chronic cognitive overload that typifies life for so many of us seems to lower our threshold for self-control. The greater the demands on our attention, it seems, the poorer we get at resisting temptations. The epidemic of obesity in developed countries, research suggests, may be due in part to our greater susceptibility, while distracted, to go on automatic and reach for sugary, fatty foods. Those who have been most successful at losing pounds and keeping them off, brain imaging studies find, exhibit the most cognitive control when facing a calorie-laden morsel.[17]

Freud's famous dictum "Where id was, there ego shall be" speaks directly to this inner tension. Id—the bundle of impulses that make us reach for the Dove Bar, buy that really-too-expensive luxury item, or click on that luscious but totally time-wasting website—constantly struggles with our ego, the mind's executive. Ego lets us lose weight, save money, and allot time effectively.

In the mind's arena, willpower (a facet of "ego") represents a wrestling match between top and bottom systems. Willpower keeps us focused on our goals despite the tug of our impulses, passions, habits, and cravings. This cognitive control represents a "cool" mental system that makes an effort to pursue our goals in the face of our "hot" emotional reactions—quick, impulsive, and automatic.

The two systems signify a critical difference in focus. The reward circuits fixate on hot cognition, thoughts with a high emotional charge, like what's tempting about the marshmallow (*it's yummy, sweet, and chewy*). The greater the charge, the stronger the impulse—and the more likely it is that our more sober-minded prefrontal lobes will be hijacked by our desires.

That prefrontal executive system, in contrast, "cools the hot," by suppressing the impulse to grab, and reappraising the temptation itself (*it's also fattening*). You (or your four-year-old) can activate this system by thinking about, for example, the shape of the marshmallow, or its color, or how it's made. This switch in focus lowers the energy charge to grab for it.

Just as he suggested for Cookie Monster, in his experiments at Stanford Mischel helped some of the kids out with a simple mental trick: he taught them to imagine that the candy is just a picture with a frame around it. Suddenly that irresistible hunk of sugar that loomed so large in their mind became something they could pretend was not real, something they could focus on or not. Changing their relationship to the marshmallow was a bit of mental judo that let kids who hadn't been able to delay their grab for the sweet more than one minute deftly resist temptation for fifteen.

Such cognitive control of impulse bodes well in life. As Mischel puts it, "If you can deal with hot emotions, then you can study for the SAT instead of watching television. And you can save more money for retirement. It's not just about the marshmallow."[18]

Intentional distractions, cognitive reappraisal, and other metacognitive strategies entered psychology's playbook in the 1970s. But similar mental maneuvers were deployed long ago by those fifth-century monks as they contemplated the body's "loathsome" parts.

A tale from those days has it that one of these monks is walking along when a gorgeous woman comes running by.[19] That morning she had a heated quarrel with her husband and she's now fleeing to her parents' house.

A few minutes later, her husband, in pursuit, shows up and asks the monk, "Venerable sir, did you by any chance see a woman go by?"

And the monk answers, "Man or woman, I cannot say. But a bag of bones passed this way."

PART III

READING OTHERS

9

THE WOMAN WHO KNEW TOO MUCH

Her father had an explosive temper, and as a child she was always terrified that he might be about to erupt. So Katrina, as I'll call her, learned to be hypervigilant, straining to sense the small cues—a rise in his tone of voice, the lowering of his eyebrows into a glower—that signaled he was heading toward another rampage.

That emotional radar grew more sensitive as Katrina grew older. In graduate school, for example, just by reading their body language she realized that a fellow student had secretly slept with a professor.

She saw how their bodies synchronized in a subtle dance. "They would shift together, move in unison," Katrina told me. "When she wiggled, he wiggled. When I saw they were intimately attuned at the body level, like lovers, I had the thought, *Oh, creepy . . .*

"Lovers don't know they're doing it, but you both become superresponsive to each other at a primal level," she added.

Only months later did the student confide the clandestine affair to Katrina, who adds, "Their affair had stopped, but their bodies were still together."

Whenever she's with someone, Katrina says, "I'm hyperaware of dozens of streams of information people don't usually sense—things like the lift of an eyebrow, the movement of a hand. It's disruptive—I know way too much and it kills me. I'm overly aware."

What Katrina senses—and sometimes spills into the open—not only upsets other people; it can throw her off, too. "I came late to a meeting and made everyone wait. They were all being perfectly friendly in what they said—but what they were telling me with their bodies was not. I could see by their postures and the way they would not meet my eyes that everyone there was angry. I felt a rush of sadness and a lump in my throat. The meeting didn't go great.

"I'm always seeing things I'm not supposed to—and it's a problem," she added. "I poke into private stuff without meaning to. For a long time I didn't realize I do not have to share every telling thing I know."

After getting feedback from people on her team that she was being too intrusive, Katrina began working with an executive coach. "The coach told me I have a problem leaking emotional cues—when I pick up this stuff I'm not supposed to notice, I react in a way that makes people think I'm angry all the time. So now I have to be careful about that, too."

People like Katrina are social sensitives, keenly attuned to the most minimal emotional signals, with an almost uncanny knack for reading cues so subtle that other people miss them. A slight dilation of your iris, lift of your eyebrow, or shift of your body is all they need to know how you feel.

This means trouble if, like Katrina, they can't handle such data well.

But these same talents can make us socially astute, sensing when not to broach a touchy topic, when someone needs to be alone, or when people would welcome words of comfort.

A trained eye for the subtle cue offers advantage in many life arenas. Take top players in sports like squash and tennis, who can sense where an opponent's serve will land by noting subtle shifts in his posture as he positions himself to hit the ball. Many of baseball's great hitters, like Hank Aaron, would watch films over and over of the pitchers they would face in their next game, to spot telling cues that revealed which pitch would come next.

Justine Cassell, director of the Human-Computer Interaction Institute at Carnegie Mellon University, applies a similar well-trained empathy in the service of science. "Observing people was a game we played in our family," Cassell told me. That childhood propensity was refined when as a graduate student she spent hundreds of hours studying hand movements in videos of people describing a cartoon they had just seen.

Working with thirty-frames-per-second slices of the video, she'd annotate a hand's shape as it changed, as well as the stream of shifts in its orientation, placement in space, and trajectory of movement. And to check her accuracy, she'd then work back from her notes to see if she could precisely reproduce the movement of the hand.

Cassell more recently has done similar work with tiny movements of the facial muscles, with eye gaze, eyebrow raises, and head nods, all scored second by second and checked. She's done that for hundreds of hours—and does it to this day with grad students in her lab at Carnegie Mellon.

"Gestures always occur just before the most emphasized part of what you're saying," Cassell tells me. "One reason why some politicians may look insincere is that they have been taught to make particular gestures, but have not been taught the correct timing, and so when they produce those gestures after the word, they give us the sense that something fake is going on."

The timing of the gesture interprets its meaning. If your timing is off, a positive statement can have negative impact. Cassell gives this example: "If you say, 'She's a great candidate for the job' and raise your eyebrows, nod, and emphasize the word *great* all at the same time, you send a very positive emotional message. But if as you say the same sentence your head nod and eyebrow raise come in the short silence after *great*, then it shifts the emotional meaning to sarcasm—you're really saying she's not all that great."

Such readings of meta-messages in nonverbal channels occur to us instantly, unconsciously, and automatically. "We cannot *not* make meaning of what someone tells us," says Cassell, whether in words or just gestures, or both together. Everything we attend to in another person generates meaning at an unconscious level, and our bottom-up circuitry constantly reads it.

In one study, listeners remembered having "heard" information they only saw in gesture. For example, somebody who heard "He comes out the bottom of the pipe" but saw the speaker's hand formed into a fist and bouncing up and down said that he had heard "and then goes down stairs."[1]

Cassell's work makes visible what typically whizzes by us in microseconds. Our automatic circuitry gets the message, but our top-down awareness misses almost all of it.

These hidden messages have powerful impacts. Marital researchers have long known, for instance, that if one of the partners repeatedly makes fleeting facial expressions for disgust or contempt during conflicts, the odds are great against that couple staying together.[2] In psychotherapy, if the therapist and client move in synch with one another, there are likely to be better therapeutic outcomes.[3]

While Cassell was a professor at MIT's Media Lab, one way she deployed this extremely precise analysis of how we express ourselves was in developing a system that guides professional animators in the art of nonverbal behavior. The system—called BEAT—allows animators to type in a segment of dialogue and get back an automatically animated cartoon person with the right gestures, head and eye movement, and posture, which they can then tweak for artistic value.[4]

Getting the "feel" just right of a virtual actor's remarks, tone of voice, and gestures seems to demand a top-down grasp of bottom-up processes. These days Cassell is building similarly animated cartoons where, she says, images of children "act as virtual peers to elementary school students, using social skills to build rapport, and then using that rapport to facilitate learning."

When we met over coffee while on a break at a conference, Cassell explained how those hundreds of hours of parsing nonverbal messages have fine-tuned her sensitivity. "Now I automatically track this when I'm with anyone," she told me—which, I confess, made me a bit self-conscious (even more so when I realized she probably noticed that, too).

10

THE EMPATHY TRIAD

Supersensitive reading of emotional signals represents a zenith of *cognitive* empathy, one of three main varieties of the ability to focus on what other people experience.[1] This variety of empathy lets us take other people's perspective, comprehend their mental state, and at the same time manage our own emotions while we take stock of theirs. These can be top-down mental operations.[2]

In contrast, with *emotional* empathy we join the other person in feeling along with him or her; our bodies resonate in whatever key of joy or sorrow that person may be going through. Such attunement tends to occur through automatic, spontaneous—and bottom-up—brain circuits.

While cognitive or emotional empathy means we recognize what another person thinks and resonate with their feelings, it does not necessarily lead to sympathy, concern for others' welfare. The third variety, empathic concern, goes further: leading us to care about them, mobilizing us to help if need be. This compassionate attitude builds on bottom-up primal systems for caring and attachment deep down in the brain, though these mix with more reflective, top-down circuits that evaluate how much we value their well-being.

Our circuitry for empathy was designed for face-to-face moments. Today, working together online poses special challenges for empathy. Take, for example, that familiar moment in a meeting when everyone has reached a tacit consensus, and one person then articulates aloud what everyone already knows but has not said: "Okay, then we all agree on this." Heads nod.

But coming to such consensus in an online text-based discussion requires flying blind, without relying on the continuous cascade of nonverbal messages that in a real meeting let someone announce aloud the as-yet-unspoken agreement. We can base our reading of others only on what they have to say. Beyond that, there's reading between the lines: online we rely on cognitive empathy, the variety of mind-reading that lets us infer what's going on in someone else's mind.

Cognitive empathy gives us the ability to understand another person's ways of seeing and of thinking. Seeing through the eyes of others and thinking along their lines helps you choose language that fits their way of understanding.

This ability, as cognitive scientists put it, demands "additional computational mechanisms": we need to think about feelings. Justine Cassell's researchers routinely employ this variety of empathy in their work.

An inquisitive nature, which predisposes us to learn from everybody, feeds our cognitive empathy, amplifying our understanding of other people's worlds. One successful executive who exemplifies this attitude put it this way: "I've always just wanted to learn everything, to understand anybody that I was around—why they thought what they did, why they did what they did, what worked for them, and what didn't work."[3]

The earliest roots in life of such perspective-taking trace to the ways infants learn the basic building blocks of emotional life, such as how their own states differ from other people's and how people react to the feelings they express. This most basic emotional understanding marks the first time an infant can take another person's point of view, entertain several perspectives, and share meaning with other people.

By age two or three, toddlers can put words to feelings and name a face as "happy" or "sad." A year or so later, kids realize that how another child perceives events will determine how the other child will react. By adolescence, another aspect, accurately reading a person's feelings, gets stronger, paving the way for smoother social interactions.

Tania Singer, director of the social neuroscience department at the Max Planck Institute for Human Cognitive and Brain Sciences in Leipzig, Germany, has studied empathy and self-awareness in alexythimics—people who have great difficulty understanding their own feelings and putting these into words. "You need to understand your own feelings to understand the feelings of others," she says.

The executive circuits that allow us to think about our own thoughts and feelings let us apply the same reasoning to other people's minds. "Theory of mind," the understanding that other people have their own feelings, desires, and motives, lets us reason about what someone else might be thinking and wanting. Such cognitive empathy shares circuitry with executive attention; it first blooms around the years between two and five and continues to develop right through the teen years.

EMPATHY RUN AMOK

A muscle-bound inmate in a New Mexico prison was being interviewed by a psychology student. The inmate was so dangerous that the office was equipped with a button for the interviewer to press if things got out of control. The inmate told the psychology student in graphic detail the gruesome way he had killed his girlfriend—

but did so in such a charming fashion that the student found it difficult not to laugh along with him.

About a third of professionals whose job requires they interview criminal sociopaths like that murderer report feeling their skin crawl, a creepy sensation that some think signifies the triggering of a primitive defensive empathy.[4]

A darker side of cognitive empathy emerges when someone uses it to spot weakness in others and so takes advantage of them. This strategy typifies sociopaths, who use their cognitive empathy to manipulate. They feel no anxiety, and so the threat of a punishment does not deter them.[5]

The classic work on sociopaths (they were known as "psychopaths" back then), the 1941 book *The Mask of Sanity*, by Hervey M. Cleckley, describes them as concealing "an irresponsible personality" behind "a perfect mimicry of normal emotion, fine intelligence, and social responsibility."[6] The irresponsible part emerges in a history of pathological lying, living off others as a parasite, and the like. Tellingly, other indicators signal deficits in attention, such as bored distractibility, poor impulse control, and a lack of emotional empathy or of sympathy for others in distress.

Sociopathy is thought to occur in about 1 percent of the population; if so, the working world harbors millions of what clinicians call "successful sociopaths" (Bernie Madoff once in jail exemplifies an unsuccessful one). Sociopaths, like their close cousins "Machiavellian personalities," are able to read others' emotions but register facial expressions in a different part of their brain than the rest of us do.

Instead of registering emotion in their brain's limbic centers, sociopaths show activity in the frontal areas, particularly the language centers. They tell themselves *about* emotions, but do not feel them directly as other people do; instead of a normal bottom-up emotional reaction, sociopaths "feel" top-down.[7]

This is strikingly true for fear—sociopaths seem to have no apprehension whatever about the punishment their crimes will bring. One theory: they suffer a particular lack in cognitive control for impulse, what amounts to an attention deficit that leaves them focusing on the thrill at hand and blinds them to the consequences of what they do.[8]

EMOTIONAL EMPATHY: I FEEL YOUR PAIN

"This machine can save lives," an ad trumpets. It features a hospital setting where a wheeled platform holds a video monitor and keyboard, with a shelf for blood pressure cuffs and the like.

I encountered that very "lifesaving" apparatus when I had a visit with a physician the other day. As I sat on an exam table to have my blood pressure read, the platform was tucked away to my right and behind me. The nurse stood by my side, facing that video monitor—not me. As she took my readings, she read mechanically through a list of health status questions from the screen, typing in my answers.

Our eyes never met, save for a moment as she left the room and said (rather ironically, considering), "Nice to see you."

It *would* have been nice to see her, if we had had the opportunity. That lack of eye contact makes an encounter anonymous, draining it of emotional connection. The paucity of warmth meant I (or she) may as well have been a cyborg.

I'm not alone. Studies in medical schools find that if a doctor looks you in the eye, nods as she listens, touches you gently if you are in pain, and asks, for example, if you're warm enough on the exam table, she gets high patient ratings. If she mainly looks at her clipboard or computer screen, the ratings are low.[9]

While the nurse may have had some cognitive empathy for me,

there was little chance for her to tune in to my feelings. Emotional empathy, sensing what other people feel and caring about them, has ancient roots in evolution; we share this circuitry with other mammals, who like us need a keen attention to an infant's signal of distress. Emotional empathy operates bottom-up: much of the neural wiring for directly sensing the feelings of others lies beneath the cortex in ancient parts of the brain that "think fast," but not deeply.[10] These circuits tune us in by arousing in our own body the emotional state picked up in the other person.

Take listening to a gripping story. Brain studies show that when people listen to someone telling such a story, the brains of the listeners become intimately coupled with that of the storyteller. The listener's brain patterns echo those of the storyteller with precision, though lagging by a second or two. The more overlap in neural coupling of the two brains, the better the listener's understanding of the story.[11] And the brains of those with the very best understanding—who are fully focused and comprehend most—do something surprising: certain patterns of their brains' activities *anticipate* that of the storyteller by a second or two.

The ingredients of rapport begin with total shared focus between two people, which leads to an unconscious physical synchrony, which in turn generates good feeling. Such a shared focus with the teacher puts a child's brain in the best mode for learning. Any teacher who has struggled to get a class to pay attention knows that once everyone quiets down and focuses, the students can start to comprehend that lesson in history or math.

The circuits for emotional empathy begin to operate in early infancy, giving a primal taste of resonance between ourselves and someone else. In the brain's development, we are wired to feel another's joy or pain before we can think about it. The mirror neuron system, a part of the wiring for this resonance (but by no means the only wiring), kicks in as early as six months.[12]

Empathy depends on a muscle of attention: to tune in to others' feelings requires we pick up the facial, vocal, and other signals of their emotion. The anterior cingulate, a part of the attention network, tunes us to someone else's distress by tapping our own amygdala, which resonates with that distress. In this sense, emotional empathy is "embodied"—we actually feel in our physiology what's going on in the body of the other person.

When volunteers had their brains imaged while they watched another person get a painful shock, their own pain circuitry lit up in what amounts to a neural simulation of the other person's suffering.[13]

Tania Singer has found that we empathize with others' pain via our anterior insula—the same area that we use to sense how our own pain feels. So we first sense another's emotions within ourselves, as our brain applies to the other person's feelings the identical system used to read our own feeling states.[14] Empathy builds on our capacity for sensing visceral feelings within our own body.

So does synchrony, that nonverbal meshing of how we move and what we do that signals an interaction in rapport. You see it in jazz musicians, who never rehearse exactly what they do, but just seem to know when to take center stage, when to fade into the background. When jazz artists were compared with classical musicians in brain function, they showed more neural indicators of self-awareness.[15] As one jazz artist put it, "In jazz you have to tune in to how your body is feeling so you know when to riff."

The brain's very design seems to integrate self-awareness with empathy by packing the way we pick up information about ourselves and about others within the same far-flung neural networks. One clever part: as our mirror neurons and other social circuitry re-create in our brain and body what's going on with the other person, our insula summates all that. Empathy entails an act of self-awareness: we read other people by tuning in to ourselves.

Take, for instance, von Economo neurons, or VENs. These unique brain cells, remember, are crucial for self-awareness. But they are situated in areas that activate in moments of anger, grief, love, and lust—as well as tender moments like when a mother hears her baby crying or at the sound of the voice of a loved one. When these circuits tag an event as salient, they direct our focus there.

These spindly cells allow a super-quick connection between the prefrontal cortex and the insula—areas active during both introspection and empathy. These circuits monitor our interpersonal world for what matters to us, doing so super-quickly, helping us react on the fly. The brain's basic circuitry for attention interweaves with that for social sensitivity and for understanding other people's experiences and how they see things—in short, for empathy.[16] This social superhighway in the brain lets us know—and so reflect on and manage—our own emotions, and those of others.

EMPATHIC CONCERN: I'M HERE FOR YOU

A woman staggered into her surgeon's waiting room, blood seeping from every visible orifice. Instantly the doctor and her staff sprang into action to handle the emergency, rushing the woman into a treatment room to stanch her bleeding, calling an ambulance, and canceling all the appointments of other patients for the remainder of the day.

The patients who had been waiting to see their doctor understood that, of course, this woman's dire need trumped their own. All, that is, save one woman who was indignant because her appointment had been canceled. Outraged, she shouted at the receptionist, "I took the day off work! How dare you cancel me!"

The surgeon who tells me the story says such indifference to suffering and the needs of others has become more prevalent in her practice. It was even the topic of a meeting for all surgeons in her state.

The biblical parable of the Good Samaritan tells of a man who stopped to help a stranger who had been beaten and robbed and was lying in pain by the side of the road. Two others had seen the injured man and, fearing danger, had crossed to the other side of the road and passed him by.

Martin Luther King Jr. observed that those who failed to offer their aid asked themselves the question: "If I stop to help this man, what will happen to me?"

But the Good Samaritan reversed the question: "If I do not stop to help this man what will happen to *him*?"

Compassion builds on empathy, which in turn requires a focus on others. If self-absorbed, we simply do not notice other people; we can walk by utterly indifferent to their predicament. But once we notice them we can tune in, sense their feelings and needs, and act on our concern.

Empathic concern, which is what you want in your physician, boss, or spouse (not to mention yourself), has substrates in the neural architecture for parenting. In mammals, this circuitry compels attention and concern toward babies and the young, who can't survive without their parents.[17] Watch where people's eyes go when someone brings an adorable baby into a room, and you see the mammalian brain center for caring leap into action.

Empathic concern first emerges early in infancy: when one baby hears another cry she, too, starts crying. This response is triggered by the amygdala, the brain's radar for danger (as well as a site for primal emotions both negative and positive). One neural theory holds that the amygdala drives bottom-up circuits in the brain of the baby who hears the crying to feel the same sadness and upset. Simultaneously top-down circuits release oxytocin, the chemical for caring, which stirs a rudimentary sense of concern and goodwill in the second baby.[18]

Empathic concern, then, is a double-edged feeling. On the one hand there is implicit discomfort from the direct experience in one person of the distress of the other combined with the same concern a parent feels toward her child. But we also add to our caring instinct a social equation that weighs how much we value the other person's well-being.

Getting this bottom-up/top-down mix right has great implications. Those in whom the stirring of sympathetic feelings becomes too strong can suffer themselves—in the helping professions this can sometimes lead to emotional exhaustion and compassion fatigue. And those who protect themselves against sympathetic distress by deadening feeling can lose touch with empathy. The neural road to empathic concern takes top-down management of personal distress but without numbing us to the pain of others.

While volunteers listened to tales of people subjected to physical pain, brain scans revealed that their own brain centers for experiencing such pain lit up instantly. But if the story was about *psychological* suffering, it took relatively longer to activate the higher brain centers involved in empathic concern and compassion. As the research team put it, it takes time to tell "the psychological and moral dimensions of a situation."

Moral sentiments derive from empathy, and moral reflections take thinking and focus. One cost of the frenetic stream of distractions we face today, some fear, is an erosion of empathy and compassion.[19] The more distracted we are, the less we can exhibit attunement and caring.

Perceiving pain in others reflexively draws our attention—the expression of pain is a crucial biological signal to evoke help. Even rhesus monkeys do not pull a chain to get a banana if that also gives a shock to another rhesus monkey (suggesting, perhaps, one root of civility).

But there are exceptions. For one, pain empathy ends if we don't like the people in pain—for instance, if we think they have been unfair—or if we see them as part of a group we dislike.[20] Then pain empathy can easily be transformed into its opposite, feelings of "schadenfreude."[21]

When resources are scarce the need to compete for them can sometimes suppress empathic concern, and competition is part of life in almost any social group, whether for food, mates, or power—or an appointment with a doctor.

Another exception is understandable: our brains resonate less with another person's pain when the pain has a good reason—say, getting a helpful medical treatment. Finally, where we focus matters: our emotional empathy grows stronger if we attend to the intensity of the pain, and lessens as we look away.

Such constraints aside, one of the subtle forms of caring occurs when we simply use our reassuring, loving presence to help calm someone. The mere presence of a loved one, studies show, has an analgesic property, quieting the centers that register pain. Remarkably, the more empathic the person who is present with someone in pain, the greater the calming effect.[22]

THE EMPATHY BALANCE

"You know, when you discover a lump in your breast, you kind of feel—well, kind of . . . ," the patient says, her words tapering off. She looks down, tears forming in her eyes.

"When did you actually discover the lump?" her doctor asks softly.

The patient replies, absently, "I don't know. It's been a while."

The doctor responds, "That sounds frightening."

The patient answers, "Well, yeah, sort of."

"Sort of frightening?" the doctor asks.

"Yeah," says the patient, "and I guess I'm feeling like my life is over."

"I see. Worried and sad, too."

"That's it, Doctor."

Contrast that exchange with one where right after the patient gets teary talking about the lump in her breast, the doctor starts running briskly through a checklist of impersonal, detailed clinical questions—with not so much as a nod toward her teary feelings.

The patient in that second encounter will be likely to leave feeling unheard and uncared about. But after that first, more empathic interaction, the patient—despite having had the same amount of distress—would feel better: understood and cared for.

Those two scenarios were used to illustrate this crucial difference in an article for physicians on how to build empathy with their patients.[23] The title of the article features an empathy-building phrase: "Let me see if I have this right . . ." It argues that taking just a few moments to pay attention to how a patient feels about her illness builds emotional connection.

Not listening is at the top of the list of complaints patients have about their physicians. For their part, many physicians complain they are not given the time they need with their patients and so the human side of their interaction gets short shrift. The barrier to human contact rises as physicians—mandated to keep digital records—tap notes on a computer keyboard during patient interviews, and so end up communing with their laptop rather than with the patient.

Yet personal moments with patients, many physicians say, are the most satisfying part of their day. Such rapport between doctor and patient greatly increases diagnostic accuracy and how the patients comply with their doctor's instructions, and enhances patients' satisfaction and loyalty.

"Empathy, the ability to connect with patients—in a deep sense, to listen, to pay attention—lies at the heart of medical practice," the article tells its medical audience. Orienting to the patient's emotions builds rapport. Tuning out feelings and focusing only on clinical details builds a wall.

Physicians who are sued for malpractice in the United States generally make no more medical errors than those who are not sued. The main difference, research shows, often comes down to the tenor of the doctor-patient relationship. Those who are sued, it turns out, have fewer signs of emotional rapport: they have shorter visits with patients, fail to ask about the patients' concerns or make sure their questions are answered, and have more emotional distance—there's little or no laughter, for example.[24]

But attention to patients' distress may pose a particular challenge to physicians giving excellent technical care—say when it demands keen concentration on performing a medical procedure perfectly despite the patient's agony.

The same network that activates when we see someone in pain also fires when we see anything aversive: *That's scary—I should get out of here* is the primal thought. Ordinarily, when people see someone else being pricked with a pin, their brain emits a signal indicating that their own pain centers are echoing that distress.

Physicians do not. Their brains are unique in blocking even such automatic responses to someone else's pain and discomfort, according to findings from a study led by Jean Decety, professor of psychology and psychiatry at the University of Chicago.[25] This attentional anesthetic seems to deploy the temporal-parietal junction (or TPJ) and regions of the prefrontal cortex, a circuit that boosts concentration by tuning out emotions. The TPJ protects focus by walling off emotions along with other distractions, and helps keep a distance between oneself and others.

This same neuronal network kicks into action in any of us when we see a problem and look for a solution. So if you're talking with someone who is upset, this system helps you understand the person's perspective intellectually by shifting from heart-to-heart emotional rapport to the head-to-heart connection of cognitive empathy.

The TPJ maneuver insulates the brain from experiencing the wash of emotion—it's the brain basis for the stereotype of someone with cool rationality amid emotional turmoil. A shift into the TPJ mode creates a boundary so you're immune to emotional contagion, freeing your brain from being affected by the other person's emotions while you're focusing.

Sometimes that's a crucial advantage: you can stay calm and concentrated when those around you are falling apart. Sometimes it's not: it also means you may tune out of emotional cues and so lose the thread of empathy.

This damping down of emotional entrainment has obvious benefits for someone who has to keep focused amid flinch-inducing procedures: injections into eyeballs, suturing bloody wounds, scalpels rending open flesh.

"I was on the team of the first doctors to respond to the earthquake in Haiti—we were there within the first few days," Dr. Mark Hyman tells me. "When we got to the one hospital in Port-au-Prince, which miraculously was largely intact, there was no food, no water, no power, almost no supplies, and just one or two hospital staff. There were hundreds of dead bodies rotting in the sun, stacked in the hospital morgue, and being loaded onto trucks to go to a mass grave. There were about fifteen hundred people in the courtyard desperately needing help—legs hanging by a thread, bodies cut nearly in half. It was traumatic. Yet we immediately got to work and focused on what we could do."

When I spoke to Dr. Hyman, he had just returned from several weeks in India and Bhutan, where he again volunteered his medical help to needy patients. "The act of service gives you the ability to transcend the pain all around you," Dr. Hyman said. "In Haiti, it was hyperreal, totally in the moment. It's weird to say, but there was a level of equanimity and calm—even peace and clarity—in the midst of all that chaos. Everything else but what we were doing fell away."

The TPJ response seems to be acquired rather than innate. Medical students learn this reaction during their socialization into the profession, as they encounter patients under duress. The cost of being too empathic is having upsetting, intrusive thoughts that compete for attention with medical imperatives.

"If you can't do anything in a situation like that," said Dr. Hyman about Haiti, "you're paralyzed. Sometimes the hurt and pain all around you would break through in moments of fatigue, heat exhaustion, and hunger. But mostly my mind put me in a state where I could function despite the horror."

As William Osler, the father of medical residency training, wrote in 1904, a doctor should be so detached that "his blood vessels don't constrict and his heart rate remains steady when he sees terrible sights."[26] Osler recommended doctors have the attitude of a "detached concern."

This could mean simply damping down emotional empathy—but in practice it can sometimes lead to blockading empathy entirely. The challenge for a physician in a daily medical practice is to maintain cool focus while staying open to the patient's feelings and experience—and to let her patient know she understands and cares.

Medical care can fail when patients do not follow what their physician tells them; about half of all the medicines doctors prescribe for patients are never taken. The strongest predictor of patients following such instruction is whether they feel their doctor is genuinely concerned about them.[27] Within the same week recently, two deans of major medical schools independently told me they face a dilemma in admitting students: how to spot those who will have empathic concern for their patients.

None other than Jean Decety, the University of Chicago neurobiologist who led the study of TPJ and patient pain, put it this way: "I want my doctor to look at me if I'm in pain—to be there, be present to me, the patient. Empathic—but not too sensitive to treat my pain well."

BUILDING EMPATHY

In one survey, about half of young physicians say their empathy for patients declined over the course of their training (only about a third say it increased).[28] And that lost art of connection persists into their career for many. That gets us back to the TPJ, the circuitry that dampens down a doctor's physiological reaction to seeing someone in pain and helps her keep calm and clear while treating what's causing it.

The buffering from distress probably helps medical residents as they learn to perform painful procedures on patients. But once learned, that damping down of bodily resonance seems to become automatic, sometimes at the cost of a more general empathy.

Yet compassionate care embodies a core value in medicine; boosting empathy is among the mandated learning objectives for medical schools. While few medical schools specifically teach the art of empathy, now that neuroscience reveals its underlying circuitry some well-designed coaching might just boost this human art.

That's the hope of Dr. Helen Riess of Massachusetts General Hospital, the mother ship of Harvard Medical School. Dr. Riess, director of the Empathy and Relational Science Program there, designed an educational program to enhance empathy for medical residents and interns that significantly improved patients' perception of their physicians' empathy.[29]

In the standard mold of medical school, some of this training was purely academic, reviewing the neuroscience of empathy in a language doctors know and respect.[30] A series of videos showed the physiological changes (as revealed by their sweat response) in doctors and their patients during difficult encounters—like when a doctor was arrogant or dismissive—revealing how upset their patients became. And, as the videos made graphically clear, when the doctors tuned in to their patients with empathy, both doctor and patient became more relaxed and in synch biologically.

To help the physicians monitor themselves, they learned to focus using deep, diaphragmatic breathing, and to "watch the interaction from the ceiling" rather than being lost in their own thoughts and feelings. "Suspending your own involvement to observe what's going on gives you a mindful awareness of the interaction without being completely reactive," says Dr. Riess. "You can see if your own physiology is charged up or balanced. You can notice what's transpiring in the situation."

If the doctor notices she's feeling irritated, for instance, that's a signal that the patient might be bothered, too. "By being more self-aware," Riess points out, "you can see what's being projected onto you, and what you're projecting onto your patients."

Training in picking up nonverbal cues includes reading patients' emotions from their tone of voice, their posture, and, to a large extent, their facial expression. Using the work of emotions expert Paul Ekman, who has identified with precision how the facial muscles move during every major emotion, the program teaches doctors how to recognize patients' fleeting feelings from reading their faces.

"If you act in a compassionate and caring way—when you deliberately look the patient in the eye and notice their emotional expressions, even when you don't feel like it at first—you start to feel more engaged," Dr. Riess told me. This "behavioral empathy" may begin with going through the motions but it makes the interaction more connected. That, she adds, can help counter a resident's emotional exhaustion in the emergency room at 2 a.m., when he has to see yet another patient and thinks, *Why couldn't he wait to come in until later in the morning?*

A direct lesson in a specific skill for being empathic—reading emotions from the face—proved to be among the most potent parts of the entire training. The more the doctors in training learned to read subtle emotional expressions, the more their actual patients reported feeling empathic care.

Dr. Riess expected the finding. "The more you can pick up the subtle cues of emotion," she told me, "the more empathic understanding you are able to have."

There are no doubt ways an empathic physician can juggle both the laptop and connecting with patients—for instance if she can manage to type on her computer and still look up from time to time and maintain meaningful eye contact. Or she could share the screen at apt moments with the patient: "I'm looking at your lab results—here, let me show you," and review them together.

Still, many physicians are afraid of getting behind schedule and that these touches will add too much time. "We are trying to dispel that myth," says Dr. Reiss. "Empathy actually saves time in the long run."

11

SOCIAL SENSITIVITY

Years ago I occasionally used the services of a freelance editor. But every time we'd get in a casual conversation, it would go on . . . and on . . . and on. I'd send him *let's-wrap-this-up* cues in my pacing and tone of voice—which he'd ignore. I'd say, "I've got to run now," and he'd just keep talking. I'd take my car keys out and head for the door—and he'd come along with me to the car without missing a beat. I'd tell him, "See you later," and he'd just go on chatting.

I've known several people like that editor, each with the same blindness to the cues a conversation was ending. That very tendency, in fact, is one of the diagnostic indicators of social dyslexia. Its opposite, social intuition, tells us how accurate we are at decoding the stream of nonverbal messages people constantly send, silent modifiers of what they are saying.

This steady stream of nonverbal exchanges rushes to and from everyone we interact with, whether in a routine hello or a tense negotiation, transmitting messages received every bit as powerfully as whatever we might be saying. Perhaps *more* powerfully.

In job interviews, for example, if the applicant moves in synch with the interviewer (not intentionally—it has to occur naturally as a by-product of brain synchronization), she's more likely to be hired. That's a problem for those who are "gesturally dysfunctional," a term coined by scientists to refer to people who just can't seem to get right the movements that annotate what we are saying.

Queen Elizabeth II's husband, Prince Philip, well-known for his social gaffes, describes himself as expert in "dontopedalogy," the science of putting your foot in your mouth.

Take what was a momentous event in Nigeria: the first visit in forty-seven years by a British monarch. Queen Elizabeth and her royal consort, Prince Philip himself, came to open a conference of Commonwealth nations. The country's president, proudly decked out in traditional Nigerian robes, met them at the airport.

"You look," said Prince Philip to the president with disdain, "like you're ready for bed."

The prince once wrote to a family friend, "I know you will never think very much of me. I am rude and unmannerly and I say many things out of turn, which I realize afterwards must have hurt someone. Then I am filled with remorse and I try to put matters right."[1]

Such lack of politesse reflects deficient self-awareness: People who are tuned out not only stumble socially, but are surprised when someone tells them they have acted inappropriately. Whether it's by talking too loudly in a restaurant or inadvertent rudeness, they tend to make others feel uneasy.

One brain test for social sensitivity, used by Richard Davidson, looks at the neural zone for recognizing and reading faces—the "fusiform face area"—while people are shown photos of faces. If we are asked to tell what emotion the person feels, our fusiform face area lights up in a brain scanner. Those who are highly socially intuitive show, as you might expect, high levels of activity when they do this. On the other hand, those whose focus just cannot pick up the emotional wavelength show low levels.

Those with autism show little fusiform action, but lots in the amygdala, which registers anxiety.[2] Looking at faces tends to make them anxious, particularly looking at a person's eyes, a rich source of emotional data. The crow's-feet wrinkles around people's eyes, for example, tell us when they are genuinely feeling happy; smiles lacking those crinkles signal faked joy. Ordinarily, small children learn much about emotions by looking at the other person's eyes, while those with autism avoid the eyes and so fail to get those lessons.

But everyone falls somewhere on this dimension. A manager at a financial advisory company had been accused of sexual harassment three times in as many years—and, I'm told, each time the manager had been stunned because he had no idea that he had been acting inappropriately. Such gaffe-prone people fail to notice the implicit ground rules for a situation—and don't pick up the social signals that they are making other people uneasy. Their insula is out of the loop. These are the folks who blithely check for text messages while there's a solemn moment of silence for a colleague who passed away.

Remember the woman who knew too much—who could read supersubtle nonverbal messages, and then would blurt out something about them that was embarrassing? She tried mindfulness meditation to help her gain more inner awareness.

After a few months of practicing mindfulness, she reported, "I already see places where I feel as if I am able to make a little bit of a choice about my reaction to events—places where I can still see what people are saying with their bodies, but don't need to react right away. It's a good thing!"

GETTING THE CONTEXT

Then there are the situations where most anyone will be "off," at least at first. We are inevitably prone to inadvertent gaffes when we travel to a new culture, where we start out blind to the fresh set of ground rules. I remember being in a monastery in the hills of Nepal, when a pert European trekker walked through in short shorts—a transgression from the Nepali perspective, but one she hadn't a clue she was committing.

Those who do business with diverse sets of people in a global economy need particular sensitivity to such unspoken norms. In Japan, I learned the hard way that the moment of exchanging business cards signals an important ritual. We Americans are prone to casually pocketing the card without looking, which there indicates disrespect. I was told you should take the card carefully, hold it in both hands, and study it for a while before putting it away in a special case (this advice came a bit too late—I had just stuffed a card into my pocket without giving it a glance).

The cross-cultural talent for social sensitivity appears related to cognitive empathy. Executives good at such perspective-taking, for example, do better at overseas assignments, presumably because they can pick up implicit norms quickly as they learn the unique mental models of a given culture.

Ground rules for what's appropriate can create invisible barriers when people from different cultures work together. An engineer from Austria who works for a Dutch company lamented, "Debate is highly valued in Dutch culture; you grow up with it from the time you're in primary school. They see it as necessary. But I don't like that kind of debate; I find it upsetting—it's too confrontational. For me the inner challenge is not to take it personally, and to stay connected and feel respect during the confrontation."

Culture aside, ground rules shift greatly depending on whom we are with. There are jokes you tell to your best buddies that you should never tell your boss.

Attention to context lets us pick up subtle social cues that can guide how we behave. Those who are tuned in this way act with skill no matter what situation they find themselves in. They know not only what to say and do, but also, just as vital, what *not* to say or do. They instinctively follow the universal algorithm for etiquette, to behave in ways that put others at ease. Sensitivity to how people are feeling in reaction to what we do or say lets us navigate hidden social minefields.

While we may have some conscious ideas of such norms (how to dress for casual Friday at work; eat only with your right hand in India), attention to implicit norms is largely intuitive, a bottom-up capacity. Our felt sense of what's socially appropriate comes to us as a feeling in our body—when we're "off" it's the physical manifestation of *this doesn't feel right*. We may be picking up subtle signals of embarrassment or distress from the people we're with.

If we're oblivious to these sensations of being socially off-key (or never have them in the first place) we just keep going, clueless as to how far off course we are. One brain test for context focus assesses the function of the hippocampus, which is a nexus for circuits that gauge social circumstances. The anterior zone of the hippocampus backs up against the amygdala and plays a key role in keeping what we do appropriate to the context. The anterior hippocampus, in conversation with the prefrontal area, squelches that impulse to do something inappropriate.

Those most alert to social situations, Richard Davidson hypothesizes, have stronger activity and connectivity in these brain circuits than do those who just can't seem to get it right. The hippocampus is at work, he says, to make you act differently when with your family and when at work, and differently again in the office versus with your workmates in a bar.

Context awareness also helps at another level: mapping the social networks in a group or at a new school or on the job—a skill that lets us navigate those relationships well. People who excel at organizational influence, it turns out, can not only sense the flow of personal connections but also name the people whose opinions hold most sway—and so, when they need to, focus on convincing those who will in turn persuade others.

Then there are those who are just tuned out of a particular social context—like the video game champ who spent so much of his life glued to his computer monitor that once when he agreed to meet a journalist at a restaurant he was mystified as to why the place should be so busy on Valentine's Day.

An extreme of being "off" in reading social context can be seen in post-traumatic stress disorder, when a person reacts to an innocent event like a car backfiring as though it were a dire emergency and dives under a table. Tellingly, the hippocampus shrinks in those with PTSD but grows larger again as symptoms abate.[3]

POWER'S INVISIBLE DIVIDE

Miguel was a day laborer, one of countless illegal immigrants from Mexico who scrape by on the meager wages they can make picking up jobs day by day—gardening, housepainting, cleaning, anything.

In Los Angeles, day laborers can be found of an early morning huddled on certain street corners sprinkled throughout the metro area, where locals will cruise up, stop their car, and make an offer for work. One day Miguel took a gardening job for a woman who, after his long and hard day's work, refused to pay him a cent.

Miguel replayed that crushing disappointment when he took part in a workshop that had him act this drama from his own life. The workshop employs methods of the "theater of the oppressed," which is designed to help a relatively privileged audience empathize with the emotional reality of victims of oppression.

After someone like Miguel depicts a scenario, a volunteer from the audience steps up to replay the scene. For Miguel, a woman repeated his performance, adding what she saw as a possible solution to his predicament.

"She depicted going to the employer and telling her how unfair she was being, reasoning with her," Brent Blair, who produced the performance, told me.

But for Miguel that was not an option: while that approach might have worked for a middle-class woman with citizenship, it would be impossible for an immigrant working as a day laborer.

Miguel watched this replay of his own story in silence, standing at the corner of the stage. Says Blair, "At the end he couldn't turn around to talk it over with the rest of us—he was weeping.

"Miguel said he didn't realize how oppressed he was until he saw his own story told by someone else."

The contrast between how that woman imagined his situation and his reality highlighted how it felt to be unseen, unheard, unfelt—a nonperson to be exploited.

When the method works, people like Miguel gain a new perspective on themselves by watching their stories as seen through another person's eyes. When audience members come up and become actors performing these scenes, ideally they share the reality of the oppressed person, "sympathizing" in the true sense of the word: having the same pathos, or pain.

"When you communicate an emotional experience, you can understand a problem through the heart and mind, and find new solutions," says Blair, who directs the Applied Theatre Arts master's program at the University of Southern California, which uses these techniques to help people in downtrodden communities. He's staged such theatrics with rape victims in Rwanda and gang members in Los Angeles.

In doing so, Blair has taken on a subtle force dividing people along otherwise invisible signs of social status and powerlessness: the powerful tend to tune out the powerless. And that deadens empathy.

Blair recounts a moment at a global conference where he ended up seeing himself through the eyes of someone more powerful. He was listening to the CEO of a giant beverage company—a man notorious for lowering workers' wages—talking about how his company was helping children become healthier.

During the question period following the CEO's talk, Blair asked an intentionally provocative question: how can you talk about healthy kids without also talking about healthy wages for their parents?

The CEO ignored Blair's question and went right on to the next one. Blair suddenly felt like a nonperson.

The ability of the powerful to dismiss inconvenient people (and inconvenient truths) by paying no attention has become the focus of social psychologists, who are finding relationships between power and the people we pay most and least attention to.[4]

Understandably, we focus on the people we value most. If you are poor, you depend on good relationships with friends and family whom you may need to turn to for help—say, when you need someone to look after your four-year-old until you get home from work. Those with few resources and a fragile perch on stability "need to lean on people," says Dacher Keltner, a psychologist at the University of California, Berkeley.

So the poor are particularly attentive to other people and their needs.

The wealthy, on the other hand, can hire help—pay for a day care center or even an au pair. This means, Keltner argues, that rich people can afford to be less aware of the needs of other people, and so can be less attentive to them and their suffering.

His research has surfaced this disdain in just a five-minute get-acquainted session.[5] The more wealthy (at least among American college students) exhibit fewer signs of engagement like making eye contact, nods, and laughing—and more of those for uninterest, like checking the time, doodling, or fidgeting. Students from wealthy families seem standoffish, while those from poorer roots appear more engaged, warm, and expressive.

And in a Dutch study, strangers told each other about distressing episodes in their lives, ranging from the death of a loved one or divorce to loss of a love or betrayal, or childhood pains like being bullied.[6] Again the more powerful person in the pairs tended to be more indifferent: to feel less of the other person's pain—to be less empathic, let alone compassionate.

Keltner's group has found similar attention gaps just by comparing high-ranking people in an organization with those at the lower tiers on their skill at reading emotions from facial expression.[7] In any interaction the more high-power person tends to focus his or her gaze on the other person less than others, and is more likely to interrupt and to monopolize the conversation—all signifying a lack of attention.

In contrast, people of lower social status tend to do better on tests of empathic accuracy, such as reading others' emotions from their faces—even just from muscle movements around the eyes. By every measure they focus on other people more than do people of higher status.

The mapping of attention on lines of power shows up in a simple metric: how long does it take person A to respond to an email from person B? The longer someone ignores an email before finally responding, the more relative social power that person has. Map these response times across an entire organization and you get a remarkably accurate chart of the actual social standing. The boss leaves emails unanswered for hours or days; those lower down respond within minutes.

There's an algorithm for this, a data mining method called "automated social hierarchy detection," developed at Columbia University.[8] When applied to the archive of email traffic at Enron Corporation before it folded, the method correctly identified the roles of top-level managers and their subordinates just by how long it took them to answer a given person's emails. Intelligence agencies have been applying the same metric to suspected terrorist gangs, piecing together the chain of influence to spot the central figures.

Power and status are highly relative, varying from one encounter to another. Tellingly, when students from wealthy families imagined themselves talking with someone of still higher status than themselves, they improved on their ability to read emotions in faces.

Where we see ourselves on the social ladder seems to determine how much attention we pay: more vigilant when we feel subordinate, less so when superior. The corollary: The more you care about someone, the more attention you pay—and the more attention you pay, the more you care. Attention interweaves with love.

PART IV

THE BIGGER CONTEXT

12

PATTERNS, SYSTEMS, AND MESSES

While he was visiting a village in India's Himalayan foothills, a fall down some stairs left Larry Brilliant confined to bed for weeks to heal a back injury. To while away the hours in that isolated hamlet, he asked his wife, Girija, to see if the local library had any books on Indian coins—he had been an avid coin collector as a kid.

That's around when I first met Dr. Larry, as his friends call him. An M.D., he had joined the World Health Organization initiative to vaccinate the world against smallpox. I remember him telling me at the time how, by immersing himself in reading about the coins of ancient India, he had started to grasp the history of the trading networks in that part of the world.

With his appetite for coin collecting renewed, once he got back on his feet, during his travels across India Dr. Larry started to visit local goldsmiths, who often sold gold and silver coins by weight. Some were ancient.

These included coins dating from the Kushans, a nation that in the second century C.E. adminstered from Kabul an empire extending from the Aral Sea to Benares. Kushan coins adopted a format borrowed from a conquered group, the Bactrians, descendants of Greek soldiers left behind to man outposts after Alexander the Great's foray into Asia. Those coins told an intriguing story.

On one side of Kushan coins was the image of their king of a given period; the flip side portrayed the image of a god. Kushans were Zoroastrian, followers of a Persian religion at the time among the world's largest. But various Kushan coins depicted not just their Persian deity, but also a wide variety of divinities, like Shiva or Buddha, borrowed from Persian, Egyptian, Greek, Hindu, and Roman pantheons—even from nations far distant from Kushan territory.

How, in the second century, could an empire centered in Afghanistan learn so much about religions—and pay tribute to their deities—ranging far beyond its borders? The answer lay in the economic systems of the day. The Kushan Empire allowed, for the first time in history, a protected linkage between the already vibrant trade routes of the Indian Ocean and the Silk Road. Kushans were in regular contact with merchants and holy men whose roots stretched from the Mediterranean basin to the Ganges, from the Arabian Peninsula to the deserts of northwestern China.

There were other such revelations. "I'd find an abundance of Roman coins in the south of India, and try to figure out how it got there," Dr. Larry told me. "It turns out the Romans, whose empire touched the Red Sea in Egypt, came around Arabia by boat to Goa to trade. You could reverse-engineer where these ancient coins were turning up and deduce the trade routes of the period."

At the time Dr. Larry had just finished working throughout South Asia on the historically successful worldwide smallpox eradication program for WHO, and he was about to embark for the University of Michigan to get a master's degree in public health. There was a surprising resonance between his exploration of trade routes and what he was to learn at Michigan.

"I had taken courses in system analysis and was studying epidemiology. This fitted my way of thinking. I realized tracking an epidemic was much like tracking the spread of an ancient civilization like the Kushans with all the archaeological, linguistic, and cultural clues along the way."

The 1918 flu pandemic, for instance, killed an estimated 50 million people worldwide. "It probably began in Kansas and was first spread by American troops traveling abroad during World War I," Dr. Larry says. "That flu marched around the world at the speed of steamships and the Orient Express. Today pandemics can spread at the speed of a 747."

Or take the case of polio, a disease known in the ancient world, but only sporadically. "What made polio become an epidemic was urbanization; in cities people shared a single, polluted water system rather than getting water from their own individual wells.

"An epidemic exemplifies system dynamics. The more you can think systemically, the more you can follow the path of coins, art, religion, or disease. Understanding how coins travel along trade routes parallels analyzing the spread of a virus."

That kind of pattern detection signals the systems mind at work. This sometimes uncanny ability lets us spot with ease the telling detail in a vast visual array (think "Where's Waldo"). If you flash a photo of lots of dots and tell people to guess how many there are, the better estimators should be better systems thinkers. The gift shows up in those best at, say, designing software or finding interventions to save failing ecosystems.

A "system" boils down to a cohesive set of lawful, regular patterns. Pattern recognition operates in circuitry within the parietal cortex, though the specific sites of a more extensive "systems brain"—if any—have yet to be identified. As it stands, there seems to be no dedicated network or circuitry in the brain that gives us a natural inclination toward systems understanding.

We learn how to read and navigate systems through the remarkable general learning talents of the neocortex. Such cortical talents—as in math or engineering—can be duplicated by computers. That sets the systems mind apart from self-awareness and empathy, which operate on dedicated, largely bottom-up, circuitry. It takes a bit of effort to learn about systems, but to navigate life successfully we need strengths in this variety of focus as well as the two that come more naturally.

MESSES AND SUPER-WICKED PROBLEMS

A systems perspective has carried over to Dr. Larry's current post as head of the Skoll Global Threats Fund, which has a mandate to safeguard humanity against dangers that include Middle East conflicts, nuclear proliferation, pandemics, climate change, and the battles that can arise over the scarcity of water.

"We find the hot spots, the points where trouble might start. Take water scarcity and the struggle among three nuclear-armed nations—Pakistan, India, and China. About ninety-five percent of water in Pakistan is used for agriculture, and India is upstream of most of its main rivers. Pakistanis think that India manipulates floodgates in India and controls when and how much water Pakistan gets. And upstream from India, Indians believe that China is controlling the water flowing out of the Third Pole, the ice and snow of the Himalayan plateau."

But no one knows how much water flows through these river systems and at what season, or how many gates control that flow, or where, or for what purpose. "This data is shrouded as a political tool by the three governments," Dr. Larry says. "So we support the gathering of that data by a trusted third party, and making it transparent. That will allow the next step: analysis of the key nodes and the 'ouch' points."

A rapid response will be essential for combating any future global flu pandemics caused by mutating strains for which no one has immunity. Yet that response will have no chance to be pretested; the situation will be unique in history (there were, for example, no 747s during the last pandemic in 1918); and the stakes are so high there is no room for error. These are among the qualifications that rank pandemics as a "wicked" problem—not in the sense of "evil," but rather meaning extremely hard to solve.

Combating global warming, on the other hand, poses a "super-wicked" problem: there is no single authority in charge of its solution, time is running out, the people who seek to solve the problem are among those (all of us) who cause it, and official policies dismiss its importance for our future.[1]

What's more, both pandemics and global warming are what are technically called "messes," where a troubling predicament interacts in a system of other interrelated problems.[2] So, as Dr. Larry points out, these are incredibly complicated dilemmas, and lots of the data we need to solve them are missing.

Systems are virtually invisible to the naked eye, but their workings can be rendered visible by gathering data from enough points that the outlines of their dynamics come into focus. The more data, the clearer the map becomes. Enter the era of big data.

Years after his coin-collecting days in India, Dr. Larry became the founding executive director of Google.org, Google's nonprofit arm. While there he brought about one of the first widely hailed applications for big data: flu-spotting. A volunteer Google team of engineers, working with epidemiologists from the Centers for Disease Control and Prevention, analyzed an enormous number of search queries for words, such as *fever* or *ache*, connected with flu symptoms.[3]

"We used tens of thousands of simultaneous computers to search every keystroke on Google over five years to create an algorithm to predict flu outbreaks," Dr. Larry recalls. The resulting algorithm identifies flu outbreaks within a day, compared with the two weeks it typically takes the CDC to notice hot spots for the disease based on reports from physicians.

Big data software analyzes voluminous amounts of information; using Google data to spot flu outbreaks was one of the early applications of big data to a mob—what's become known as "collective intelligence." Big data lets us know where the collective attention focuses.

The uses are endless. For instance, analyzing who connects to whom—via calls, tweets, texts, and the like—surfaces the human nerve system of an organization, mapping connectivity. Hyperconnected folks are typically the most influential: an organization's social connectors, knowledge holders, or power brokers.

Among the multiplying commercial applications for big data: A mobile phone company used the methodology to analyze the calls its customers made. This identified "tribal leaders," individuals who got and made the largest number of connections to a small affinity group. The company found that if such a leader adopted a new phone service the company offered, those in the tribe were highly likely to do so, too. On the other hand, if the leader dropped the phone service for another, the tribe would be likely to follow.[4]

"The focus of organizational attention has been on internal information," Thomas Davenport, who tracks the uses of big data, told me. "We've squeezed about as much juice from that fruit as we can. So we've turned to external information—the Internet, customer sentiment, supply chain risk, and the like."

Davenport, formerly director of the Accenture Institute for Strategic Change, was on the faculty at Harvard Business School when we spoke. He added, "What we need is an ecological model, where you survey the external information environment—everything happening in a company's surround that might impact it."

The information an organization gets from its computer systems, Davenport argues, can be far less useful than what comes in from other sources in the overall ecology of information, as processed by people. And a search engine may give you massive data, but no context for understanding, let alone wisdom about that information. What makes data more useful is the person curating it.[5] Ideally, the person who curates information will zero in on what matters, prune away the rest, establish a context for what the data means, and do all that in a way that shows why it is vital—and so captures people's attention.

The best curators don't just put the data in a meaningful context—they know what questions to ask. When I interviewed Davenport, he was writing a book that encourages those who manage big data projects to ask questions like these: Are we defining the right problem? Do we have the right data? What are the assumptions behind the algorithm the data gets fed into? Does the model guiding those assumptions map on reality?[6]

At an MIT conference on big data, one speaker pointed out that the financial crisis of 2008 onward was a failure of the method, as hedge funds around the world collapsed. The dilemma is that the mathematical models embodied in big data are simplifications. Despite the crisp numbers they yield, the math behind those numbers hinges on models and assumptions, which can fool those who use them into placing too much confidence in their results.

At that same conference, Rachel Schutt, a senior statistician at Google Research, observed that data science requires more than math skills: it also takes people who have a wide-ranging curiosity, and whose innovation is guided by their own experience—not just data. After all, the best intuition takes huge amounts of data, harvesting our entire life experience, and filters it through the human brain.[7]

13

SYSTEM BLINDNESS

Mau Piailug could read the stars and clouds, the ocean swells and the birds in flight, as though they were a GPS screen. Mau would take these readings and many others in the middle of the South Pacific, with nothing but sky on the horizon for weeks on end, using only the knowledge of the seas he learned from his elders on his native Caroline island of Satawal.

Mau, born in 1932, was the last surviving native practitioner of the ancient Polynesian art of "wayfinding": piloting a double-hulled canoe with only the lore in your head, traversing hundreds or thousands of miles from one island to another. Wayfinding embodies systems awareness at its height, reading subtle cues like the temperature or saltiness of seawater; flotsam and plant debris; the patterns of flight of seabirds; the warmth, speed, and direction of winds; variations in the swells of waves; and the rising and setting of the stars at night. All that gets mapped against a mental model of where islands are to be found, lore learned through native stories, chants, and dances.

That allowed Mau to pilot a Polynesian-style canoe the 2,361 miles from Hawaii to Tahiti, a 1976 voyage that made anthropologists realize ancient islanders could traverse the South Pacific routinely, in two-way traffic from distant island to distant island.

But over the half century during which Mau preserved this refined awareness of natural systems, Polynesians had turned to the navigational aids of the modern world. His was a dying lore.

Mau's epic canoe voyage stirred a revival in the study of the art of wayfinding among the native peoples of the South Pacific, a renewed interest that continues to this day. Fifty years after his own initiation as a wayfinder, Mau held the same ceremony once again for the first time, for a handful of students he had trained.

Such lore, handed down for generations from elders to the young, exemplifies the local knowledge that native peoples everywhere have relied on to survive in their particular ecological niche, letting them get basics like food, safety, clothing, and shelter.

Through human history, systems awareness—detecting and mapping the patterns and order that lie hidden within the chaos of the natural world—has been propelled by this urgent survival imperative for native peoples to understand their local ecosystem. They must know what plants are toxic, which nourish or heal; where to get drinking water and where to gather herbs and find food; how to read the signs of seasonal change.

Here's the catch. We are prepared by our biology to eat and sleep, mate and nurture, fight-or-flee, and exhibit all the other built-in survival responses in the human repertoire. But as we've seen, there are no neural systems dedicated to understanding the larger systems within which all this occurs.

Systems are, at first glance, invisible to our brain—we have no direct perception of any of the multitude of systems that dictate the realities of our lives. We understand them indirectly, through mental models (the meanings of wave swells, constellations, and the flight of seabirds are each such models) and take action based on those models. The more grounded in data those models are, the more effective our interventions (for example, a rocket to an asteroid). The less grounded in data, the less effective they will be (much education policy).

This lore stems from hard-learned lessons that become distributed knowledge, shared among a people, such as the healing property of specific herbs. And older generations pass on this accumulated lore to the younger.

One of Mau's students, Elizabeth Kapu'uwailani Lindsey, a Hawaii-born anthropologist who specialized in ethnonavigation, has become an explorer and fellow at the National Geographic Society. Her mission: ethnographic rescue, the conservation of vanishing indigenous knowledge and traditions.

"Much of the loss of native lore is due to acculturation and colonization, and governments marginalizing native wisdom," she told me. "This lore is passed on in many ways. Hawaiian dance, for example, was a code of movement and chants that told our genealogy, astronomy, and natural laws, and the backstory of our cultural history. The dancer's movements, the chants, even the sound of the *pahu* drums, held meaning.

"These were traditionally sacred practices," she added. "Then when missionaries arrived, they deemed these dances immoral. It was only during our cultural renaissance in the 1970s that ancient hula, or *hula kahiko*, emerged once more. Until then, modern hula had become entertainment for tourists."

Mau studied for years, with many teachers: his grandfather chose him to begin studies as a navigator-to-be when Mau was but five or so. From that time on, Mau joined the older men preparing their canoes to go fishing; he'd ride the seas, listening to their tales of sailing—and the navigational tips embedded in them—into the night as they drank in the canoe house. All in all he studied with a half dozen expert navigators.

Such native lore represents the root sciences, the needs-to-know that have over centuries grown into today's burgeoning multitude of scientific specialties. This growth has been self-organizing, perhaps fulfilling an innate survival drive to understand the world around us.

The invention of culture was a huge innovation for *Homo sapiens*: creating language and a shared cognitive web of understanding that transcends any individual's knowledge and life span—and that can be drawn on as needed and passed on to new generations. Cultures divide up expertise: there are midwives and healers, warriors and builders, farmers and weavers. Each of these domains of expertise can be shared, and those who hold the deepest reservoir of understanding in each are the guides and teachers for others.

Native lore has been a crucial part of our social evolution, the way cultures pass down their wisdom through time. Primitive bands in early evolution would have thrived or died depending on their collective intelligence in reading the local ecosystem: to anticipate key moments for planting, harvesting, and the like—and so the first calendars came into being.

But as modernity has provided machines to take the place of such lore—compasses, navigational guides, and, eventually, online maps—native people have joined everyone else in relying on them, forgetting their local lore, like wayfinding.

And so it has gone with almost every traditional form of expertise for attuning to nature's systems. The first contact of a native people with the outside world typically marks the start of a gradual forgetting of their lore.

When I spoke with Lindsey, she was preparing to leave for Southeast Asia to see the Moken, who are sea nomads. Just before the 2004 tsunami swept through the islands they inhabited in the Indian Ocean, the Moken "realized the birds had stopped singing and the dolphins were swimming farther out to sea," she told me. "So they all climbed in their boats and traveled to deep ocean, where the tsunami crest was minimal as it passed them. Not one Moken was hurt."

Other peoples—who had long forgotten to listen to the birds and watch the dolphins, as well as what to make of how those species behaved—perished. Lindsey is worried that the Moken are being forced to give up their gypsy life at sea and settle on land in Thailand and Burma. Such ecological intelligence can vanish from collective memory within a generation as the forms for passing it on vanish.

Lindsey—an anthropologist raised by native healers in Hawaii—told me, "I was taught by my elders that when you go into the forest to pick flowers for making leis or plants for medicine, you only take a few blossoms or leaves from each limb. When you're done, the forest should look like you had never been there. Today kids often go in with plastic garbage bags and break off branches."

This obliviousness to the systems around us has long puzzled me, particularly as I've investigated our collective cluelessness in the face of a threat to our species survival posed by our daily doings. We seem curiously unable to perceive in a way that leads us to prevent the adverse consequences of human systems, such as those for industry or commerce.

THE ILLUSION OF UNDERSTANDING

Here was the dilemma and opportunity for a major national retailer: its magazine buyers were reporting that close to 65 percent of all the magazines printed in the United States were never sold. This represented an annual cost of hundreds of millions of dollars to the system, but no one party in the system could change it alone. So the retail chain—among the biggest customers for magazines in the country—got together with a group of publishers and magazine distributors to see what they could do.

For the magazine industry, squeezed by the digital media and falling sales, the matter was urgent. For years no one could solve this problem; everyone just shrugged. Now the industry was ready to take a hard look.

"There was a huge amount of waste, whether you look at it from the perspective of sheer cost, trees cut, or carbon emitted," Jib Ellison, CEO of Blu Skye consulting, told me.

Ellison, who helped convene the group, added, "We find this in most supply chains: they were built in the nineteenth century with a view toward what can be sold, not with sustainability or reducing waste in mind. When one part of the chain optimizes for itself, it tends to suboptimize the whole."

One of the biggest dilemmas was that advertisers paid according to how many magazines their ads appeared in—not how many were sold. But a magazine "in circulation" might just sit on a shelf for weeks or months, and then be pulped. So publishers had to go back to their advertisers and explain a new basis for charging them.

The retail chain analyzed which were its best-selling magazines in what stores. It found, for example, that *Roadster* might sell well in five markets but not at all in another five. The chain was able to adjust where magazines went by where they were wanted. All in all, the various fixes reduced waste by up to 50 percent. This was not only an environmental plus; it also opened shelf space for other products while saving beleaguered publishers money.

Solving such problems takes seeing the systems that are in play. "We look for a systemic problem that no one player can solve—not a person, a government, a company," Ellison tells me. The first breakthrough in the magazine dilemma was simply getting all these players together—and getting the system into the room.[1]

"Systems blindness is the main thing we struggle with in our work," says John Sterman, who holds the Jay W. Forrester chair at MIT's Sloan School of Management. Forrester, Sterman's mentor, was a founder of systems theory, and Sterman has been the go-to systems expert at MIT for years, directing MIT's Systems Dynamics Group.

His classic textbook on system thinking applied to organizations and other complex entities makes the fundamental point that what we think of as "side effects" are misnamed. In a system there are no side effects—just effects, anticipated or not. What we see as "side effects" simply reflect our flawed understanding of the system. In a complex system, he observes, cause and effect may be more distant in time and space than we realize.

Sterman gives the example of debates over "zero-emission" electric cars.[2] They are not, in fact, "zero-emission" within a systems perspective, if they draw their electricity from an energy grid composed largely of polluting coal plants. And even if the power is generated in, say, solar farms, there's the cost to the planet of the emissions of greenhouse gases in manufacturing the solar panels and the powering of their supply chain.[3]

One of the worst results of system blindness occurs when leaders implement a strategy to solve a problem—but ignore the pertinent system dynamics.

"It's insidious," says Sterman. "You get short-term relief, and then the problem comes back, often worse than before."

Traffic jams? The shortsighted solution means building more and wider roads. The new capacity brings short-term relief in congestion. But because it's now easier to get around, those very roads mean people, stores, and workplaces spread throughout the region. Traffic over the long term increases until the jams and delays are just as bad as, or worse than, before—the traffic keeps growing until it's so unpleasant to drive that further growth in trips stops.

"Feedback loops regulate congestion," says Sterman. "Anytime you have more capacity for traffic, people take more car trips, move farther away, buy more cars. As people spread out, mass transit loses viability. You're trapped."

We think we are held up because of that traffic jam, but the jam itself emerges from the dynamics of highway systems. The disconnect between such systems and how we relate to them begins with distortions in our mental models. We blame those other drivers clogging the road but fail to take into account the systems dynamics that put them there.

"Much of the time," Sterman notes, "people attribute what happens to them to events close in time and space, when in reality it's the result of the dynamics of the larger system within which they are embedded."

The problem gets compounded by what's called the "illusion of explanatory depth," where we feel confidence in our understanding of a complex system, but in reality have just superficial knowledge. Try to explain in depth how an electric grid operates or why increasing atmospheric carbon dioxide ups the energy in storms, and the illusory nature of our systems understanding becomes clearer.[4]

In addition to mismatches of our mental models and the systems they presume to map, there are even more profound predicaments: our perceptual and emotional systems are all but blind to them. The human brain was molded by what helped us and our forerunners survive in the wild, particularly in the Pleistocene geological epoch (roughly from 2 million years ago to about 12,000 years ago, when there was the rise of agriculture).

We are finely tuned to a rustling in the leaves that may signal a stalking tiger. But we have no perceptual apparatus that can sense the thinning of the atmosphere's ozone layer, nor the carcinogens in the particulates we breathe on a smoggy day. Both can eventually be fatal, but our brain has no direct radar for these threats.

MAKING THE INVISIBLE PALPABLE

It's not just perceptual mistuning. If our emotional circuitry (particularly the amygdala, the trigger point for the fight-or-flight response) perceives an immediate threat it will flood us with hormones like cortisol and adrenaline, which ready us to hit or run. But this does not happen if we hear of potential dangers that might emerge in years or centuries to come; the amygdala hardly blinks.

The amygdala's circuitry, concentrated in the middle of the brain, operates automatically, bottom-up. We rely on it to be on the alert for dangers and tell us what we need to pay urgent attention to. But our automatic circuitry, usually so reliable in guiding our attention, have no perceptual apparatus or emotional loading for systems and their dangers. They draw a blank.

"It's easier to override an automatic, bottom-up response with top-down reasoning than it is to deal with the complete absence of a signal," Columbia University psychologist Elke Weber observes. "But that's the situation when it comes to dealing with the environment. There's nothing here in the Hudson Valley on this lovely summer day to tell me the planet is warming."

"Ideally, some of my attention should go there—it's a long-term danger," adds Weber, whose work includes advising the National Academy of Sciences on environmental decision-making.[5] "But there's no bottom-up message to pay attention to, nothing that says: 'Danger over here! Do something,' so this is much harder to address. We don't notice what's not there—and neither mental system alerts us to this. It's the same with our health or our retirement savings. When we eat some very rich dessert, we don't get a signal telling us, 'If you keep this up, you'll die three years earlier.' And when you buy that spunky second car, nothing tells you, 'You will regret this when you are old and destitute.'"

Dr. Larry, whose mandate includes fighting global warming, puts it this way: "I have to persuade you that there's an odorless, tasteless, invisible gas that's gathering in the heavens and capturing the sun's heat because of what man does in using fossil fuels. It's a heavy lift.

"Actually the most comprehensive, complex science shows this," he adds. "More than two thousand scientists put together what might be the most elegant coordination of scientific findings in history—the Intergovernmental Panel on Climate Change. They did it to convince people who are not wired for this to realize the dangers.

"But unless you live in the Maldives or Bangladesh, it seems far away," Dr. Larry observes. "The dimension of time is a huge problem—if the pace of global warming were accelerated to a few years instead of over centuries, people would pay more attention. But it's like the national debt: *I'll leave it to my grandchildren—I'm sure they'll think of some solution.*"

As Sterman observes, "Climate change will come over a long time horizon that we can't see, so it's hard to convince people. Only the leaf-rustling problems get our attention, not the big ones that will kill us."

At one time, the survival of human groups depended on ecological attunement. Today we have the luxury of living well using artificial aids. Or seem to have the luxury. For the same attitudes that have made us reliant on technology have lulled us into indifference to the state of the natural world—at our peril.

So to meet the challenge of impending system collapse we need what amounts to a prosthesis for the mind.

14

DISTANT THREATS

As the Indian yogi Neem Karoli Baba once told me, "You can plan for a hundred years, but you don't know what will happen the next moment."

On the other hand, cyberpunk author William Gibson observes, "The future is already here. It's just not evenly distributed."

What we can know of the future lies somewhere between the two views: we have glimmerings, and yet there's always the potential of a black-swan event that could wash it all away.[1]

Back in the 1980s, in her prophetic work *In the Age of the Smart Machine*, Shoshona Zuboff saw that the advent of computers was flattening the hierarchy in organizations. Where once knowledge was power, and so the most powerful hoarded their information, new tech systems were opening the gates to data for everyone.

When Zuboff wrote, that future was by no means evenly distributed—the Internet did not yet exist, let alone the cloud, YouTube, or Anonymous. But today (and certainly tomorrow) the flow of information ranges ever more freely, not just within an organization, but globally. A frustrated fruit vendor sets himself aflame in a marketplace in Tunisia, sparking the Arab Spring.

Two classic instances of not knowing what will happen the next moment: Thomas Robert Malthus's prediction in 1798 that population growth would reduce human existence to a "perpetual struggle for room and food," trapped in a downward spiral of squalor and famine; and Paul R. Ehrlich's 1968 warning about the "population bomb," which would produce vast famines by 1985.

Malthus failed to foresee the Industrial Revolution, and the ways mass production allowed more people to live longer. Ehrlich's calculations missed the coming of the "green revolution," which accelerated food production ahead of the population curve.

The Anthropocene Age, which began with the Industrial Revolution, marks the first geologic epoch in which the activities of one species—we humans—inexorably degrade the handful of global systems that support life on earth.

The Anthropocene represents systems in collision. Human systems for construction, energy, transportation, industry, and commerce daily attack the operation of natural systems like the nitrogen and carbon cycles, the rich dynamics of ecosystems, the availability of usable water, and the like.[2] What's more, within the last fifty years this onslaught has undergone what scientists call the "great acceleration," with atmospheric carbon dioxide concentrations, among other indicators of coming systems crises, increasing at an ever-greater rate.[3]

The human planetary footprint, Ehrlich saw, is a product of three forces: what each of us consumes, how many of us there are, and the methods we deploy to get the stuff we consume. Using those three measures, the United Kingdom's Royal Society tried to estimate the earth's carrying capacity for humanity—the maximum number of people the earth can support without a collapse in the systems that support life. Their conclusion: it depends.

The biggest unknown in the forecast was improvements in technology. China, for instance, worryingly expanded its capacity for generating electricity from coal—and more recently increased its use of solar and wind energy at a rapid rate. Net result: the ratio of CO_2 emitted relative to economic output in China has plummeted by around 70 percent over the last thirty years (although these numbers hide the continuing steep growth in coal-burning power plants in "the world's factory").[4] In short, technological revolutions may save us from ourselves, letting us use resources in ways that protect the planet's vital life-support systems—if we can find methods that don't just create new problems or conceal old ones.

Or at least that's the hope. But no strong economic force favors such technology revolutions in the long run. The short-term gains are made largely because companies can save money, not because of the planetary virtues of sustainability per se.

For example, during the economic crisis that began in 2008, CO_2 levels began falling in the United States not because of government mandates, but because of market forces—less demand, plus cheaper natural gas for power plants replaced coal (though the local pollution and health problems caused by fracking for that gas creates other headaches).

As we've seen, a blind spot in the human brain may contribute to this mess. Our brain's perceptual apparatus has fine-tuning for a range of attention that has paid off in human survival. While we are equipped with razor-sharp focus on smiles and frowns, growls and babies, as we've seen, we have zero neural radar for the threats to the global systems that support human life. They are too macro or micro for us to notice directly. So when we are faced with news of these global threats, our attention circuits tend to shrug.

Worse, our core technologies were invented in a day long before we had a clue about their threat to the planet. Half of industry's CO_2 emissions are due to how we make steel, cement, plastic, paper, and energy. While we can make substantial reductions in those emissions with improvements in those methods, we'd be far better off reinventing them entirely so they have zero negative impact, or even replenish the planet.

What could make that reinvention pay? A factor unnoted by

Ehrlich and others who have tried to diagnose this dilemma: ecological transparency.

Knowing where to focus in a system makes all the difference. Take the biggest mess facing our species: our slow-motion mass suicide as human systems degrade the global systems that support life on this planet. We can begin to get a more fine-tuned handle on this degradation by applying life cycle analysis (LCA) to the products and processes that cause it.

Over the course of its life cycle a simple glass jar, for instance, goes through about two thousand discrete steps. At each step the LCA can calculate a multitude of impacts, from emissions into air, water, and soil to impacts on human health or degradation of an ecosystem. The addition of caustic soda to the mix for glass—one of those steps—accounts for 6 percent of the jar's danger to ecosystems, and 3 percent of its harm to health; 20 percent of the jar's role in climate warming is from the power plants that feed the glass factory. Each of the 659 ingredients used in glassmaking has its own LCA profile. And so on, ad infinitum.

Life cycle analyses can give you a tsunami of information, overwhelming even the most ardent ecologists in the business world. An information system designed to cache all that life cycle information would spew out a bewildering cloud of millions or billions of data points. Still, digging into that data can pinpoint, for instance, exactly where in the history of that object changes can most readily reduce its ecological footprint.[5]

The need to focus on a less complicated order (whether in organizing our closets, developing a business strategy, or analyzing LCA data) reflects a fundamental truth. We live within extremely complex systems, but engage them lacking the cognitive capacity to understand or manage them completely. Our brain has solved this problem by finding means to sort through what's complicated via simple decision rules. For instance, navigating our lives within the intricate social world of all the people we know gets simpler if we use trust as an organizing rule of thumb.[6]

To simplify that LCA tsunami, promising software zeroes in on the four biggest impacts four levels down in a product's supply chain.[7] This offers up the roughly 20 percent of the causes that account for about 80 percent of effects—the ratio known as the Pareto principle, that a small amount of variables account for the largest portion of effect.

Such heuristics determine whether a flood of data offers up a "Eureka!" or we suffer from information overload. That decision (*Got it!* versus *Too much information*) emanates from a thin strip in the brain's prefrontal area, the dorsolateral circuits. The arbiter of this cognitive tipping point resides in the same neurons that keep the turbulent impulses of the amygdala damped down. When we hit cognitive overwhelm, the dorsolateral gives up, and our decisions and choices get worse and worse as our anxiety rises.[8] We've reached the pivot where more data leads to poor choices.

Better: Zero in on a manageable number of meaningful patterns within a data torrent and ignore the rest. Our cortical pattern detector seems designed to simplify complexity into manageable decision rules. One cognitive capacity that continues to increase as the years go on is "crystallized intelligence": recognizing what matters, the signal within the noise. Some call it wisdom.

WHAT'S YOUR HANDPRINT?

I'm as trapped in these systems as anyone. Yet I find it hard to write about this without sounding shrill; our impacts on the planet are inherently guilt-inducing and depressing. And that's my point. Focusing on what's wrong about what we do activates circuitry for distressing emotions. Emotions, remember, guide our attention. And attention glides away from the unpleasant.

I used to think that complete transparency about the negative impacts of what we do and buy—knowing our eco-footprints—would in itself create a market force that would encourage us all to vote with our dollars by buying better alternatives.[9] Sounded like a good idea—but I neglected a psychological fact. Negative focus leads to discouragement and disengagement. When our neural centers for distress take over, our focus shifts to the distress itself, and how to ease it. We long to tune out.

So instead we need a positive lens. Enter www.handprinter.org, a website that encourages anyone to take the lead in environmental improvements. Handprinter draws on LCA data to guide us in assessing our habits (such as in cooking, travel, heating, and cooling) to get a baseline for our carbon footprints. But that's just the beginning.

Then Handprinter takes all the helpful things we do—use renewable energy, ride a bike to work, turn the thermostat down—and gives us a precise metric for the *good* we do by lessening our footprint. The sum total of all our good habits yields the value for our handprint. The key idea: keep making improvements, so that our handprint becomes bigger than our footprint. At that point we become a net positive for the planet.

If you can get other people to follow your lead and adopt the same changes, your handprint grows accordingly. Handprinter is a natural for social media; it's already an app on Facebook. Families, stores, teams, and clubs, even towns and companies, can increase their handprint together.

So can schools. That's one venue where Gregory Norris, who developed Handprinter, sees special promise. Norris is an industrial ecologist who studied with John Sterman while at MIT, and then taught life cycle analysis there. Now he's working with an elementary school in York, Maine, to help it grow its handprint.

Norris got the head of sustainability at Owens-Corning, the giant glass products corporation, to donate three hundred fiberglass blankets for water heaters to the school. In Maine, those blankets can reduce carbon emissions by a significant amount—and save households around seventy dollars a year in utility bills.[10] Houses that get the blankets will share part of their fuel savings with the school, which can use that cash to make improvements at the school and still have plenty left over to buy water blankets to give away to two other schools.[11]

Those two schools will repeat the process, each giving blankets to two other schools, in an ever-expanding sequence. The math of such a geometric progression augurs a ripple effect throughout the region and, potentially, far beyond.

In the first round, every participating school gets credited in its handprint with a reduction of some 130 tons of CO_2 emissions per year, for an expected blanket life of at least ten years. But Handprinter also gives it successive credits for every other school in the chain; in just six rounds that should include 128 schools, a carbon reduction of around 16,000 tons of CO_2. Assuming new "rounds" every three months, that would be 60,000 tons by the start of the third year, and 1 million by the fourth.

"The LCA calculation for one house's heater wrap starts off negative, when you assess the wrap's supply chain and life cycle," says Norris. "But once you get into the impacts of its use, at a certain point it becomes progressively positive for greenhouse gases" as a home draws less power from coal-burning power plants or uses less fuel oil.[12]

Handprints put the negatives (our footprint) in the background and positives in the foreground. When we are motivated by positive emotions, what we do feels more meaningful and the urge to act lasts longer. It all stays longer in attention. In contrast, fear of global warming's impacts may get our attention quickly, but once we do one thing and feel a little better, we think we're done.

"Twenty years ago few people paid attention to how their activities mattered for carbon emissions," Columbia's Elke Weber observes. "There was no way to measure it. Now the carbon footprint gives us a metric for what we do, making these decisions easier: you can diagnose where you stand. What we measure we pay more attention to and have goals around.

"But a footprint is a negative metric, and negative emotions are poor motivators. For example, you can get women's attention about getting breast exams by scaring them about what might happen if they don't get examined. This tactic captures attention in the short term, but because fear is a negative feeling, people will take just enough action to change their mood for the better—then ignore it.

"For long-term change you need sustained action," Weber added. "A positive message says, 'Here are better actions to take and with this metric you can see the good you're doing—as you keep going, you can continually feel better about how you are doing.' That's the beauty of handprints."

SYSTEMS LITERACY

Raid on Bungeling Bay, an early video game, put the player in a helicopter that was attacking a military enemy. You could bomb factories, roads, docks, tanks, planes, and ships.

Or, if you understood that the game was mapping the enemy's supply chain, you could win with a smarter strategy: bombing his supply boats first.

"But most people just flew around and blew up everything as fast as they could," says the game's designer, Will Wright, better known as the brain behind SimCity and its successive universes of multiplayer simulations.[13] One of Wright's early inspirations in designing these virtual worlds was the work of MIT's Jay Forrester

(John Sterman's mentor and a founder of modern systems theory), who in the 1950s was among the first to try to simulate a living system on a computer.

While there are reasonable concerns about the social impacts of games on kids, a little-recognized benefit of games is acquiring the knack for learning the ground rules of an unknown reality. Games teach kids how to experiment with complex systems. Winning demands acquiring an intuitive sense of the algorithms built into the game and figuring out how to navigate through them, as Wright points out.[14]

"Trial and error, reverse-engineering stuff in your mind—all the ways kids interact with games—that's the kind of thinking schools should be teaching. As the world becomes more complex," Wright adds, "games are better at preparing you."

"Kids are natural systems thinkers," says Peter Senge, who brought systems thinking to organizational learning, and has more recently been teaching this perspective in schools. "You'll get three six-year-olds looking at why they have so many fights on the playground, and they'll realize they have a feedback loop where calling names leads to hurt feelings, which leads to calling names, with more hurt feelings—and it all builds to a fight."

Why not embed this understanding in the general education our culture passes on to our children, like Mau's tutorial in celestial navigation? Call it systems literacy.

Gregory Norris has become part of the Center for Health and the Global Environment at the Harvard School of Public Health, where he long taught a course in LCA. He and I did some brainstorming about what a curriculum for kids in systems and LCA might look like.

Take those particulates that are emitted less by power plants if homes use a water heater blanket. There are two main kinds, both damaging to the lungs: tiny particles that go into the lungs' deepest recesses, and some that start as the gases nitrous oxide or sulfur dioxide and transform into particles that do the same damage.

These particles are an enormous problem in public health, particularly in urban areas like Los Angeles, Beijing, Mexico City, and New Delhi, where highly polluted days are frequent. The World Health Organization estimates that outdoor air pollution causes about 3.2 million deaths yearly worldwide.[15]

Given such data, a health or math class could calculate for a smoggy day in a city the resulting "disability adjusted life years" (or DALY; one DALY unit equals the loss of a year of good health)—computing the days of healthy life lost due to particulate emissions. This can be calculated for even a tiny amount of exposure and translated into its role in increased disease rates.

Different topics would analyze these systems in their own way. Biology would explore, for example, the mechanisms involved when particulates in the lungs lead to asthma, cardiovascular disease, or emphysema. A chemistry class could focus on the conversion of the gases nitrous oxide and sulfur dioxide into those particles. Social policy, civics, or environmental studies could discuss the issues of how today's systems of energy, transportation, and construction routinely pose such threats to the public's health—and how these systems could be changed to lower those health risks.

Embedding this learning in school lesson plans erects the conceptual scaffolding for systems thinking that can be elaborated on more explicitly as children at higher grades engage the specifics in greater detail.[16]

"It takes a panoramic attention to appreciate system-level interactions," says Richard Davidson. "You need to be attentionally flexible, so you can expand and contract your focus, like a zoom lens, to see elements big and small." Why not teach children these basic skills in reading systems?

Education upgrades mental models. Helping students master

the cognitive maps for, say, industrial ecology as part of their overall education means these insights will become part of their decision rules in adulthood.

For consumers, this would affect thinking about what brands to buy and which to avoid; for decision-makers at work it would come up in everything from where to invest to manufacturing processes and material sourcing, to business strategy and risk avoidance. Most especially this way of thinking should lead some among our younger generations to become avid about research and development, particularly along the lines of bio-mimicry—doing things the way nature does them.

Virtually all of today's industrial platforms, chemicals, and manufacturing processes were developed in an earlier era when no one knew or cared about environmental impacts. Now that we have the LCA lens with systems thinking, we need to rethink them all—a huge entrepreneurial opportunity for the future.

At a closed-door meeting of several dozen heads of sustainability, I was encouraged to hear them tick off lists of improvements their company had made, ranging from energy-saving solar-powered factories to sourcing sustainably grown raw materials. But I was equally depressed to hear a chorus of complaints boiling down to this: "But our customers don't care."

This education initiative should help solve that problem in the long run. The young inhabit a world of social media, where the forces emerging from digital hyperconnections can sway markets and minds. If a method like Handprints goes viral, it could help create the now-missing economic force that makes it imperative for companies to change how they do business.

The more well-informed minds the better. When we confront an immense system, attention needs to be widely distributed. One set of eyes can see only so far; a swarm grasps much more. The most robust entity takes in the greatest amount of relevant information, understands it most deeply, and responds most nimbly. We, collectively, can become that entity.

Add systems literacy to the long and growing list of what people around the world are already doing to avoid a planetary meltdown. The more, the better: there may be no single fulcrum for change, but rather many widely dispersed ones. That's the argument made by Paul Hawken in his book *Blessed Unrest*. When the 2009 Copenhagen climate meeting (like all the others) failed to come up with an agreement, Hawken said it was "irrelevant because I don't think that's where change comes from."

Hawken's perspective: "Imagine 50,000 people in Copenhagen exchanging antennae and notes and cards and contacts and ideas and so forth and then spreading back all over the world to 192 countries. Energy and climate is a system; this is a systemic problem. That means everything we're doing is part of the healing of the system and that there is no Archimedean point in the system where we're either failing or, if we pull harder, we're going to succeed."[17]

PART V

SMART PRACTICE

15

THE MYTH OF 10,000 HOURS

The Iditarod may be the world's most grueling race: sled dogs compete over a gauntlet of more than eleven hundred miles of Arctic ice, running for more than a week. Typically the dogs and musher go all day and rest at night, or go all night with rest during the day.

Susan Butcher reinvented the Iditarod by running and resting alternately in four-to-six-hour chunks throughout the night and day instead of twelve hours on and twelve off. It was a risky innovation—for one, it gave her less chance to sleep (while her dogs slept she would have to prepare for the next leg). But she and her sled dogs had practiced that way, and from the first time she tried, Butcher just knew in her heart the all-out regimen could work.

Butcher went on to win the Iditarod four times. She died from leukemia (which had claimed her brother in her childhood) a decade after her racing days. In her honor, the state of Alaska proclaimed the first day of the Iditarod to be Susan Butcher Day.

Butcher, a veterinary technician, was a leader in humane treatment of her dogs, making year-round care and training the standard for mush teams rather than an exception. She was attuned to the biological limits of what her dogs could withstand. Poor treatment of dogs has been the main criticism of the race.

Butcher trained her dogs much as a marathoner prepares for a race, realizing that rest is as important as running. "For Susan, dog care was the number-one priority," her husband, David Monson, told me. "She regarded her dogs as year-round professional athletes, giving them the highest-quality veterinary care, training, and nutrition."

Then there was her personal preparation. "Most people can't imagine the complexity of going on a thousand-mile expedition in the ice and snow that might last for up to fourteen days," Monson told me. "The temperature varies from forty above to sixty below; you're at the mercy of blizzards. You've got to bring repair kits, and food and medicine for yourself and your dogs, and make the right strategic decisions. It's like preparing for an expedition up Everest.

"For instance, there are ninety or a hundred miles between checkpoints where you've cached food and supplies for the next segment, and you need a pound of dog food for each dog every day. But if the next area might have a blizzard, you need to take extra food and shelter for the dogs. And that adds weight."

Butcher had to make such life-and-death decisions—plus stay vigilant and attentive—while getting just one or two hours of sleep a day. While the dogs rested as much as they ran, during their breaks she would be busy caring for and feeding the dogs and herself, and making any needed repairs. "Keeping your attention up during a highly exhausting and stressful time means you have to be methodical and well practiced, so you make the right decisions under duress," Monson says.

She spent hours and hours fine-tuning her mushing skills, studying the subtleties of snow and ice, and bonding with her dogs. But it was her self-discipline that was most prominent in her training regimen.

"She was really able to focus," said Joe Runyan, another Iditarod winner. "And that's what made her really good at the sport."

The "10,000-hour rule"—that this level of practice holds the secret to great success in any field—has become sacrosanct gospel, echoed on websites and recited as litany in high-performance workshops.[1] The problem: it's only half true.

If you are a duffer at golf, say, and make the same mistakes every time you try a certain swing or putt, 10,000 hours of practicing that error will not improve your game. You'll still be a duffer, albeit an older one.

No less an expert than Anders Ericsson, the Florida State University psychologist whose research on expertise spawned the 10,000-hour rule of thumb, told me, "You don't get benefits from mechanical repetition, but by adjusting your execution over and over to get closer to your goal."[2]

"You have to tweak the system by pushing," he adds, "allowing for more errors at first as you increase your limits."

Apart from sports like basketball or football that favor physical traits such as height and body size, says Ericsson, almost *anyone* can achieve the highest levels of performance with smart practice.

Iditarod mushers at first dismissed Susan Butcher's chances of ever winning the race. "In those days," David Monson recalls, "the Iditarod was considered a man's cowboy-type sport—rough-and-tumble. You did it because you were tough. Other racers said Susan could never win—she babies her dogs. Then when she won year after year, people realized her dogs were better suited than others for the rigors of the race. That fundamentally changed how folks prepare for and run in the race now."

Ericsson argues that the secret of winning is "deliberate practice," where an expert coach (essentially what Susan Butcher was for her dogs) takes you through well-designed training over months or years, and you give it your full concentration.

Hours and hours of practice are necessary for great performance, but not sufficient. How experts in any domain pay attention while practicing makes a crucial difference. For instance, in his much-cited study of violinists—the one that showed the top tier had practiced more than 10,000 hours—Ericsson found the experts did so with full concentration on improving a particular aspect of their performance that a master teacher identified.[3]

Smart practice always includes a feedback loop that lets you recognize errors and correct them—which is why dancers use mirrors. Ideally that feedback comes from someone with an expert eye—and so every world-class sports champion has a coach. If you practice without such feedback, you don't get to the top ranks.

The feedback matters and the concentration does, too—not just the hours.

Learning how to improve any skill requires top-down focus. Neuroplasticity, the strengthening of old brain circuits and building of new ones for a skill we are practicing, requires our paying attention: When practice occurs while we are focusing elsewhere, the brain does not rewire the relevant circuitry for that particular routine.

Daydreaming defeats practice; those of us who browse TV while working out will never reach the top ranks. Paying full attention seems to boost the mind's processing speed, strengthen synaptic connections, and expand or create neural networks for what we are practicing.

At least at first. But as you master how to execute the new routine, repeated practice transfers control of that skill from the top-down system for intentional focus to bottom-up circuits that eventually make its execution effortless. At that point you don't need to think about it—you can do the routine well enough on automatic.[4]

And this is where amateurs and experts part ways. Amateurs are content at some point to let their efforts become bottom-up operations. After about fifty hours of training—whether in skiing or driving—people get to that "good-enough" performance level, where they can go through the motions more or less effortlessly. They no longer feel the need for concentrated practice, but are content to coast on what they've learned. No matter how much more they practice in this bottom-up mode, their improvement will be negligible.

The experts, in contrast, keep paying attention top-down, intentionally counteracting the brain's urge to automatize routines. They concentrate actively on those moves they have yet to perfect, on correcting what's not working in their game, and on refining their mental models of how to play the game, or focusing on the particulars of feedback from a seasoned coach. Those at the top never stop learning: if at any point they start coasting and stop such smart practice, too much of their game becomes bottom-up and their skills plateau.

"The expert performer," says Ericsson, "actively counteracts such tendencies toward automaticity by deliberately constructing and seeking out training in which the set goal exceeds their current level of performance." Moreover, "The more time expert performers are able to invest in deliberate practice with full concentration, the further developed and refined their performance."[5]

Susan Butcher was training herself and her sled dogs to operate as a high-performing unit. Throughout the year she and her dogs would go through a twenty-four-hour cycle of running and resting periods, then take two days off—rather than risk her dogs slowing down from being over-raced at the then-standard twelve hours. By the time they got to the Iditarod, she and her dogs were at peak conditioning.

Focused attention, like a strained muscle, gets fatigued. Ericsson finds world-class competitors—whether weight lifters, pianists, or a dog sled team—tend to limit arduous practice to about four hours a day. Rest and restoring physical and mental energy get built into their training regimen. They seek to push themselves and their bodies to the max, but not so much that their focus gets diminished in the practice session. Optimal practice maintains optimal concentration.

ATTENTION CHUNKS

When the Dalai Lama speaks to large audiences on his world tours, often at his side will be Thupten Jinpa, his main English-language interpreter. Jinpa listens with rapt attention while His Holiness speaks in Tibetan; he only occasionally jots a quick note. Then when there's a pause, Jinpa repeats what was said in English, in his elegant Oxbridge accent.[6]

Those times that I've lectured abroad with the help of an interpreter, I've been told to speak only a few sentences before pausing for the interpreter to repeat my words in the local language. Otherwise there's too much to remember.

But I happened to be present when this Tibetan duo was in front of a crowd of thousands, and the Dalai Lama seemed to be speaking in longer and longer chunks before pausing for the translation to English. At least once he went on in Tibetan for a full fifteen minutes before pausing. It seemed an impossibly long passage for any interpreter to track.

After the Dalai Lama finished, Jinpa was silent for several moments, as the audience stirred with palpable consternation at the memory challenge he faced.

Then Jinpa started his translation, and he, too, went on for fifteen minutes—without hesitation or even a pause. It was a breathtaking performance, one that moved the audience to applaud.

What's the secret? When I asked Jinpa, he attributed his memory strengths to training he got as a young monk in a Tibetan Buddhist monastery in the south of India, where he was required to memorize long texts. "It starts when you're just eight or nine," he told me. "We tackle texts in classical Tibetan, which we don't yet understand—it would be like memorizing Latin for a European monk. We memorize by the sound. Some of the texts are liturgical chants—you'll see monks recite those chants completely from memory."

Some of the texts young monks memorize are up to thirty pages long, with hundreds of pages of commentary. "We'd start with twenty lines we'd memorize in the morning, then repeat several times during the day with the text as a prompt. Then at night we'd recite the lines in the dark, completely from memory. The next day we'd add another twenty lines, and recite all forty—until we could recite the entire text."

Smart practice maven Anders Ericsson has taught a similar talent to American college students, who by dint of sheer persistence learned to repeat back correctly up to 102 random digits (that level of digit recall took four hundred hours of focused practice). As Ericsson found, a keen attention lets learners find smarter ways to perform—whether at the keyboard or in the maze of the mind.

"When it comes to this application of attention," Jinpa confided, "it takes some doggedness. You need persistence even though it may be boring."

Such remarkable memorization *seems* to expand the capacity of working memory, where for a few seconds we store whatever we are paying attention to as we pass it on to long-term memory. But that seeming increase is not a true stretching of what we can hold in attention at any one moment. The secret is chunking—a form of smart practice.

"While His Holiness speaks," Jinpa told me, "I know the gist of what he's saying, and most of the time I know the particular text he's talking about. I make a shorthand note for the key points, though I rarely consult the notes when I speak." That shorthand indicates chunking.

As Herbert Simon, the late Nobel laureate and professor of computer science at Carnegie Mellon University, told me some years ago, "Every expert has acquired something like this memory ability" within her specialty. "Memory is like an index; experts have approximately 50,000 chunks of familiar units of information they recognize. For a physician, many of those chunks are symptoms."[7]

IN THE MENTAL GYM

Think of attention as a mental muscle that we can strengthen by a workout. Memorization works that muscle, as does concentration. The mental analog of lifting a free weight over and over is noticing when our mind wanders and bringing it back to target.

That happens to be the essence of one-pointed focus in meditation, which, seen through the lens of cognitive neuroscience, typically involves attention training. You're told to keep your focus on one thing, such as a mantra or your breath. Try it for a while and inevitably your mind wanders off.

So the universal instructions are these: when your mind wanders—and you notice that it has wandered—bring it back to your point of focus and sustain your attention there. And when your mind wanders off again, do the same. And again. And again. And again.

Neuroscientists at Emory University used functional magnetic resonance imaging (fMRI) to study the brains of meditators going through this simple movement of mind.[8] There are four steps in this cognitive cycle: the mind wanders, you notice it's wandering, you shift your attention to your breath, and you keep it there.

During mind wandering the brain activates the usual medial circuitry. At the moment you notice your mind has wandered, another attention network, this one for salience, perks up. And as you shift focus back to your breath and keep it there, prefrontal cognitive control circuits take over.

As in any workout, the more reps the stronger the muscle becomes. More-experienced meditators, one study found, were able to deactivate their medial strip more rapidly after noticing mind wandering; as their thoughts become less "sticky" with practice, it becomes easier to drop thoughts and return to the breath. There was more neural connectivity between the region for mind wandering and those that disengage attention.[9] The increased connectivity in the brains of the long-term meditators, this study suggests, are analogous to those competitive weight lifters with the perfect pecs.

Muscle builders know you won't get a six-pack belly by lifting free weights—you need to do a particular set of crunches that work the relevant muscles. Specific muscles respond to particular training regimens. So it is with attention training. Concentration on one point of focus is the basic attention builder, but that strength can be applied in many different ways.

In the mental gym, as in any fitness training, the specifics of practice make all the difference.

ACCENTUATE THE POSITIVE

Larry David, creator of the hit sitcoms *Seinfeld* and *Curb Your Enthusiasm*, hails from Brooklyn but has lived most of his life in Los Angeles. On a rare stay in Manhattan to film episodes for *Curb*—in which he plays himself—David went to see a ball game at Yankee Stadium.

During a lull in the game, cameras sent his image up to gigantic Jumbotron screens. The entire stadium of fans stood to cheer him.

But as David was leaving later that night, in the parking lot someone leaned out of a passing car and yelled "Larry, you suck!"

On the way home, Larry David obsessed about that one encounter: "Who's that guy? What was that? Who would do that? Why would you say something like that?"

It was as though those fifty thousand adoring fans didn't exist—there was just that one guy.[10]

Negativity focuses us on a narrow range—what's upsetting us.[11] A rule of thumb in cognitive therapy holds that focusing on the negatives in experience offers a recipe for depression. Cogitive therapy treatments might well encourage someone like Larry David to bring to mind his good feelings when the crowd went crazy for him, and hold his focus there.

Positive emotions widen our span of attention; we're free to take it all in. Indeed, in the grip of positivity, our perceptions shift. As psychologist Barbara Fredrickson, who studies positive feelings and their effects, puts it, when we're feeling good our awareness expands from our usual self-centered focus on "me" to a more inclusive and warm focus on "we."[12]

Focusing on the negatives or positives offers us a bit of leverage in determining how our brain operates. When we're in an upbeat, energized mood, Richard Davidson has found, our brain's left prefrontal area lights up. The left area also harbors circuitry that reminds us how great we'll feel when we finally reach some long-sought goal—the circuitry that helps keep a graduate student slogging away at a daunting dissertation.

At the neural level, positivity reflects how long we can sustain this outlook. One technical measure, for instance, assesses how long people hold a smile after seeing someone help a person in distress or after watching an exuberant toddler prancing about.

This sunny outlook shows up in attitudes: for example, that moving to a new city or meeting new people is an adventure opening up exciting possibilities—wonderful places to discover, new friends—rather than a scary step. When life brings a surprising positive moment, such as a warm conversation, the pleasant mood lasts and lasts.

As you might expect, people who experience life in this light focus on the silver lining, not just the clouds. The opposite, cynicism, breeds pessimism: not just a focus on the cloud, but the conviction that there are even darker ones lurking behind. It all depends on where you focus: the one mean fan, or the fifty thousand cheering ones.

In part positivity reflects the brain's reward circuitry in action. When we're happy, the nucleus accumbens, a region within the ventral striatum in the middle of the brain, activates. This circuitry seems vital for motivation and having a sense that what you're doing is rewarding. Rich in dopamine, these circuits are a driver of positive feeling, striving toward our goals, and desire.

This combines with the brain's own opiates, which include endorphins (the runner's-high neurotransmitters). The dopamine may fuel our drive and persistence, while the opiates tag that with a feeling of pleasure.

These circuits remain active while we stay positive. In a telling study comparing people with depression and healthy volunteers, Davidson found that after seeing a happy scene those with depression could not maintain the resulting positive feelings—their reward circuitry shut off much sooner.[13] Our executive area can trigger this circuit, making us better able to sustain positive feeling, as in keeping going despite setbacks, or just grinding away toward a goal that makes us smile when we picture what reaching it will be like. And positivity, in turn, has great payoffs for performance, energizing us so we can focus better, think more flexibly, and persevere.

Here's a question: If everything worked out perfectly in your life, what would you be doing in ten years?

That query invites us to dream a little, to consider what really matters to us and how that might guide our lives.

"Talking about your positive goals and dreams activates brain centers that open you up to new possibilities. But if you change the conversation to what you should do to fix yourself, it closes you down," says Richard Boyatzis, a psychologist at the Weatherhead School of Management at Case Western Reserve University (and a friend and colleague since we met in graduate school).

To explore these contrasting effects in personal coaching, Boyatzis and colleagues scanned the brains of college students being interviewed.[14] For some, the interview focused on positives like that question about what they'd love to be doing in ten years, and what they hoped to gain from their college years. The brain scans revealed that during the positively focused interviews there was greater activity in the brain's reward circuitry and areas for good feeling and happy memories. Think of this as a neural signature of the openness we feel when we are inspired by a vision.

For others the interview focus was more negative: how demanding they found their schedule and their assignments, difficulties making friends, and fears about their performance. As the students wrestled with the more negative questions their brain activated areas that generate anxiety, mental conflict, sadness.

A focus on our strengths, Boyatzis argues, urges us toward a desired future and stimulates openness to new ideas, people, and plans. In contrast, spotlighting our weaknesses elicits a defensive sense of obligation and guilt, closing us down.

The positive lens keeps the joy in practice and learning—the reason even the most seasoned athletes and performers still enjoy rehearsing their moves. "You need the negative focus to survive, but a positive one to thrive," says Boyatzis. "You need both, but in the right ratio."

That ratio would do well to flip far more to the positive than the negative, in light of what's known as the "Losada effect," after

Marcial Losada, an organizational psychologist who studied emotions in high-performing business teams. Analyzing hundreds of teams, Losada determined that the most effective had a positive/negative ratio of at least 2.9 good feelings to every negative moment (there's an upper limit to positivity: above a Losada ratio of about 11:1, teams apparently become too giddy to be effective).[15] The same ratio range holds for people who flourish in life, according to research by Barbara Fredrickson, who is a psychologist at the University of North Carolina (and a former research associate of Losada).[16]

Boyatzis makes the case that this positivity bias applies as well to coaching—whether by a teacher, a parent, a boss, or an executive coach.

A conversation that starts with a person's dreams and hopes can lead to a learning path yielding that vision. This conversation might extract some concrete goals from the general vision, then look at what it would take to accomplish those goals—and what capacities we might want to work on improving to get there.

That contrasts with a more common approach that focuses on a person's weaknesses—whether bad grades or missing quarterly targets—and what to do to remedy them. This conversation focuses us on what's wrong with us—our failings and what we have to do to "fix" ourselves—and all the feelings of guilt, fear, and the like that go along. One of the worst versions of this approach occurs when parents punish a child for bad grades until he improves. The anxiety associated with being punished actually hampers the child's prefrontal cortex while he is trying to concentrate and learn, creating further impediment to improvement.

In the courses he teaches at Case for MBA students and mid-career executives, Boyatzis has been applying dreams-first coaching for many years. To be sure, dreams alone are not enough: you have to practice any new needed abilities at every naturally occurring opportunity. In a given day that might mean anything from zero to a dozen chances to practice the routine you're trying to master on the way to your dream. Those moments add up.

One manager, an executive MBA student, wanted to build better relationships. "He had an engineering background," Boyatzis told me. "Give him a task and all he saw was the task, not the people he worked with to get it done."

So his learning plan became: "Spend time thinking about how the other person feels." To get regular, low-risk opportunities for this practice outside his work and the habits he had there, he helped coach his son's soccer team and tried to focus on the players' feelings while he coached.

Another executive took up tutoring for the same learning agenda, volunteering in a high school in a poor neighborhood. He used this opportunity, says Boyatzis, "to help himself learn to be more attuned and 'gentle' when helping others"—a new habit he brought into his workplace. He enjoyed tutoring so much he signed on for several more rounds.

To get data on how well this works, Boyatzis does systematic ratings of those going through the course. Coworkers or others who know them well anonymously rate the students on dozens of specific behaviors that display one or another of the emotional intelligence competencies typical of high-performers (for example: "Understands others by listening attentively"). Then he tracks the students down years later and has them rated again by those who now work with them.

"By now we've done twenty-six separate longitudinal studies, tracking people down wherever they work now," Boyatzis tells me. "We've found that the improvements students make in their first round hold up as long as seven years later."

Whether we're trying to hone a skill in sports or music, enhance our memory power, or listen better, the core elements of smart practice are the same: ideally, a potent combination of joy, smart tactics, and full focus.

As we've explored the three varieties of focus, we've also heard about ways to enhance each. Smart practice gets to a more fundamental level, cultivating the basics of attention upon which the triple focus builds.

16

BRAINS ON GAMES

Daniel Cates, a world champion, began his dedicated training routine at age six. That was when he first discovered his natural affinity for the video game Command & Conquer, which in those days came free, bundled with Microsoft Windows. From then on Cates disdained playing with other kids, preferring to spend hours commanding and conquering in the basement of his family's suburban home.[1]

At the math-and-science high school he attended, Cates would cut class and find his way to the computer room to play the puzzle game Minesweeper. The game requires locating mines hidden in an opaque grid and flagging them—without exposing one and getting blown up. Although he was just so-so when he started playing the game, endless hours of practice made Cates able to clear all the mines within ninety seconds—a feat that seemed impossible to him when he started learning the game (and utterly inconceivable to me when I just tried to play the game online; give it a go and you'll see).

At sixteen, he discovered his métier: online poker. In just eighteen months Cates went from losing five-dollar games in live-action kitchen poker to winning up to $500,000 online poker purses (and just in time—within a few years online poker became the target of laws against it, at least in the United States). By the time he was twenty, Cates had won $5.5 million at the game, $1 million more than the second-highest player's reported earnings that year.[2]

Cates earned that remarkable sum by "grinding" (as in grinding away), playing not just game after game, but multiple simultaneous games, with all comers, including the most expert. Online poker lets you play as many opponents as you can handle simultaneously, with instant win-lose feedback, which fast-tracks the learning curve. A teenager who can play a dozen online hands at a time accrues as much cumulative practice at the game's subtleties in a few short years as a lifetime gambler in his fifties who plays only the tables in Vegas.

Cates's gift for poker very likely built on the cognitive scaffolding started back when he dived into Command & Control as a first grader. Winning that battle game requires speedy cognitive processing of factors like how your troops can be deployed against your opponent's, vigilance in picking up cues of when your enemy has just begun to weaken, and mercilessly attacking. Just before his switch to poker Cates was a world champion at Command & Control; the attention skills and killer instinct that made him a champ transferred readily to the card game.

But in his twenties Cates woke up to the barrenness of his social world and nonexistent romantic life. He began a search for a lifestyle that would let him enjoy his winnings. What would that mean?

"Exercise. Girls," as he put it.

Being world class in the online zone offers little help on singles night at the local bar. Video game strengths like rampant aggression at an opponent's first sign of weakness transfer poorly to the dating scene.

Last I heard, Cates was reading my book *Social Intelligence*. I wish him well. The book argues that interactions like those during online poker lack a vital learning loop for the interpersonal circuits of the brain that help us connect and, say, make a good impression on a first meeting.

"Neurons that fire together wire together," as psychologist Donald Hebb neatly put it back in the 1940s. The brain is plastic, constantly resculpting its circuitry as we go through our day. Whatever we are doing, as we do it our brain strengthens some circuits and not others.

In face-to-face interactions our social circuitry picks up a multitude of cues and signals that help us connect well, and wire together the neurons involved. But during thousands of hours spent online, the wiring of the social brain gets virtually no exercise.

BOOSTS TO BRAIN POWER OR DAMAGE TO THE MIND?

"The majority of our socialization is flowing through machines," says Marc Smith, a founder of the Social Media Research Foundation, "and that opens up great opportunities and many concerns."[3] While "majority" seems an overstatement, debates rage about both the opportunity and the concerns, with video games an epicenter of debate.

A running stream of studies proclaim on the one hand that such games damage the mind, or on the other that they boost brainpower. Are those who argue the games give kids a sinister training in aggression right? Or, as others propose, do the games train vital attention skills? Or both?

To help settle the matter, the prestigious journal *Nature* convened half a dozen experts to sort out the benefits from the harms.[4] Turns out it's like the effects of food—it all depends: some are nutritious; too much of others can be toxic. For video games the answers hinge on the specifics of which game strengthens what brain circuitry in a given way.

Take, for instance, those hyperactive auto races and rapid-fire battles. The data on such action games shows enhancements in visual attention, speed of processing information, object tracking, and switching from one mental task to another. Many such games even seem to offer a silent tutorial in statistical inference—that is, sensing the odds that you can beat the enemies given your resources and their numbers.

And more generally, various games have been found to improve visual acuity and spatial perception, attention switching, decision-making, and the ability to track objects (though many of those studies do not let us know if people drawn to the games are already a bit better at such mental skills, or whether the games improved them).

Games that offer increasingly harder cognitive challenges—more accurate and challenging judgments and reactions at higher speeds, fully focused attention, increasing spans of working memory—drive positive brain changes.

"When you constantly need to scan the screen to detect little differences (because they may signal an enemy) and then orient attention to that area, you become better at those attentional skills," says Douglas Gentile, a cognitive scientist at the Media Research Lab at Iowa State University.[5]

But, he adds, these skills do not necessarily transfer well to life outside the video screen. Though they might have great value for specific jobs, such as air traffic controllers, they are no help when it comes to ignoring the fidgety kid sitting next to you so you can focus on your reading. Fast-paced games, some experts argue, might acclimate some children to a stimulation rate quite unlike that in the classroom, a formula for even more than usual school boredom.

Although video games may strengthen attention skills like rapidly filtering out visual distractions, they do little to amp up a more crucial skill for learning, sustaining focus on a gradually evolving body of information—such as paying attention in class and understanding what you're reading, and how it ties in to what you learned last week or year.

There's a negative correlation between the hours a kid spends gaming and how well he does in school, very likely in direct ratio to time stolen from studies. When 3,034 Singaporean children and adolescents were followed for two years, those who became extreme gamers showed increases in anxiety, depression, and social phobia, and a drop in grades. But if they stopped their gaming habit, all those problems decreased.[6]

Then there's the downside of playing countless hours of games that fine-tune the brain for a rapid, violent response.[7] Some dangers here, the expert panel says, have been exaggerated in the popular press: violent games may increase low-level aggression, but such games in themselves are not going to turn a well-raised kid into a violent one. Yet when the games are played by children who, for example, have been the victim of physical abuse at home (and so are more prone to violence themselves), there might be a dangerous synergism—though no one can as yet predict with any certainty in which child this toxic chemistry will occur.

Still, hours spent battling hordes intent on killing you understandably encourage "hostile attribution bias," the instant assumption that the kid who bumped you in the hallway has a grudge. Just as troubling, violent gamers show lessened concern when witnessing people being mean, as in bullying.

Given that the paranoid vigilance such games encourage can occasionally mix tragically with the agitation and confusion of the mentally disturbed, do we want to be feeding our young from this mental menu?

The recent generations raised on games and otherwise glued to video screens, one neuroscientist told me, amount to an unprecedented experiment: "a massive difference in how their brains are plastically engaged in life" compared with previous generations. The long-term question is what such games will do to their neural wiring, and so to the social fabric—and how this might either develop new strengths or warp healthy development.

On the upside, the demand that a player keep focused despite snazzy distracting lures enhances executive function, whether for sheer concentration now or resisting impulse later. If you add to the game's mix a need to cooperate and coordinate with other players, you've got a rehearsal of some valuable social skills.

Kids who play games that require cooperation show more helpfulness in the course of a day. Perhaps those purely violent, me-against-all games could be redesigned so that a winning strategy demanded coming to the aid of those in trouble and finding helpers and allies—not just a hostile scan.

SMART GAMES

The popular app Angry Birds lures millions of people into cumulative billions of hours of concentrated finger-flicking. If neurons that fire together wire together, you have to wonder just what mental skills, if any, are getting fine-tuned when your kids (or you) spend all that time lost in Angry Birds.

The brain learns and remembers best when focus is greatest. Video games focus attention and get us to repeat moves over and over, and so are powerful tutorials. That presents an opportunity for training the brain.

Michael Posner's group at the University of Oregon gave children four to six years old five days of attention training, in sessions lasting up to forty minutes each. Part of the time they were playing a game where they used a joystick to control a cat on a screen that was trying to catch small moving objects.

Although these three-plus hours of practice seem fairly short to track a change in the neural networks for attention, brain wave data suggested a shift in the activity of the circuitry for executive attention, toward levels seen in adults.[8]

The conclusion: target kids with the poorest attention for such training—those with autism, attention deficit, and other learning problems—since they stand to benefit the most. And beyond remedial lessons, Posner's group proposes that attention training should be part of the education of every child, giving a boost in learning across the board.

Those who, like Posner, see such potential brain training benefits propose that specially designed games could improve everything from visual tracking in "lazy eye" (known technically as amblyopia) to the hand-eye coordination of surgeons. A deficiency in the alerting network, research suggests, underlies attention deficit disorder; problems in orienting are seen in the fixations of autism.[9]

In the Netherlands, eleven-year-olds with ADHD played a computer game demanding heightened attention: they had to be vigilant for enemy bots popping up, for instance, and stay alert to when their own avatar's energy was getting too low.[10] After just eight one-hour sessions they were better able to focus despite distractions (and not just while playing the game).

At their best, "video games are controlled training regimens delivered in highly motivating" ways that result in "enduring physical and functional neurological remodeling," says Michael Merzenich, a neuroscientist at the University of California, San Francisco, who has led the design of games meant to retrain the brains of older people with neurological deficits like memory loss and dementia.[11]

Ben Shapiro, who was in charge of worldwide drug discovery—including neuroscience—at Merck Research Laboratories, has joined the board of a company designing games that increase concentration and minimize distractions. He sees advantages in using smart practice rather than medication for such purposes. "Games like this could slow the loss of key cognitive functions with aging," Shapiro tells me.

He adds, "If you want to make people's mental lives better, work directly with mental targets, rather than molecular ones—drugs are a shotgun approach, since nature uses the same molecules for many different purposes."

Dr. Merzenich puts little stock in the rather random—and decidedly mixed—benefits of off-the-shelf games, preferring to tailor ones that target a specific set of cognitive skills. A new generation of brain training apps, Douglas Gentile proposes, would apply smart practice techniques familiar to superb teachers:

- clear objectives at progressively more difficult levels
- adapting to the pace of the specific learner
- immediate feedback and graduated practice challenges to the point of mastery
- practicing the same skills in different contexts, encouraging skill transference

One day in the future, some predict, brain training games will be a standard part of schooling, with the best ones gathering data about the players as they simultaneously fine-tune themselves into the exact game needed—an empathic cognitive tutor. In the meantime, experts ruefully admit, the money spent on such education apps pales compared with budgets of gaming corporations—and so at present even the best brain training tools are sad echoes of the pizzazz of a Grand Theft Auto. But there are signs that may be changing.

I just watched my four grandchildren, one by one, play the beta version of a game for the iPad called *Tenacity*. The game offers you a leisurely journey through any of a half dozen scenes, from a barren desert to a fantasy staircase spiraling heavenward.

The challenge: Every time you exhale, you tap the iPad screen with one finger. And for every fifth exhalation you tap with two fingers—at least at the beginning level.

At the time, the grandchildren ranged in age from six, eight, and a newly minted twelve to an about-to-be fourteen. They offer what amounts to a natural experiment in brain maturation and attention.

The six-year-old goes first. He picks the desert scene, which puts him on a slow amble along a path through sand dunes, palms, and mud-daubed domiciles. The first try he had to be reminded of what to do; by the third he had gotten pretty good at coordinating his taps with his breath—though he still sometimes forgot the double taps.

Even so, he was delighted to see a field of roses slowly emerge from the desert sand every time he got it right.

A staircase spiraling through the sky was the choice of our eight-year-old. As the staircase unwound itself upward, there were occasional distractions: a helicopter flies into view, does a flip, and flies off; later a plane, a flock of birds—and at the highest altitude, various satellites. She stays intent on her tapping for the full ten minutes, despite having a bit of a fever that day.

The next grandchild, just turned twelve, picks a staircase in space, where the distractions include planets, asteroid showers, and meteorites. While her younger two siblings had helped get their taps right by controlling their breathing and counting aloud, she just breathes naturally.

And the last, soon to be fourteen, picks the desert scene and executes the whole routine effortlessly. At the end, she tells me, "I feel calm and relaxed—I like this game."

Indeed, all of them had immediately become enrapt, attuning to their breathing and the rhythm of their finger taps. "I felt really focused," the twelve-year-old reported. "I want to do it again."

That's exactly what the game designers hoped for. *Tenacity*, Davidson tells me, was developed by an award-winning game design group at the University of Wisconsin, with his input. "We took what we were learning about focus and calming in our contemplative neuroscience studies, and put it into a game so kids could get the benefits."

Tenacity strengthens selective attention, "the building block for all other kinds of learning," he added. "The self-regulation of attention lets you focus on explicit goals and resist distraction," a key to success in any domain.

"If we can create a game kids want to play, it will be an efficient way to train attention, given how much time kids spend playing and how naturally it comes to them," says Davidson, who heads the University's Center for Investigating Healthy Minds. "They'll love doing the homework."

Stanford University has a Calming Technology Lab, which focuses on gadgets that embed mindful, quieting focus. With one such calmer, "breathware," you wear a belt that detects your breath rate. Should a chock-full inbox trigger what the developer calls "email apnea," an iPhone app guides you through focusing exercises that calm your breath—and mind.

Stanford's Institute of Design offers a graduate course called "Designing Calm." As one of the teachers, Gus Tai, says, 'A lot of Silicon Valley tech is oriented toward distracting. But with calming tech, we're asking how we can bring more balance to the world."[12]

17

BREATHING BUDDIES

Drive to the dead end at the farthest reach of a street on the east side of New York City's Spanish Harlem and you find an elementary school, P.S. 112, snuggled between the FDR Drive, a Catholic church, a parking lot for big-box stores, and the massive Robert F. Wagner low-income housing compound.

The kindergartners through second graders who attend P.S. 112 come from hardscrabble homes, many in those low-income apartments. When a seven-year-old there mentioned in class that he knew someone who had been shot, the teacher asked how many other children knew a shooting victim. Every hand went up.

As you enter P.S. 112, you sign in at a desk manned by a police officer, albeit a kindly older woman. But if you walk down the halls as I did one morning, what's most striking is the atmosphere: looking into classrooms I found the children sitting still, calm and quiet, absorbed in their work or listening to their teacher.

When I drop by Room 302, the second-grade classroom of co-teachers Emily Hoaldridge and Nicolle Rubin, I witness one ingredient in the recipe for the halcyon atmosphere: breathing buddies.

The twenty-two second graders sit doing their math, three or four to a table, when Miss Emily strikes a melodious chime. On cue, the kids silently gather on a large rug, sitting in rows, cross-legged, facing the two teachers. One girl goes over to the classroom door, puts a DO NOT DISTURB sign on the outside knob, and closes it.

Then, still in silence, the teachers hold up Popsicle sticks one by one, each with a student's name—a signal for the pupils to go individually over to their cubbies and bring back their special, fist-sized stuffed animals: striped tigers, a pink pig, a yellow puppy, a purple donkey. The boys and girls find a spot on the floor to lie down, put their stuffed animal buddy on their belly, and wait, hands to their sides.

They follow the directions of a man's friendly voice leading them through some deep belly breathing, as they count to themselves, "one, two, three," while they take a long exhalation and inhalation.[1] Then they squeeze and relax their eyes; stretch their mouth wide open, sticking out their tongue; and squeeze their hands into a ball, relaxing each in turn. It ends with the voice saying, "Now sit up, and feel relaxed," and as they do, they all seem to be just that.

Another chime, and still in silence the kids on cue take their places in a circle on the rug, and report on what they experienced: "It feels nice inside." "I felt very lazy because it calmed my body." "It made me have happy thoughts."

The orderliness of the exercise and the calm focus in the classroom make it hard to believe eleven of the twenty-two kids are classified as having "special needs": cognitive impairments like dyslexia, speech difficulties or partial deafness, attention deficit hyperactivity disorder, points on the autism spectrum.

"We've got many kids with problems, but when we do this, they don't act out," says Miss Emily. But the week before, a glitch in the school day meant Room 302 skipped this ritual. "It was like they were a different class," says Miss Emily. "They couldn't sit still; they were all over the place."

"Our school has some kids who are highly distractible," says the school principal, Eileen Reiter. "This helps them relax and focus.

We also give them regular movement breaks—all these strategies help."

For example, says Reiter, "Instead of using time-outs, we teach kids to take 'time-ins,' to manage their feelings," part of an emphasis on teaching the students to self-regulate rather than relying on punishments and rewards. And when children do have problems, she adds, "We'll ask them what they could do differently next time."

Breathing buddies is part of the Inner Resilience Program, a legacy of the attacks on the World Trade Center on September 11, 2001. Thousands of children in schools near the twin towers were evacuated as the buildings went up in flames. Many hiked miles up the emptied West Side Highway, their teachers walking backward to be sure the children were not looking at the horrific specter behind.

In the months afterward, the Red Cross asked Linda Lantieri—whose conflict resolution program had already been successful in many schools—to design a program to help the children (and teachers) regain their composure after 9/11. The Inner Resilience Program, along with a range of social and emotional learning methods, "has transformed the school," Reiter says. "It's a very calm place. And when kids are calm, they learn better.

"The biggest piece is getting the kids to self-regulate," principal Reiter adds. "Because we are an early childhood school, we help students learn how to put their problems in perspective and develop strategies to resolve them. They learn to size up how big a problem is, like getting teased or bullied—it's big when someone hurts your feelings. Or middle-sized, like being frustrated with your schoolwork. They can match the problem to a strategy."

The classrooms in P.S. 112 all have a "peace corner," a special place where any child who needs to can retreat for time alone to calm down. "Sometimes they just need a break, a few moments alone," Reiter adds. "But you'll see a child who is really frustrated or upset go over to the peace corner and apply some strategies they've learned. The big lesson is to tune in and know what to do to care for yourself."

While five- to seven-year-olds get instruction in the breathing buddies exercise, from eight and up they practice mindfulness of breathing, which has proven benefits both for sustaining attention and for the circuitry that calms us down. This combination of calm and concentration creates an optimal inner state for focus and learning.

Evaluations of a one-semester version of the program found that the children who need greatest help—those at "high risk" for derailing in life—benefited the most: significant boosts in attention and perceptual sensitivity, and drops in aggressiveness, downbeat moods, and frustration with school.[2] What's more, teachers who used the program increased their sense of well-being, auguring well for the learning atmosphere of their classrooms.

THE STOPLIGHT

In a preschool, songs play as eight three-year-olds sit at a low table, each one coloring in the thick outline of a clown. Suddenly the music stops—and so do the kids.

That moment captures a learning opportunity for any three-year-old's prefrontal cortex, the site where executive functions like squelching an unruly impulse take root. One of those abilities, cognitive control, holds a key to a well-lived life.

Stopping on cue is the holy grail of cognitive control. The better children are at stopping when the music stops—or making the right move and not the wrong one while playing Simon Says—the stronger their prefrontal wiring for cognitive control becomes.

Here's a test of cognitive control. Quick now, in what direction is the middle arrow pointing in each row?

→ → → ← ←

→ ← ← ← ←

→ → ← → →

When people take this test under laboratory conditions there are detectable differences (as measured in thousandths of a second—not so detectable by you or me) between them in the speed with which they name the middle arrow's direction. The test, called the "Flanker" for the distracting arrows that flank the target one, gauges a child's susceptibility to distractions disrupting concentration. Focusing on the middle arrow going to the left and ignoring all the others headed right takes lots of cognitive control for a youngster, especially over the arduous course of a series of arrays like this.

Kids gone wild—the ones whom frustrated teachers kick out of their class, or want to—suffer from a deficit in these circuits; their whims dictate their acts. But rather than punishing kids for this, why not give them lessons that help them manage themselves better? For instance, preschoolers who had sessions learning to focus on their breath showed more accurate and faster performance on the Flanker.[3]

Perhaps no mental skill—as the New Zealand study found—matters as much in life success as executive control. Kids who can ignore impulse, filter out what's irrelevant, and stay focused on a goal fare best in life. There's an education app for that. It's called "social and emotional learning," or SEL.

When second and third graders in a Seattle school are getting upset, they're told to think of a traffic signal. Red light means stop—calm down. Take a long, deep breath and as you calm down a bit, tell yourself what the problem is and how you feel.

The yellow light reminds them to slow down and think of several possible ways they might solve the problem, then choose which is best. The green light signals them to try out that plan, and see how it works.

I first encountered stoplight posters when I was touring the New Haven, Connecticut, public schools while writing an article for the *New York Times*—well before I appreciated the crucial attention training the poster guides kids through. The stoplight rehearses the shift from bottom-up, amygdala-driven impulse to top-down, prefrontal executive-driven attention.

The stoplight exercise was the brainchild of Roger Weissberg, a psychologist then at Yale who in the late 1980s developed a pioneering program called "social development" for New Haven's public schools. Now that same image can be found on the walls of countless thousands of classrooms worldwide.

And for good reason. Back then there was only spotty data suggesting that getting kids to respond this way to their anger and anxiety had positive impact. But now that case has become about as strong as any in social science.

A meta-analysis of more than two hundred schools with social and emotional learning programs like New Haven's social development curriculum compared them with similar schools without such programs.[4] The findings for those with the programs: classroom disruption and misbehavior down 10 percent, attendance and other positive behavior up 10 percent—and achievement test scores boosted by 11 percent.

In that Seattle school the stoplight exercise was coupled with another. The second and third graders were regularly shown cards of faces with different expressions and their names. The kids talked about what it's like to have one of those feelings—to be mad or scared or happy.

These "feeling face" cards tone up a seven-year-old's emotional self-awareness; they connect the word for a feeling with its image, and then with their own experience. That simple cognitive act has neural impact: the brain's right hemisphere recognizes the feelings depicted, while the left understands the name and what it means.

Emotional self-awareness requires putting all that together via cross-talk in the corpus callosum, the tissue that connects the brain's left and right sides. The stronger the connectivity across this neural bridge, the more fully we can understand our emotions.

Being able to name your feelings and put that together with your memories and associations turns out to be crucial for self-control. Learning to speak, developmental psychologists have found, lets children call on their inner *don't* to replace the voice of their parents' in managing unruly impulses.

As a duo the stoplight and the feeling cards build two synergistic neural tools for impulse control. The stoplight strengthens circuitry between the prefrontal cortex—the brain's executive center, just behind the forehead—and the midbrain limbic centers, that cauldron of id-driven impulses. The feeling faces encourage connectivity across the two halves of the brain, boosting the ability to reason about feelings. This up-down, left-right linkage knits a child's brain together, seamlessly integrating systems that, if left to themselves, create the chaotic universe of a three-year-old.[5]

In younger children these neural connections are still budding (these brain circuits don't finally finish maturing until the mid-twenties), which explains kids' zany, sometimes maddening antics, where their whims drive their actions. But between ages five and eight, children's brains have a growth spurt in their impulse control circuits. The ability to think about their impulses and just say "no" to them makes third graders less wild than those boisterous first graders down the hall. The Seattle project's design took full advantage of this neural building boom.

But why wait until grade school? These inhibitory circuits start to develop from birth. Walter Mischel taught four-year-olds how to resist those luscious marshmallows by seeing them differently—for example, focusing on their color. And Mischel is the first to say that even a four-year-old who just can't wait and grabs the marshmallow right off the bat can still learn to delay gratification—impulsivity is not necessarily something he's stuck with for life.

In a day when online shopping and instant messages encourage gratification now, kids need more help with that practice. One strong conclusion by the scientists who studied the Dunedin, New Zealand, kids was the need for interventions that boost self-control, particularly during early childhood and the teen years. The SEL programs fill the bill, covering the years from kindergarten through high school.[6]

It's intriguing that Singapore has become the first country in the world to require every one of its students go through an SEL program. The tiny city-state represents one of the great economic success stories of the last fifty years, as a paternalistic government built a diminutive nation into an economic powerhouse.

Singapore has no natural resources, no great army, no special political sway. Its secret lies in its people—and the government has intentionally cultivated these human resources as the driver of its economy. Schools are the incubator for Singapore's outstanding workforce. With an eye toward the future, Singapore has partnered with Roger Weissberg, now president of the Collaborative for Academic, Social, and Emotional Learning, to design emotional intelligence–based lesson plans for its schools.

And for good reason: one conclusion by economists involved in the Dunedin study was that teaching all kids these skills could shift an entire nation's income up a few notches, with added gains in their health and a lower crime rate.

MINDFULNESS-BASED EMOTIONAL INTELLIGENCE

The attention training that kids get at P.S. 112 mixes well with the rest of the Inner Resilience Program, which stands as a model of best practices in the social and emotional learning movement. I became a cofounder of the Collaborative for Academic, Social, and Emotional Learning—the group that has facilitated these programs' spread to thousands of school districts throughout the world—while writing my book *Emotional Intelligence.*

I saw lessons in emotional intelligence—that is, in self-awareness, self-management, empathy, and social skills—as synergistic with standard academic courses. Now I'm realizing that the basics of attention training are a next step, a low-tech method for boosting neural circuitry at the heart of emotional intelligence.

"I've done SEL for years," Linda Lantieri tells me. "When I added the mindfulness piece, I saw a dramatically quicker embodiment of calming ability and the readiness to learn. It happens at earlier ages, and earlier in the school year."

There seems to be a natural synergy between SEL and attention training like mindfulness. When I spoke with Weissberg, he told me the organization had just undertaken a review of the impacts of mindfulness in SEL programs.

"Cognitive control and executive function seem crucial for self-awareness and self-management, as well as academics," Weissberg said.

Deliberate, top-down attention holds a key to self-management. The parts of the brain for such executive function mature rapidly from the preschool years to about second grade (and the growth of these neural networks continues into early adulthood). These circuits manage both "hot" processing of emotional moments and "cool" processing of more neutral information, like academics.[7]

This circuitry seems surprisingly plastic throughout childhood, suggesting that interventions like SEL can enhance it.

One study taught attention skills to four- and six-year-olds in just five sessions of playing games that exercise visual tracking (guessing where a duck swimming underwater will surface), spotting a target cartoon character within an array of distractions, and inhibiting impulse (clicking if a sheep comes out from behind a bale of hay, but not if a wolf emerges).[8]

The finding: the neural scaffolding for both emotional and cognitive abilities was enhanced. The brains of four-year-olds who got this brief training resembled those of six-year-olds, and those of the trained six-year-olds were well on their way to neural executive function seen in adults.

Though a gene controls the maturation of the brain regions that handle executive attention, such genes are in turn regulated by experience—and this training seems to have sped their activity. The circuitry that manages all this—which runs between the anterior cingulate and the prefrontal areas—is active in both emotional and cognitive varieties of attention regulation: managing emotional impulse as well as aspects of IQ like nonverbal reasoning and fluid thinking.

An older dichotomy in psychology between "cognitive" and "noncognitive" abilities would put academic skills in a separate category from social and emotional ones. But given how the neural scaffolding for executive control underlies both academic and social/emotional skills, that separation seems as antiquated as the Cartesian split between mind and body. In the design of the brain they are highly interactive, not fully independent. Kids who can't pay attention can't learn; they also can't manage themselves well.

"When you have elements like regular quiet time," says Lantieri, "a Peace Corner where kids can go on their own when they need to calm down, and mindfulness, you get more calmness and self-management on the one hand, and enhanced focus and the ability to sustain it on the other. You change their physiology and self-awareness."

By teaching kids the skills that help them calm down and focus, "we lay a foundation of self-awareness and self-management on which you can scaffold the other SEL skills like active listening, identifying feelings, and so on.

Back when SEL started, Lantieri tells me, "We were expecting kids to use their SEL skills when they were hijacked, but they couldn't access them. Now we realize they need a more basic tool first: cognitive control. That's what they get with breathing buddies and mindfulness. Once they experience how this can help them, they get the confidence, 'I can do this.'

"Some kids use it during tests—they wear a Biodot," a small plastic dot that changes color as skin temperature (and so blood flow to that area) shifts. This "tells them when they are getting too anxious to think well on the test. If it says they need to, they use the mindfulness to calm and focus themselves, and then go back to the test when they can think more clearly.

"The kids understand that when they don't do well on a test, it's not because they are stupid, but that 'When I'm super-nervous it's in there but I can't access it. But I know how to focus and calm—then I'll get to it.' They have the attitude I'm in charge of myself now—I know what to do that can help."

The Inner Resilience Program is in schools from Youngstown, Ohio, to Anchorage, Alaska. "It works best," Lantieri says, "when combined with an SEL program—all these places do that."

CUTTING THROUGH THE HODGEPODGE

The scientific literature on the effects of meditation amounts to a hodgepodge of bad, good, and remarkable results in a mix of questionable methodologies, so-so designs, and gold-standard studies. So I asked the dean of contemplative neuroscience, Wisconsin's Richard Davidson, to sort through it all and summarize the clear benefits for attention of mindfulness practice. He immediately ticked off two big ones.

"Mindfulness," he said, "boosts the classic attention network in the brain's fronto-parietal system that works together to allocate attention. These circuits are fundamental in the basic movement of attention: disengaging your focus from one thing, moving it to another, and staying with that new object of attention."

Another key improvement is in selective attention, inhibiting the pull of distractors. This lets us focus on what's important rather than be distracted by what's going on around us—you can keep your focus on the meaning of these words instead of having it pulled away by, say, checking this endnote.[9] This is the essence of cognitive control.

Though so far there are just a few well-designed studies of mindfulness in children, "[i]n adults there seems to be strong data on mindfulness and attention networks," according to Mark Greenberg, professor of human development at Pennsylvania State University.[10] Greenberg, who himself is leading studies of mindfulness in young people, is cautious but optimistic.[11]

One of the bigger benefits for students is in understanding. Wandering minds punch holes in comprehension. The antidote for mind wandering is meta-awareness, attention to attention itself, as in the ability to *notice that you are not noticing* what you should, and correcting your focus. Mindfulness makes this crucial attention muscle stronger.[12]

Then there are the well-established relaxation effects, such as the calm emanating from a breathing buddies classroom. This physiological impact suggests a downshift in the set point for arousal in the vagus nerve circuitry, the key to staying calm under stress and recovering quickly from upsets. The vagus nerve manages a host of physiological functions, most notably heart rate—and so the quickness of recovery from stress.[13]

Higher vagal tone, which can result from mindfulness and other meditations, leads to greater flexibility in many ways.[14] People are better able to manage both their attention and their emotions. In the social realm they can more easily create positive relationships and have effective interactions.

Beyond such benefits, mindfulness meditators show symptom lessening in a remarkable range of physiological disorders, from sheer jitters to hypertension and chronic pain. "Some of the biggest effects found with mindfulness are biological," says Davidson, adding, "It's surprising for an exercise that trains attention."

Jon Kabat-Zinn founded the Mindfulness-Based Stress Reduction program, which triggered a worldwide wave of mindfulness deployed in thousands of hospitals and clinics, and in society at large, from prisons to leadership development. He tells me, "Our patients typically come in because they're overwhelmed by stress or pain. But there's something about paying attention to your own inner states, and seeing what needs to change in your life. People on their own stop smoking or change the way they eat and start losing weight, though as a rule we never say anything directly about these."

Almost any variety of meditation, in essence, retrains our habits of attention—particularly the routine default to a wandering mind.[15] When three kinds of meditation were tested—concentration, generating loving-kindness, and open awareness—each technique quieted the areas for mind wandering.

So while gaming offers one promising venue for enhancing cognitive skills, mindfulness and similar attention-training methods present an alternative or complement. The two training approaches may be merging, as in the breathing game *Tenacity*. When I spoke to Davidson he told me, "We're taking what we can learn from meditation research and adapting it for games, so the benefits can spread more widely. Our research on attention and calming informs the games' design."

Still, methods like mindfulness seem to offer an "organic" way to teach focusing skills without the risks that endless hours of gaming pose for de-skilling kids in the social realm.[16] Indeed, mindfulness seems to prime brain circuitry that makes us engage the world more, not withdraw.[17] Whether a well-designed game can do the same for the brain's social circuitry remains to be seen.[18]

Psychiatrist Daniel Siegel of the University of California, Los Angeles, describes the wiring that links attuning to ourselves and attuning to others as a "resonance circuit" that mindfulness practice strengthens.[19] A well-connected life, Dr. Siegel argues, begins with the circuitry for mindfulness in the brain's prefrontal executive centers, which do double duty: they are also at play when we attune in rapport.

Mindfulness strengthens connections between the prefrontal executive zones and the amygdala, particularly the circuits that can say "no" to impulse—a vital skill for navigating through life (as we saw in part 2).[20]

Enhanced executive function widens the gap between impulse and action, in part by building meta-awareness, the capacity to observe our mental processes rather than just be swept away by them. This creates decision points we did not have before: we can squelch troublesome impulses that we usually would act on.

MINDFULNESS AT WORK

Google is a citadel of the high IQ. I had heard that no applicants get a job interview there unless they can show test scores putting them in the top 1 percent of intellect. So when I gave a talk on the emotional kind of intelligence at Google some years ago, I was surprised to find an overflow crowd in one of the biggest meeting rooms at the Googleplex, with monitors broadcasting my talk to people in overflow rooms. That enthusiasm was later channeled into a mindfulness-based emotional intelligence course at Google University called Search Inside Yourself.

To create that course, Google's employee No. 107, Chade-Meng Tan, teamed with my old friend Mirabai Bush, founder of the Center for Contemplative Mind in Society, to design an experience that enhances self-awareness—for example, by using a body scan meditation to tune in to feelings. An inner compass helps greatly at Google, where many business innovations have come from the company's policy of giving its employees one free day a week to pursue their own pet projects. But Meng, as he's known widely, has a larger vision: to make the course available far beyond Google, particularly to leaders.[21]

Then there's the newly formed Institute for Mindful Leadership, which is located in Minneapolis and which has trained leaders from Target, Cargill, Honeywell Aerospace, and a host of other companies around the world. Another mecca has been Center for Mindfulness-Based Stress Reduction at the University of Massachusetts Medical School, in Worcester; it has a training center for executives. Miraval, a posh resort in Arizona, has offered an annual CEO mindfulness retreat for several years, taught by Jon Kabat-Zinn, whose work at the center he founded unleashed the mindfulness movement.

Mindfulness programs have been deployed by groups as diverse as the chaplaincy unit of the U.S. Army, Yale Law School, and General Mills, where more than three hundred executives are applying mindful leadership methods.

What difference does it make? At a biotech firm where the Google Search Inside Yourself program was delivered, early data suggests mindfulness boosts both self-awareness and empathy.

Those who took part in the training showed increases in specific mindfulness skills, including a greater ability to observe and describe their own experience, and to act with awareness, said Philippe Goldin, a psychologist at Stanford, who assessed the program's effects.

"The participants said they had become better able to use self-regulation strategies—like redirecting their attention to less upsetting aspects of loaded situations—in the heat of the moment when their attention was being hijacked," Goldin added. "They're building the muscle of attention deployment so they can choose what aspect of experience to attend to. It's a volitional redirection of attention. And they're more able to use these attention skills when they are really needed.

"We also found a boost in empathic concern for others, and being able to listen better," Goldin said. "One is an attitude, the other the actual skill, the muscle. These are vitally important in the workplace."

One division head at General Mills came to the mindfulness course there to get a breather from feeling overwhelmed. She brought a taste of mindfulness back to work, where she asked her direct reports to take a reflective pause before asking her to a meeting. The aim of that pause was to question the need for the division head to spend her time at that meeting in the first place.

The result: What had been a nine-to-five schedule of back-to-back meetings opened up into three hours daily for her own priorities.

These questions are designed to provoke a person to reflect on his or her level of mindfulness:[22]

- Do you have trouble remembering what someone has just told you during a conversation?
- Have no memory of your morning commute?

- Not taste your food while eating?
- Pay more attention to your iPod than the person you're with?
- Are you skimming this book?

The more "yes" answers, the greater the likelihood you zone out rather than tune in. Mindfulness gives us a greater level of choice in focus.

Mindlessness, in the form of mind wandering, may be the single biggest waster of attention in the workplace. Focus on our experience in the here and now—like the task at hand, the conversation we're having, or the building of consensus in a meeting—demands that we tune down the all-about-myself murmurs of mind stuff irrelevant to what's going on right now.[23]

Mindfulness develops our capacity to observe our moment-to-moment experience in an impartial, nonreactive manner. We practice letting go of thoughts about any one thing and open our focus to whatever comes to mind in the stream of awareness, without getting lost in a torrent of thoughts about any one thing. This training generalizes, so that in those moments at work when we need to pay attention to *this* and drop our stream of thought about *that*, we can let go of the one and focus on the other.

Mindfulness training decreases activity in me-circuitry centering on the medial prefrontal cortex—and the less self-talk, the more we can experience in the moment.[24] The longer people have been mindfulness practitioners, the more their brain can decouple the two kinds of self-awareness and activate circuits that foster a here-and-now presence for the task at hand free of the mind's "me" chatter.[25]

Building executive control helps especially for those of us for whom every setback, hurt, or disappointment creates endless cascades of rumination. Mindfulness lets us break the stream of thoughts that might otherwise lead to wallowing in misery, by changing our relationship to thought itself. Instead of being swept away by that stream we can pause and see that *these are just thoughts*—and choose whether or not to act on them.

In short, mindfulness practice strengthens focus, particularly executive control, working memory capacity, and the ability to sustain attention. Some of these benefits can be seen with as little as twenty minutes of practice for just four days (though the longer the training, the more sustained the effects).[26]

Then there's multitasking, the bane of efficiency. "Multitasking" really means switching what's filling the capacity of working memory—and routine disruptions from a given focus at work can mean minutes lost to the original task. It can take ten or fifteen minutes to regain full focus.

When human resources professionals were trained in mindfulness, then tested on a simulation of their daily frenzy—scheduling meetings for conference attendees, locating available meeting rooms, proposing a meeting agenda, and so on, while receiving random phone calls, texts, and emails telling them what's possible—the mindfulness training improved their concentration noticeably. What's more, they stayed on task longer and more efficiently.[27]

I was at a meeting in the office of More Than Sound (a production company run by one of my sons) when our focus meandered: there were parallel conversations going on, and some people discreetly checked their email. That disintegration of our shared focus was a moment familiar from hundreds of other meetings—a signal that the group's efficiency was tanking. But suddenly one of the people there said, "Time for some mindful moments," got up, and rang a small gong.

We all sat there together in silence for a few minutes until the gong rang again, and then resumed our meeting—but with renewed energy. A remarkable moment for me, but not at More Than

Sound, where, it seems, the team assembles at irregular intervals to share some minutes of mindfulness, signaled by that ringing gong. The group pause, they say, clears their heads and gives them a new burst of energized focus.

It's no surprise this small publisher recognizes the value of mindfulness; when I dropped by it had just released *Mindfulness at Work*, an audio instruction by Mirabai Bush, the woman who introduced mindfulness to Google.

SEEING THE BIGGER PICTURE

Business leaders are increasingly pressured by the acceleration of complexity in the systems they need to navigate: there's the globalization of markets, suppliers, and organizations; the hyperspeed of evolving information technologies; impending ecological dangers; products coming to market and becoming obsolete faster. It can make your head spin.

"Most leaders just don't pause," a seasoned leadership coach tells me. "But you need the time to reflect."

His boss, the head of a mega-sized investment management firm, put it this way: "If I don't protect that kind of time, I really get thrown off."

Former Medtronic CEO Bill George agrees. "Today's leaders are besieged. They're scheduled every fifteen minutes throughout the day, with thousands of interruptions and distractions. You need to find some quiet time in your day just to reflect."

Setting aside some regular reflective time in the daily or weekly schedule might help us get beyond the firefight-of-the-day mentality, to take stock and look ahead. Very diverse thinkers, from Congressman Tim Ryan to Columbia University economist Jeffrey D. Sachs, are calling for mindfulness as a way to help leaders see the bigger picture.[28] They propose we need not just mindful leaders, but a mindful society, one where we bring a triple focus: to our own well-being, that of others, and the operations of the broader systems that shape our lives.

Mindfulness of self, Sachs argues, would include a more accurate reading of what makes us truly happy. Global economic data shows that once a country reaches a modest level of income—enough to meet basic needs—there is zero connection between happiness and wealth. Intangibles like warm connections with people we love and meaningful activities make people far happier than say, shopping or work.

But we can be poor judges of what will make us feel good. Sachs argues that if we are more mindful of how we use our money we will be less likely to fall prey to seductive ads for products that will not make us any happier. Mindfulness would lead us to more modest material desires and to spend more time and energy fulfilling our deeper, more satisfying needs for meaning and connection.

Mindfulness of others at the societal level, Sachs says, means paying attention to the suffering of the poor and to the social safety net, which is badly fraying in the United States and many other advanced economies. He argues that while now the poor are helped just enough to barely survive, that simply creates intergenerational poverty. What's needed is a one-generation boost in education and health for the poorest children so they can go through life with higher levels of skills and so not need the same kind of help their families did.

To that end I'd add programs, like mindfulness, that boost the brain's executive control. In Dunedin the kids who happened to improve their self-control over the course of childhood derived the same earnings and health benefits for life success as those who always were adept in delaying gratification. But those impulse control upgrades were due to happenstance, not achieved by plan. Wouldn't it make sense to teach these skills to every child?

Then there's awareness of systems at the global level, like the human impact on the planet. Solving systems-level problems takes systems focus. Mindfulness of the future means taking into account the long-term consequences of our own actions for our children's generation and their children's, and beyond.

PART VI

THE WELL-FOCUSED LEADER

18

HOW LEADERS DIRECT ATTENTION

"Death by PowerPoint" refers to those endless, meandering presentations that this software tool seems to encourage. Those presentations can be painful when they reflect a lack of focused thinking, and a poor sense of what matters. One sign of the ability to pinpoint what's salient is how someone answers the simple question, What's your main point?

When a meeting is coming up, I hear, Steve Balmer, CEO at Microsoft (birthplace of the dread PowerPoint), bans such presentations. Instead he asks to see the material beforehand so that when he's face-to-face he can cut to the chase and ask the questions that matter most right off the bat, rather than taking a long, winding road to get there. As he says, "It gives us greater focus."[1]

Directing attention toward where it needs to go is a primal task of leadership. Talent here lies in the ability to shift attention to the right place at the right time, sensing trends and emerging realities and seizing opportunities. But it's not just the focus of a single strategic decision-maker that makes or breaks a company: it's the entire array of attention bandwidth and dexterity among everyone.[2]

Sheer numbers of people make an organization's cumulative attention far more distributable than an individual's, with a division of labor in who pays attention to what. This multiple focus powers an organization's attention capacity for reading and responding to complex systems.

Attention in organizations, as with individuals, has a limited capacity. Organizations, too, have to choose where to allocate attention, focusing on this while ignoring that. An organization's core functions—finance, marketing, human resources, and the like—describe how a particular group focuses.

Signs of what might be called organizational "attention deficit disorder" include making flawed decisions because of missing data, no time for reflection, trouble getting attention in the marketplace, and inability to focus when and where it matters.

Take getting noticed in the marketplace, where customers' focus is hard currency. The bar for attracting attention rises continually; what was dazzling last month seems boring today. While one strategy for grabbing eyeballs tweaks our bottom-up systems with surprising, attention-compelling tech effects, there's been a renaissance in an older method: telling a good story.[3] Stories do more than grab our attention: they keep it. This is a lesson not lost in the "attention industries" like media, TV, film, music, and advertising—all of which play a zero-sum game for our attention, where one's victory is the other's loss.

Attention tends to focus on what has meaning—what matters. The story a leader tells can imbue a particular focus with such resonance, and so implies a choice for the others on where to put their attention and energy.[4]

Leadership itself hinges on effectively capturing and directing the collective attention. Leading attention requires these elements: first, focusing your own attention, then attracting and directing attention from others, and getting and keeping the attention of employees and peers, of customers or clients.

A well-focused leader can balance an inner focus on the climate and culture with an "other focus" on the competitive landscape, and an outer focus on the larger realities that shape the environment the outfit operates in.

A leader's field of attention—that is, the particular issues and goals she focuses on—guides the attention of those who follow her, whether or not the leader explicitly articulates it. People make their choices about where to focus based on their perception of what matters to leaders. This ripple effect gives leaders an extra load of responsibility: they are guiding not just their own attention but, to a large extent, everyone else's.[5]

Take, as a case in point, strategy. An organization's strategy represents the *desired* pattern of organizational attention, what every unit should share a degree of focus on, each in its particular way.[6] A given strategy makes choices about what to ignore and what matters: Market share or profit? Current competitors or potential ones? Which new technologies? When leaders choose strategy, they are guiding attention.

WHERE DOES STRATEGY COME FROM?

Kobun Chino, a master of *kyudo*, Zen archery, was once invited to demonstrate his skills at Esalen Institute, the famed adult learning center in Big Sur, California, just down the road from the San Francisco Zen Center's Tassajara retreat.

Comes the day and someone sets up an archery target on a grassy knoll atop a tall cliff at the edge of the Pacific Ocean. Chino positions himself a good distance away from the target, places his feet in the traditional archer's stance, straightens his back, very slowly draws the bow, waits a while, and then lets the arrow fly.

The arrow zooms far over the target, arcs against the open sky, and falls into the Pacific Ocean far below. Everyone watching is aghast.

Then Kobun Chino shouts with glee, "Bull's-eye!"

"Genius," Arthur Schopenhauer observed, "hits the target others do not see."

Kobun Chino was the Zen teacher of Apple Computer's legendary CEO, the late Steve Jobs. Among unseen targets Jobs hit was the then-radical concept of a computer that anyone could understand and use with ease, not just geeks—an idea that had somehow eluded every computer company of the day. After creating the first Apple desktop he and his team transferred that user-friendly vision to the iPod, iPhone, and iPad, each a handy product that we hadn't realized we needed—or imagined in the first place—until we saw it.

When Steve Jobs returned to Apple in 1997, after having been ousted in 1984, he found a company with a sea of products—computers, peripheral products for computers, twelve different types of Macintosh. The company was floundering. His strategy was simple: focus.

Instead of dozens of products, Apple would concentrate on just four: one computer and one laptop each for two markets, consumer and professional. Just as in his Zen practice, where recognizing you've become distracted helps you concentrate, he saw that "[deciding what *not* to do is as important as deciding what to do."[7]

Jobs was relentless in filtering out what he considered irrelevancies, both personally and in his professionl life. But he knew that in order to simplify effectively you need to understand the complexity that you are reducing. A single decision to simplify, like Jobs's dictum that Apple products allow a user to do anything in three clicks or less, demanded a deep understanding of the function of the commands and buttons being given up, and finding elegant alternatives.

More than a century before Apple existed, another radical vision made the Singer sewing machine an enormous commercial success worldwide. The disruptive assumption was that housewives could operate a mechanical contraption—a radical thought in the nineteenth century, long before women in the United States won the right to vote. And Singer made it easy for women to buy the machines by extending them credit, another innovative move.

In 1876 alone, Singer sold 262,316 machines, an enormous number in those days. One of its founders built the Dakota, a landmark Manhattan apartment building where luminaries like Yoko Ono and John Lennon have lived. In 1908, the brand-new forty-seven-story company headquarters, the Singer building, was the world's tallest.

My mother, who was born in 1910 (and passed away two months short of her hundredth birthday), owned a Singer from her teen years. I can remember as a child going with her to the local pattern store; women of her era routinely made many of their own and their family's clothes. But by the time I arrived—her late-in-life third child—she bought my clothes.

Culture shifts like housewives taking to sewing machines—and then later buying their family ready-made clothes, which then were increasingly made by cheap labor abroad—constantly open possibilities: new groups of customers, ways to buy, evolving needs, technologies, distribution channels, or information systems. Every advance opens doors to a host of potential winning strategies.

Apple and Singer left fresh footprints in the snow that their competitors followed in a desperate game of catching up. Today a mini-industry of consultants stands ready to guide companies through a standard playbook of strategic choices. But those off-the-shelf strategies fine-tune an organization's tactics—they don't change the game.

The original meaning of *strategy* was from the battlefield; it meant "the art of the leader"—back then, generals. Strategy was how you deployed your resources; tactics were how battles were fought. Today, leaders need to generate strategies that make sense in whatever larger systems they operate in—a task for outer focus.

A new strategy means reorienting from what's now business as usual to a fresh focus. Coming up with a radically innovative strategy demands perceiving a novel position, one your competitors do not see. Winning tactics are available to everyone, yet are overlooked by all but a few.

Armies of consultants offer elaborate analytic tools for fine-tuning a strategy. But they stop cold when it comes to answering the big question: Where does a winning strategy come from in the first place? A classic article on strategy makes this offhand remark and leaves it at that: to find winning strategies "requires creativity and insight."[8]

Those two ingredients take both inner and outer focus. When Marc Benioff, founder and first CEO of Salesforce, realized the potential for cloud computing, he was monitoring the evolution of a system-changing technology—an outer focus—along with his own gut sense of how a company offering such services would do. Salesforce uses the cloud to help companies manage their customer relationships, and it staked out an early position in this competitive space.

The best leaders have systems awareness, helping them answer the constant query, Where should we head and how? The self-mastery and social skills built on self and other focus combine to build the emotional intelligence that drives the human engine needed to get there. A leader needs to check a potential strategic choice against everything she knows. And once the strategic choice gets made, the leader needs to communicate it with passion and skill, drawing on cognitive and emotional empathy. But those personal skills alone will founder if leaders lack strategic wisdom.

"If you think in a systems way," says Larry Brilliant, "that drives how you deal with values, vision, mission, strategy, goals, tactics, deliverables, evaluation, and the feedback loop that restarts the whole process."

THE TELLING DETAIL ON THE HORIZON

By the mid-2000s, the BlackBerry had become the darling of corporate IT. Companies loved that the system ran on its own closed network, reliable, fast, and secure. They handed BlackBerrys out to employees by the thousands, and the word *crackberry* (for the addiction of users) entered the lexicon. The maker rose to market dominance on four key strengths: ease of typing, excellent security, long battery life, and wireless data compression.

For a time the BlackBerry was a winning technology, changing the rules of the game by displacing competitors (in this case, some functions of PCs and laptops, and, entirely, that era's mobile phones). But even as BlackBerrys dominated the corporate market and were fast becoming a consumer fad, the world was changing. The iPhone ushered in an epoch where more and more workers bought their own brands of smartphones—not necessarily BlackBerrys—and companies adapted by letting employees bring their devices to the company network. Suddenly BlackBerrys' lock on the corporate market evaporated as they had to compete with everyone else.

Research in Motion (RIM), the Canadian-based maker of the BlackBerry, was slow to catch up. When RIM introduced a touchscreen, for example, it was no match for those long on the market. BlackBerry's closed network, once an asset, became a liability in a world where phones themselves—the iPhone, and those based on the Android operating system—had become platforms for their own worlds of apps.

RIM was run by co-CEOs who were both engineers, and the brand's initial success was built on superior engineering. After these co-CEOs were forced out by their board, RIM announced it would once again focus on companies as its prime market, even though most of its growth had come on the consumer side.

As Thorsten Heins, the new CEO, put it, RIM had missed major paradigm shifts in its ecological niche. It had ignored the move in the United States to fourth-generation (4G) wireless networks, failing to build devices for 4G even as its competitors seized that market. It underestimated how popular the iPhone's touchscreen would become, and stuck to the keyboard.

"If you have a great touch interface, people are actually willing to sacrifice battery life," Heins says. "We thought that wouldn't happen. Same thing with security," as companies changed their standards to allow workers to join corporate networks with their own smartphones.[9]

While once the BlackBerry brand had seemed revolutionary, now, as one analyst put it, they "seemed clueless about what customers wanted."[10]

Though it continued to lead in markets like Indonesia, just five years after the BlackBerry dominated the American market RIM had lost 75 percent of its market value. As I write this, RIM has announced a last-ditch attempt to recoup market share with a new phone. But RIM may have entered a chapter in a company's life that could be fatal—a "valley of death."

That phrase comes from Andrew Grove, the legendary founding CEO of Intel, who recounts a near-death moment in his company's history. In its early years Intel made silicon chips for what was then the fledgling computer industry. As Grove tells it, top managers were oblivious to messages coming from their own sales force telling them that customers were shifting in droves to cheaper chips being made in Japan.

If Intel had not happened to have a side business in microprocessors—which became the ubiquitous "Intel Inside" in the heyday of laptops—the company would have died. But back then, Grove admits, Intel suffered from a "strategic dissonance," in shifting from making memory chips—its first business success—to designing microprocessors.

The name of Grove's book—*Only the Paranoid Survive*—tacitly nods to the necessity of vigilance, scanning for the telling detail on the horizon. This holds true in particular for the tech sector, where super-short product cycles (compared with, say, refrigerators) make the pace of innovation brutal.

The rapid-fire cycle of product innovations in the tech sector makes it a handy source of case studies (somewhat akin to the role that frenetically procreating, short-lived fruit flies play in genetics). In gaming, Nintendo's remote controller Wii grabbed the market from Sony's PlayStation 2; Google blew away Yahoo's supremacy as the favored portal to the Web. Microsoft, which at one point had a 42 percent market share for mobile phone operating systems, saw iPhone earnings mushroom to dwarf the total revenue of Microsoft. Innovations rearrange our sense of what's possible.

When Apple launched the iPod, it took Microsoft four or five years to release Zune, its version of a portable digital media player—and another six years to kill the failed product.[11] Microsoft's fixation on its cash cow, the Windows software family, analysts say, accounts for the company failing to match Apple's march to market supremacy through the iPod, iPhone, and iPad.

As Clay Shirky observes of the failure to disengage focus from comfort zones, "First the people running the old system don't notice the change. When they do, they assume it's minor. Then it's a niche, then a fad. And by the time they understand that the world has actually changed, they've squandered most of the time they had to adapt."[12]

THINK DIFFERENT

RIM during its difficult days offers a textbook example of organizational rigidity, where a company that thrives by being the first to market a new technological twist falls behind successive tech waves because its focus fixates on the old new thing, not the next. An organization that focuses inwardly may execute superbly. But if it has not attuned to the larger world in which it operates, that execution may end up in the service of a failed strategy.

Any business school course on strategy will tell you about two approaches: exploitation and exploration. Some people—and some businesses like RIM—succeed through a strategy of exploitation, where they refine and learn how to improve an existing capacity, technology, or business model. Others find their road to success through exploration, by experimenting with innovative alternatives to what they do now.

Companies with a winning strategy tend to refine their current operations and offerings, not explore radical shifts in what they offer. A mental balancing act—exploring the new while exploiting what's working—does not come naturally. But those companies that can both exploit and explore—as Samsung has done with smartphones—are "ambidextrous": they separate each strategy into units, with very different ways of operating and cultures. At the same time they have a tight-knit team of senior leaders who keep an eye on the balance of inner, outer, and other focus.[13]

What works at the organizational level parallels the individual mind. The mind's executive, the arbiter of where our focus goes, manages both the concentration that exploitation requires and the open focus that exploration demands.

Exploration means we disengage from a current focus to search for new possibilities, and allows flexibility, discovery, and innovation. Exploitation takes sustained focus on what you're already doing, so you can refine efficiencies and improve performance.

Those who exploit can find a safer path to profits, while those who explore can potentially find a far greater success in the next new thing—though the risks of failure are greater, and the horizon of payback is further away. Exploitation is the tortoise, exploration the hare.

The tension between these two operates in every decision-maker's mind. Do you stay with the battery technology your company has been getting better and better at making pay? Or do you pursue, say, R&D on a new energy storage technique that could make batteries obsolete (or not)? These are the hands-on strategic decisions that make or break a company, as Stanford's strategy theory maven, James March, has been arguing for years.[14]

The best decision-makers are ambidextrous in their balance of the two, knowing when to switch from one to the other. They can lead switch-hitting organizations, which are, for instance, good at seeking growth by simultaneously innovating and containing costs—two very different operations. Kodak was superb at analog photography but stumbled in the new competitive reality of digital cameras.

Danger here abounds during a business downturn, when companies understandably focus on surviving and meeting their numbers by cutting costs—but often at the expense of caring for their people or keeping up with how the world has changed. Being in survival mode narrows our focus.

But prospering is no guarantee of ambidexterity, either. That switch can be hardest for those caught in what Intel's Grove calls the "success trap." He observes that every company will face a point when it will have to change dramatically to survive, let alone raise its performance. "Miss the moment," he warns, "and you start to decline."

For too long, Grove says, Intel still had its best development people working on memory chips—even as the company's survival had begun to depend on microprocessors, which over the next decade were to become a huge growth engine. Intel was having trouble unsticking from exploitation to exploration.

Apple's slogan "Think different" dictates a switch to exploration. Moving into new territory rather than hunkering down to increase efficiency is more than a contrast in stances—at the level of the brain the two represent entirely different mental functions and neural mechanisms. Attention control holds the key for decision-makers needing to make the switch.

Brain scans of sixty-three seasoned business decision-makers as they pursued either exploitive or exploratory strategies in a simulation game—or switched between the two—revealed the specific circuitry underlying each kind of focus.[15] Exploitation was accompanied by activity in the brain's circuitry for anticipation and for reward—it feels good to coast along in a profitable, familiar routine. But exploration mobilized activity in the brain's executive centers and those for controlling attention; searching for alternatives to a current strategy, it seems, demands intentional focus.

The first movement to new territory entails disengaging from pleasing routine and fighting the inertia of ruts; this small act of attention demands what neuroscience calls "cognitive effort." That effortful dab of executive control frees attention to roam widely and pursue fresh paths.

What keeps people from making this small neural effort? For one, mental overload, stress, and sleep deprivation (not to mention drinking) deplete the executive circuitry needed to make such a cognitive switch, keeping us in our mental ruts. And the stress of overload, sleeplessness, and turning to substances that calm you down are all too prevalent among those in high-demand jobs.

19

THE LEADER'S TRIPLE FOCUS

When he was just eleven years old Steve Tuttleman started reading the *Wall Street Journal* with his grandfather, a habit that some four decades later has been gravitating toward his tablet. Each day he checks over twenty websites, in addition to news and opinion feeds stripped by an RSS reader. Starting the moment he wakes up and then a half dozen times over the course of the day he checks breaking news, mainly on sites of the *New York Times*, the *Wall Street Journal*, and Google News. A web app organizes contents of the twenty-six magazines he currently subscribes to so that he can flag relevant articles to read later. Says Tuttleman, "If the piece is of high importance, or takes some study, or needs to be saved for reference, then I come back to it when I can devote myself."

Then there are the sector-specific publications, each tied to a particular business interest. *National Restaurant News* relates to a chain of Dunkin' Donuts franchises he holds a stake in; *Bowler's Journal* keeps him up to speed for managing Ebonite, a manufacturing company he owns that sells balls and the like for bowlers. The *Journal of Practical Estate Planning*, along with a half dozen similar publications, helps keep him abreast of what might be relevant to his role as a director of Hirtle Callaghan, which manages assets for philanthropies, universities, and high-net-worth individuals. And *Private Equity Investor* helps track conditions for the business he leads as president of Blue 9 Capital.

"It's a big scan, that's for sure," Tuttleman tells me. "Sometimes I feel it takes too much time. But I'm always making connections with what I read. It gives me a foundation for what I do."

When Tuttleman was approached in 2004 to invest in a retail chain called Five Below, he says, "They shared projections for a model store, and the numbers were right for costs and margins."

But Tuttleman went beyond the numbers, visiting one of the chain's six stores, where he checked his inner signals against how others were reacting. "They offered an appealing selection of goods, one with a point of view. Their target customers are twelve to fifteen, and in the stores you mostly see moms with their kids. But mainly I saw people liked the store, and *I* liked the store."

Over the next several years Tuttleman put more money into Five Below. What had been a six-store chain in 2004 had grown to 250 by the end of 2012, and the company had gone through a successful IPO. The company went public in the wake of the Facebook IPO debacle, but it did well nonetheless.

"People bring investment opportunities to me all the time," says Tuttleman. "They give me a 'book' that details the numbers for a company that's on the market. But I've got to weigh that in a broader context of what's happening in society, the culture, and the economy. I'm always scanning for what's happening in the broader world; you need a bigger field of view."

Way back in 1989 Tuttleman bought stock in Starbucks, Microsoft, Home Depot, and Wal-Mart. He still owns the same stocks. Why did he buy them? "I bought what *I* liked," he explains. "I go by my gut."

When we make a decision like that, subcortical systems operate outside conscious awareness, gathering the decision rules that guide us and store our life wisdom—and deliver their opinion as a felt sense. That subtle stirring—*This feels right*—sets our direction even before we can put that decision into words.

The most successful entrepreneurs gather data that might be relevant to a key decision far more widely—and from a larger variety of sources—than most people would think relevant. But they also realize that when facing a major decision, gut feelings are data, too.

The subcortical circuits that know such gut truths before we have words for them include the amygdala and the insula. A scholarly review of gut intuitions concludes that using feelings as information is a "generally sensible judgmental strategy," rather than a perennial source of error, as the hyperrational might argue.[1] Tuning in to our feelings as a source of information taps into a vast amount of decision rules that the mind gathers unconsciously.

Tuttleman's tutorial for his gut sense very likely has roots in those early years going over the *Wall Street Journal* with his grandfather, who as a Russian immigrant had gotten a job in a grocery store and ended up buying the store, then buying the distributor who supplied the store. Selling that company, he became a stock market investor.

Like his father and grandfather before him, says Tuttleman, "I always knew I would be an investor. Our dinner table conversation was always about business as I grew up. I've been in this business for almost thirty years, and always had a portfolio of companies. Every company has its own issues that I'm constantly dealing with. I'm still building that inner database."

The sweet spot for smart decisions, then, comes not just from being a domain expert, but also from having high self-awareness. If you know yourself as well as your business, then you can be shrewder in interpreting the facts (while, hopefully, safeguarding against the inner distortions that can blur your lens).[2]

Otherwise we're left with cold rationality as embodied, for instance, in decision trees (applications of what's known as "expected utility theory"), where we weight and compute the pros and cons of all relevant factors. One problem: life rarely arranges itself so neatly. Another: our bottom-up mind harbors crucial information that our top-down brain can't access directly, let alone put into that decision tree. What looks good on paper may not be so great in actuality: say, unregulated markets for subprime derivatives or invading Iraq.

"The most successful leaders are constantly seeking out new information," says Ruth Malloy, global director of Hay Group's leadership and talent practice. "They want to understand the territory they operate in. They need to be alert to new trends, and to spot emerging patterns that might matter to them."

When we say a leader has "focus" we typically are referring to one-pointedness on business results, or on a particular strategy. But is such single-pointedness enough? What about the rest of the repertoire of attention?

Tuttleman's business choices integrate the numbers with inputs from a wide outer scan, attuning to his gut reactions, and reading how other people feel. There's a strong case that leaders need the full range of inner, other, and outer focus to excel—and that a weakness in any one of them can throw a leader off balance.

LEADERS WHO INSPIRE

Consider two leaders. Leader #1 works as a high-level executive in a construction engineering firm. During Arizona's housing boom in the early 2000s (and well before the resulting crash), he switched jobs over and over, each time getting a higher-level position. His agility in climbing the corporate ladder, though, was not matched by his abilities as an inspiring leader. When asked to come up with a vision statement for his company to guide it into the future, he fumbled the task. "Being better than our competition" was the best he could do.

Leader #2 directed a nonprofit corporation that offered health and social services to Hispanic communities in the Southwest. His vision statement flowed freely, and focused squarely on greater goals: "to create a good environment for this community, which has been nurturing our company all these years, to make it a profit-sharing endeavor . . . and to benefit from our products." His vision was positive and embraced an expanded view of stakeholders.

In the following weeks, employees who worked directly for each leader were asked in confidence to evaluate how inspiring they found their boss. Leader #1 had one of the lowest ratings among the fifty leaders evaluated; leader #2 was among the highest.

More intriguingly, each leader had been assessed on a brain measure of "coherence," the degree to which circuits within a region interconnect and coordinate their activity. The specific region was in the prefrontal area of the right side of the brain, in a zone active in integrating thought and emotion, as well as in understanding the thoughts and emotions of others. The inspiring leaders showed a high level of coherence in this key area for inner and other awareness, the dull leaders very little.[3]

Leaders who inspire can articulate shared values that resonate with and motivate the group. These are the leaders people love to work with, who surface the vision that moves everyone. But to speak from the heart, to the heart, a leader must first know her values. That takes self-awareness.

Inspiring leadership demands attuning both to an inner emotional reality and to that of those we seek to inspire. These are elements of emotional intelligence, which I've had to rethink a bit in light of our new understanding of focus.

Attention gets talked about only indirectly in the emotional intelligence world: as "self-awareness," which is the basis of self-management; and as "empathy," the foundation for relationship effectiveness. Yet awareness of our self and of others, and its application in managing our inner world and our relationships, is the essence of emotional intelligence.

Acts of attention are woven throughout the very fabric of emotional intelligence because at the level of brain architecture the dividing line between emotion and attention blurs. The neural circuits for attention and those for feelings overlap in many ways, sharing neural pathways or interacting.

Because the brain interweaves its circuits for attention and for emotional intelligence, it turns out that some of this shared neural circuitry also sets these skills apart from the more academic variety, as measured by IQ.[4] That means a leader can be very smart but not necessarily have the focusing skills that come with emotional intelligence.

Take empathy. The common cold of leadership is poor listening. Here's how one CEO candidly assessed his own trouble with this form of empathy: "My brain races too much, so even if I've listened to everything somebody said, unless you show that you've digested it, people don't think they are being well heard. Sometimes you really don't hear because you're racing. And so, if you really want to get the best out of people, you have to really hear them and they have to feel like they've been really heard. So I've got to learn to slow down and improve in that dimension, both to make me better and to make the people around me better."[5]

A London-based executive coach tells me, "When I give people their feedback from others, very often it says an executive does not listen attentively. When I coach them on getting better at paying attention to people I often hear an executive say, I can do this."

I point out, "You *can*, but the question is how *often* you do this."

We pay careful attention in moments that matter most to us. But amid the din and distraction of work life, poor listening has become epidemic.

Still, attentive listening pays dividends. One CEO told me about a time when his company was locked in a struggle with a state agency over the purchase of a large tract of forest land. Rather than just leaving the matter to lawyers, the CEO made an appointment with the head of the agency.

At the meeting, the agency head launched a tirade of complaints about the CEO's company, and how the land needed to be conserved rather than developed. The CEO simply listened attentively for fifteen minutes. By then, he saw, his company's needs and those of the agency could be made compatible. He proposed a compromise where the company would develop only a small portion of the tract, and put the rest into a conservation trust for perpetual protection.

The meeting ended with the two shaking hands on a deal.

BLINDED BY THE PRIZE

She was a partner at a huge law firm who drove her team crazy. She micromanaged, constantly second-guessing them, rewriting reports that didn't meet her standards even though they were perfectly fine. She could always find something to criticize, but nothing to praise. Her steadfast focus on the negative demoralized her team—a star member quit and others were looking to move laterally in the firm.

Those who, like that too critical lawyer, have this high-achieving, super-focused style are called "pacesetters," meaning they like to lead by example, setting a fast pace they assume others will imitate. Pacesetters tend to rely on a "command and coerce" leadership strategy where they simply give orders and expect obedience.

Leaders who display just the pacesetting or command style—or both—but not any others create a toxic climate, one that dispirits those they lead. Such leaders may get short-term results through personal heroics, like going out and getting a deal themselves, but do so at the expense of building their organizations.

"Leadership Run Amok" was *Harvard Business Review*'s title for an article about the dark side of pacesetting, written by Scott Spreier and his colleagues at Hay Group. "They're so focused on the prize," Spreier told me, "they're blinded to their impact on the people around them in the room."

Spreier's article offered up that hard-driving law partner as a prime example of pacesetting at its worst. Such leaders don't listen, let alone make decisions by consensus. They don't spend time getting to know the people they work with day in and out, but relate to them in their one-dimensional roles. They don't help people develop new strengths or refine their abilities, but simply dismiss their need to learn as a failing. They come off as arrogant and impatient.

And they are spreading. One tracking study finds that the number of people in organizations of all kinds who are overachievers has been climbing steadily among those in leadership positions since the 1990s.[6] That was a period when economic growth created an atmosphere where raise-the-bar-at-any-cost heroics were lionized. The downsides of this style—for example, lapses in ethics, cutting corners, and running roughshod over people—were too often winked at.

Then came a series of flameouts and burst bubbles, from the collapse of Enron and the dot-com debacle on. This more sober business reality put a spotlight on the underside of pacesetters' single-minded focus on fiscal results at the expense of other leadership basics. During the financial crisis of 2008 and onward, "many companies promoted strong, top-down leaders, who are good for handling emergencies," Georg Vielmetter, a consultant in Berlin, told me. "But it changes the heart of the organization. Two years later those same leaders have created a climate where trust and loyalty evaporate."

The failure here is not in reaching the goal, but in connecting with people. The just-get-it-done mode runs roughshod over human concerns.

Every organization needs people with a keen focus on goals that matter, the talent to continually learn how to do even better, and the ability to tune out distractions. Innovation, productivity, and growth depend on such high-performers.

But only to a point. Ambitious revenue targets or growth goals are not the only gauge of an organization's health—and if they are achieved at a cost to other basics, the long-term downsides, like losing star employees, can outweigh short-term successes as those costs lead to later failures.

When we're fixated on a goal, whatever is relevant to that point of focus gets priority. Focus is not just selecting the right thing, but also saying no to the wrong ones. But focus goes too far when it says no to the right things, too. Single-pointed fixation on a goal morphs into *over*achievement when the category of "distractions" expands to include other people's valid concerns, their smart ideas, and their crucial information. Not to mention their morale, loyalty, and motivation.

The roots of this research go back to Harvard professor David McClelland's studies of how a healthy drive to achieve fuels entrepreneurship. But from the start he noted some high-achieving leaders "are so fixated on finding a shortcut to the goal that they may not be too particular about the means they use to reach it."[7]

"Two years ago I got some sobering performance feedback," confides the CEO of a global office real estate firm. "I was great on business expertise, but lacking when it came to inspirational leadership and empathy. I had thought I was fine, so at first I denied it.

Then I reflected and realized I often was empathetic but shut down the moment people were not doing their job well. I get very cool, even mean.

"I realized my biggest fear is of failure. That's what's driving me. So when someone on my team disappoints me, that fear kicks in."

When fear hijacks him that CEO falls back on pacesetting. "If you don't have self-awareness when you get hooked by the drive to achieve a goal," says Scott Spreier, who coaches senior leaders, "that's when you lose empathy and go on autopilot."

The antidote: realizing the need to listen, motivate, influence, cooperate—an interpersonal skill set that pacesetting leaders are typically not familiar with using. "At their worst, pacesetters lack empathy," George Kohlrieser, a leadership maven at IMD, a Swiss business school, told me. Kohlrieser teaches leaders from around the world to become "secure base" leaders, whose emotionally supportive and empathic style encourages the people they lead to work at their best.[8]

"We're all pacesetters here," the CEO of one of the world's largest financial firms admits a bit ruefully. But having a pack of pacesetters need not be damaging to morale: it can work if everyone there has been selected for a high level of talent and drive to succeed—that is, pacesetting.

But as one financial analyst described a bank where a pacesetting culture led to brash treatment of its customers, "I wouldn't put my money there—but I'd recommend buying the stock."

MANAGING YOUR IMPACT

In the spring of 2010, in the first weeks after the disastrous BP oil spill in the Gulf of Mexico, as countless sea animals and birds were dying and residents of the Gulf were decrying the catastrophe, BP executives were a textbook example of how not to manage a crisis.

The height of their folly came when BP CEO Tony Hayward infamously declared, "There's no one who wants this thing over more than I do. I'd like my life back."

Rather than showing the least concern for the spill's victims, he seemed annoyed by the inconvenience. He went on to claim the disaster was not BP's fault, blamed its subcontractors, and took no responsibility.[9] Widely circulated photos showed him at the peak of the crisis blithely sailing on a yacht, taking a vacation.

As a BP media relations exec put it, "The only time Tony Hayward opened his mouth was to change feet. He didn't understand the animal that is the media. He didn't understand the public's perception."[10]

Signe Spencer, coauthor of one of the first books on workplace competence, tells me there is a recently identified capability seen in some high-level leaders—called "managing your impact on others"—by skillful leveraging of their visibility and role to have a positive impact.[11]

Tony Hayward, blind to his impact on others, let alone to public perception of his company, set off a firestorm of antagonism, including front-page articles demanding to know why he hadn't been fired yet, and even President Obama declaring he would have fired him. Hayward's exit from BP was announced the following month.

The disaster has since cost BP up to $40 billion in liabilities, saw four executives charged with negligence, and led to the U.S. government forbidding BP further business—including new oil leases in the Gulf—because of "lack of business integrity."

Tony Hayward offers a textbook case of the costs of a leader with deficits in focus. "To anticipate how people will react, you have to read people's reactions to you," says Spencer. "That takes self-awareness and empathy in a self-reinforcing cycle. You become more aware of how you're coming across to other people."

With high self-awareness, she adds, you can more readily develop good self-management. "If you manage yourself better, you will influence better," Spencer says. Hayward during the oil spill crisis seems to have failed in each of these areas—and flunked managing his impact.

This triple focus demands attention juggling, and leaders who fail at that do so to their own and their organization's detriment.

20

WHAT MAKES A LEADER?

Back when I was his graduate student at Harvard, David McClelland created a minor storm by publishing a controversial article in the main journal of our profession, the *American Psychologist*. McClelland reviewed data questioning a hallowed assumption: that doing well in school in itself predicted career success.

He recognized the strong evidence that IQ is the best predictor of what kind of job any given high school student can eventually hold; the score sorts people into workplace roles quite well. Academic abilities (and the IQ they roughly reflect) signal what level of cognitive complexity someone can handle, and so what kind of job. You need to be approximately a standard deviation above average in intelligence (an IQ of 115) to be a professional or high-level executive, for instance.

But what's little discussed (at least in academic circles, where it's less apparent) is that once you are at work among a pool of colleagues who are about as smart as you are, your cognitive abilities alone do not make you outstanding—particularly as a leader. There's a floor effect for IQ when everyone in the group is at the same high level.

McClelland argued that once you were in a given job, specific competencies like self-discipline, empathy, and persuasion were far stronger forces in success than a person's ranking in academics. He proposed the methodology that has become competence modeling—now common in world-class organizations—for identifying the key abilities that made someone a star performer in a specific organization.

The article, "Testing for Competence Rather Than Intelligence," was well received among those in organizations who day to day actually evaluated on-the-job performance and had to decide whom to promote, who was the most effective leader, and what talents to groom promising people for. They had hard business metrics for success and failure, and knew that people's grades and the prestige of the schools they went to had little or nothing to do with their actual effectiveness.

As the former head of a major bank told me, "I was hiring the best and the brightest, but I was still seeing a bell-shaped curve for success and wondering why." McClelland had the explanation.

But the article was controversial among many academics, some of whom could not grasp that doing well in their courses had little to do with how their students would perform once in a job (unless that job was, say, being a college professor).[1]

Now, decades after that controversial article, competence models tell a clear story: nonacademic abilities like empathy typically outweigh purely cognitive talents in the makeup of outstanding leaders.[2] In a study done at Hay Group (which has absorbed McBer, the company McClelland himself founded, and which calls a research division the McClelland Institute), leaders who showed strengths in eight or more of these noncognitive competencies had created highly energizing, top-performing climates.[3]

But Yvonne Sell, the Hay Group's director of the leadership and talent practice in the United Kingdom, who did the study, found such leaders are rare: only 18 percent of executives attained this level. Three-quarters of leaders with three or fewer strengths in people skills created *negative* climates, where people felt indifferent or demotivated. Lame leadership seems all too prevalent—more than half of leaders fell within this low-impact category.[4]

Other studies point to the same hard case for soft skills. When Accenture interviewed one hundred CEOs about the skills they needed to run a company successfully, a set of fourteen abilities emerged, from thinking globally and creating an inspiring shared vision to embracing change and tech savvy.[5] No one person could have them all. But there was one "meta" ability that emerged: self-awareness. Chief executives need this ability to assess their own strengths and weaknesses, and so surround themselves with a team of people whose strengths in those core abilities complement their own.

And yet self-awareness rarely shows up in those lists of competencies that organizations come up with by analyzing the strengths of their star performers.[6] This subtle variety of focus may be too elusive, though abilities reflecting high cognitive control, which builds on this foundation of self-awareness, are frequent, and include persistence, resilience, and the drive to achieve goals.

Empathy in its many forms, from simple listening to reading the paths of influence in an organization, shows up more often in leadership competence studies. Most of the competencies for high-performing leaders fall into a more visible category that builds on empathy: relationship strengths like influence and persuasion, teamwork and cooperation, and the like. But these most visible leadership abilities build not just on empathy, but also on managing ourselves and sensing how what we do affects others.

The singular focusing ability that allows systems understanding goes under names that vary from organization to organization and competence model to model: big-picture view, pattern recognition, and systems thinking among them. It includes the ability to visualize the dynamics of complex systems and foresee how a decision at one point will ramify to create an effect at a distant one, or sense how what we do today will matter in five weeks, or in months, years, or decades.

The challenge for leaders goes beyond having strengths in all three kinds of focus. The key is finding balance, and using the right one at the right time. The well-focused leader balances the data streams each offers, weaving these strands into seamless action. Putting together data on attention with that on emotional intelligence and performance, this triple focus emerges as a hidden driver of excellence.

FINDING THE RIGHT BALANCE

Take any working group and ask the members, "Who is the leader?" and they'll be likely to name whoever has the fitting job title.

Now ask them, "Who is the most *influential* person in your group?" The answer to that identifies the informal leader, and tells you how that group actually operates.

These informal leaders are more self-aware than their teammates: they tend to have the smallest gap between their own ratings of their abilities and those by others.[7] University of New Hampshire psychologist Vanessa Druskat, who did this study, says, "Informal leaders often emerge in a temporary way, and switch in and out. For our research we ask, 'Who would you say is the informal leader most of the time?'"

If that informal leader has strengths in empathy in balance with other abilities, the research shows, the team's performance tends to be higher. "If the leader has low empathy," Druskat told me, "and a high level of achievement drive, the leader's goal-orientation drags down the team performance. But, importantly, if the leader has high levels of empathy and low levels of self-control, performance is also reduced—too much empathy gets in the way of calling people on their misbehaving."

A bank officer tells me, "I'm in financial services, and I never used the word *empathy* at work—until now. The key is tying it to our strategy: employee engagement, good customer experience. Empathy is a way to differentiate us from our competitors. Listening is key."

She's in good company; I heard the same message from the CEOs of the Mayo Clinic and the Cleveland Clinic, two of the world's preeminent hospitals.

And the CEO of one of the world's largest money management firms tells me that the most ambitious of business school grads apply for jobs at his company, motivated by visions of huge salaries. But, he lamented, he was looking for people "who care about the widows and retired firemen whose life savings we manage"—in other words, an empathic focus that includes the humanity of those whose money is at stake.

On the other hand, a single-minded focus on people is not enough. Take an executive who had started out as a forklift operator, working his way up to head of manufacturing for Asia at a global manufacturing company. Despite his lofty role, chatting with workers on the factory floor was where he felt most comfortable. He knew he should be doing strategic thinking, but he preferred being a "people person."

"He didn't have the right balance between his other focus and outer focus," says Spreier. "He was misfocused, and he wasn't coming up with strategy well. He didn't enjoy it—intellectually he knew he should, but emotionally he just was not there."

There may be a neural challenge for getting the right balance between focusing on hitting a target and sensing how others are reacting. My longtime colleague Richard Boyatzis tells me his research at Case Western Reserve shows that the neural network that engages when we focus on a goal differs from the circuitry for social scanning. "They inhibit each other," says Boyatzis. "The most successful leaders cycle back and forth between these within seconds."

Of course companies need leaders who beam in on getting better results. But those results will be more robust in the long run when leaders don't simply tell people what to do or just do it themselves, but have an other focus: they are motivated to help other people be successful, too.

They realize, for instance, that if someone lacks a given strength today, they can work to develop it. Such leaders take the time to mentor and advise. In practical terms all this means:

- Listening within, to articulate an authentic vision of overall direction that energizes others even as it sets clear expectations.
- Coaching, based on listening to what people want from their life, career, and current job. Paying attention to people's feelings and needs, and showing concern.
- Listening to advice and expertise; being collaborative and making decisions by consensus when appropriate.
- Celebrating wins, laughing, knowing that having a good time together is not a waste of time but a way to build emotional capital.

These leadership styles, used in tandem or as appropriate to the moment, widen a leader's focus to draw on inner, other, and outer inputs. That maximal bandwidth, and the wider understanding and flexibility of response it affords, can pay dividends. Research by the McClelland Institute on these leadership styles shows that more adept leaders draw on these as appropriate—each represents a unique focus and application. The wider a leader's repertoire of styles, the more energized the organization's climate and the better the results.[8]

APERTURE

The head of a health company was assessing a group of forty-plus managers whom he was directing in a new job. In a meeting where each stood up to raise issues, he noticed carefully how the other managers paid attention to the person speaking. Everyone was riveted on one manager and really listening, he saw, while when another stood up to speak peoples' eyes went down to their tables—a sure sign that he had lost them.

Emotional aperture, the ability to perceive such subtle cues in a group, operates a bit like a camera. We can zoom in to focus on one person's feelings, or zoom out to take in the collective—whether a classroom or a work group.

For leaders, aperture ensures a more accurate reading, for example, of support or antagonism for a proposal. Reading it well can mean the difference between a failed initiative and a helpful midcourse correction.[9]

Picking up telltale emotional cues such as tone of voice, facial expressions, and the like at a group level can tell you, for instance, how many in a group are feeling fear or anger, how many hope and positivity—or contempt and indifference. Those cues give a quicker and more true assessment of the group's feelings than, say, asking what they are feeling.

At work, collective emotions—sometimes called organizational climate—make a huge difference in, for example, customer service, absenteeism, and group performance in general.

A more nuanced sense of the range of emotions in a group—how many feel fear, hope, and the rest of the emotional gamut—can help a leader make decisions that transform fear to hope or contempt to positivity.

One hurdle in such a wide-aperture view, it turns out, is the implicit attitude at work that professionalism demands we ignore our emotions. Some trace this emotional blind spot to the work ethic embedded in the norms of workplaces in the West, which sees work as a moral obligation that demands suppressing attention to our relationships and what we feel. In this all-too-common view, paying attention to these human dimensions undermines business effectiveness.

But organizational research over the last decades provides ample evidence that this is a misguided assumption, and that the most adept team members or leaders use a wide aperture to gather the emotional information they need to deal well with their teammates' or employees' emotional needs.

Whether we notice the emotional forest or just zero in on one tree determines our aperture. When people saw cartoons depicting, for example, one person smiling surrounded by others frowning, eye-tracking devices revealed that most viewers narrowed their attention to just the smiling face, ignoring the others.[10]

There seems to be a bias (at least among college students in the West, who are the bulk of subjects in such studies in psychology) to ignore the larger collective. In East Asian society, by contrast, people more naturally take in broad patterns in a group—a wide aperture comes easily.

Leadership maven Warren Bennis uses the term "first-class noticers" for those who bring a finely honed attention to every situation, and a constant, sometimes infectious sense of fascination with what's going on in the moment. Great listeners are one variety of first-class noticers.

Two of the main mental ruts that threaten the ability to notice are unquestioned assumptions and overly relied-on rules of thumb. These need to be tested and refined time and again against changing realities. One way to do this is through what Harvard psychologist Ellen Langer calls environmental mindfulness: constant questioning and listening; inquiry, probing, and reflecting—

gathering insights and perspectives from other people. This active engagement leads to smarter questions, better learning, and a more sensitive early warning radar for coming changes.

THE SYSTEMS BRAIN

Consider an executive identified in a study of those in government posts whose track record marked them as innovative, successful leaders.[11]

His first job for the navy was in a ship's radio room. He soon mastered the radio system and, he said, "I knew it better than anyone on the ship. I was the one they came to with problems. But I realized that if I was going to be a success I had to master the ship."

So he applied himself to learning how the different parts of the ship worked together, and how each interacted with the radio room. Later in his career, when he got promoted to a much bigger job as a civilian working for the navy, he said, "Just as I mastered the radio room, and then the ship, I realized I had to master how the navy works."

While some of us have a knack for systems, for many or most leaders—like this executive—it is an acquired strength. But systems awareness in the absence of self-awareness and empathy will not be sufficient for outstanding leadership. We need to balance the triple focus, not depend on having just one strength.

Now consider the Larry Summers paradox: he no doubt has a genius IQ and brilliance as a systems thinker. He was, after all, one of the youngest professors to get tenure in Harvard's history. But years later Summers was, in effect, fired as Harvard president by its faculty, who were fed up with his insensitive blunders—most notably dismissing women's capabilities for science.

That pattern seems to fit what the University of Oxford's Simon

Baron-Cohen has identified as an extreme brain style, one that excels at systems analysis but flunks empathy and the sensitivity to social context that comes along with it.[12]

Baron-Cohen's research finds that in a small—but significant—number of people this strength comes coupled with a blind spot for what other people are feeling and thinking, and for reading social situations. For that reason, while people with superior systems understanding are organizational assets, they are not necessarily effective leaders if they lack the requisite emotional intelligence.

An executive at one bank explained to me how the bank has created a career ladder for those with this talent set that allows them to progress in status and salary on the basis of their solo talents as brilliant systems analysts rather than by climbing the leadership ranks. That way the bank can keep this talented crew and have them advance in their career, while recruiting leaders from a different pool. Those leaders can then consult their systems expertise as needed.

THE WELL-FOCUSED TEAM

At an international organization people were hired solely for their technical expertise, without regard for their personal or interpersonal abilities—including teamwork. Perhaps predictably, a one-hundred-member team there had a breakdown, with lots of friction and constant missed deadlines.

"The head of the team never had the chance to stop and reflect with someone," I was told by the leadership coach who was brought in to help. "He didn't have a single friend he could talk to openly. When I gave him the opportunity for reflection, we started with his dreams, then his problems.

"When we stepped back to look at his team he realized he'd

been seeing everything through a single small lens—how they were constantly disappointing him—but hadn't been thinking about *why* people were behaving the way they were. He had no perspective-taking; he couldn't see things from the team members' point of view."

The team leader focused his thinking on what was wrong with the members, their specific failings, and his indignation that they were torpedoing his own performance. He found it easy to blame their shortcomings.

But once he was able to shift his focus to the team's perspective on what wasn't working, his diagnosis of the trouble changed. He realized that resentments among team members were rampant. The theory-oriented basic scientists disdained the more pragmatic, get-it-done engineers, who in turn put down what they saw as head-in-the-clouds researchers.

Another variety of strife was nationalistic. The huge team was like a tiny United Nations, with members drawn from countries around the world—a goodly number of which were in conflict with each other—and those conflicts mapped onto many of the tensions between people.

The group rhetoric was that these divides didn't exist (and so *we can't talk about it*)—but in fact, the head of the team saw, he needed to get it out on the table. "So that's where he started to put things right," his coach said.

Vanessa Druskat finds that top-performing teams follow norms that enhance the collective self-awareness, such as by surfacing simmering disagreements and settling them before they boil over.

One resource for dealing with the team's emotions: create time and space to talk about what's on people's mind. Druskat's research, done with Steven Wolff, finds that many teams don't do this—it's the least frequently demonstrated norm of those they study. "But if a team does this," she says, "there's a large positive payoff.

"I was in North Carolina working with a team, and the resource we used to help them discuss emotion-laden issues was a large ceramic elephant," Druskat told me. "They all agreed to a norm that said, 'Anyone, anytime, can pick up the elephant and say, "I want to raise an elephant,"' meaning bring up something that's bothering them.

"Right away, one guy—and these are all top executives—did it. He started talking about how swamped he was and how the other folks on the team didn't realize it and were making too many demands on his time. He told them, 'You've got to realize this is my busy season.' His colleagues told him they had no idea, and had been wondering why he had been so unresponsive. Some had been taking it personally. After that there was a flood of others speaking up, getting things off their chest, clearing the air. In less than an hour it seemed like a completely different team."

"To harvest the collective wisdom of a group, you need two things: mindful presence and a sense of safety," says Steven Wolff, a principal at GEI Partners.[13] "You need a shared mental model that this is a safe place—Not, *If I say the wrong thing I'll get a note in my file*. People need to feel free to speak out.

"Being present," Wolff clarifies, "means being aware of what's going on and inquiring into it. I've learned to appreciate negative emotions—it's not that I enjoy them, but that they signal a pot of gold at the end of the rainbow if we can stay present to them. When you feel a negative emotion, stop and ask yourself, 'What's going on here?' so you can begin to understand the issue behind the feelings and then make what is going on within you visible to the team. But that requires the group be a safe container, so you can say what's actually going on."

This collective act of self-awareness clears the air of emotional static. "Our research," Wolff adds, "shows that is one sign of a high-performing team. They make it easy to give time to bring up and explore team members' negative feelings."

As with individuals, top teams excel in the triple focus. For a team, self-awareness means tuning in to the needs of members, surfacing issues, and being intentional about setting norms that help—like "raising the elephant." Some teams make time for a daily "check-in" at the start of a meeting to ask how each person is doing.

A team's empathy applies not just to sensitivity among members, but also to understanding the view and feelings of other people and groups the team deals with—group-level empathy.

The best teams also read the organization's dynamics effectively; Druskat and Wolff find that this kind of system awareness is strongly linked to positive team performance.

Team focus can take the form of both whom in the wider organization to help and where to get the resources and attention teams need to accomplish their own goals. Or it can mean learning what the concerns are of others in the organization who can influence the team's capabilities, or asking whether what the team is considering fits the larger strategy and goals of the outfit.

Top teams also periodically reflect on their functioning as a group to make needed changes. This exercise in group self-awareness allows frank feedback from within, which, Druskat tells me, "boosts the group effectiveness, especially at first."

They also create a positive atmosphere; having fun is a sign of shared flow. Tim Brown, CEO of IDEO, an innovations consultancy, calls it "serious play." He says, "Play equals trust, a space where people can take risks. Only by taking risks do we get to the most valuable new ideas."

PART VII

THE BIG PICTURE

21

LEADING FOR THE LONG FUTURE

My late uncle, Alvin Weinberg, was a nuclear physicist who often acted as the conscience of that sector. He was fired as director of Oak Ridge National Laboratory after twenty-five years in the job because he would not stop talking about the dangers of reactor safety and nuclear waste. He also, controversially, opposed using the type of reactor fuel that produces material for weapons.[1] Then, as founder of the Institute for Energy Analysis, he initiated one of the nation's pioneering R&D units on alternative energy—he was one of the first scientists to warn about the threat of CO_2 and global warming.

Alvin once confided to me his ambivalence about for-profit companies running nuclear power plants; he feared that the profit motive would mean they cut safety measures—a premonition of what contributed to the Fukushima disaster in Japan.[2]

Alvin was particularly troubled that the nuclear energy industry had never solved the problem of what to do with radioactive waste. He urged it to find a solution that would persist as long as the waste remained radioactive—such as an institution dedicated to guarding those stockpiles and keeping people safe from them over centuries or millennia.[3]

Decisions with the long horizon in mind raise questions like, How will what we do today matter in a century, or in five hundred years? To the grandchildren of our grandchildren's grandchildren?

In that far future the specifics of our actions today may well fade like distant shadows of forgotten ancestors. What could have more lasting consequence are the norms we establish, the organizing principles for action that live on long after their originators have gone.

There are think tanks, as well as corporate and government groups, that deeply ponder possible future scenarios. Consider these projections for the world in 2025, made by the U.S. National Intelligence Council:[4]

- Ecological impacts of human activity will create scarcity of resources like farmable soil.
- The economic demand for energy, food, and water will outstrip readily available sources—water shortages loom soon.
- These trends will create shocks and disruptions to our lives, economies, and political systems.

When that report was delivered, the federal government ignored the results. There is no agency, office, or particular government position charged with acting for the long term. Instead politicians focus on the short term—what it takes to get reelected, particularly—with virtually no attention paid to what needs to be done now to protect future generations. For too many politicians saving their jobs commands more of their attention than saving the planet or the poor.

But it's not just politicians—most of us prefer immediate solutions. Cognitive psychologists find that people tend to favor now in decisions of all kinds—as in, *I'll have the pie à la mode now, and maybe diet later.*

This pertains, too, to our goals. "We attend to the present, what's needed for success now," says Elke Weber, the Columbia

University cognitive scientist. "But this is bad for farsighted goals, which are not given the same priority in the mind. Future focus becomes a luxury, waiting for current needs to be taken care of first."

In 2003, New York mayor Michael Bloomberg decreed that smoking was banned in bars. His decision got huge opposition—bar owners said it would ruin their business; smokers hated it. He said, You might not like it, but you'll thank me in twenty years.

How long does it take before the public reaction becomes positive? Elke Weber looked at Bloomberg's smoking ban, among other such decisions, to answer that question: "We did case studies of how long it took for a change that was initially unpopular to become the new, accepted status quo. Our data shows the range is nine to six months."

That smoking ban? "Even smokers liked it after a while," Weber adds. "They got to enjoy hanging out with other smokers outdoors. And everyone likes that bars didn't reek of stale smoke."

Another case study: The provincial government of British Columbia imposed a tax on carbon emissions. It was revenue neutral: the fees collected were distributed among the province's citizens. At first there was tremendous opposition to the new tax. But after a while people liked getting their checks. Fifteen months later the tax was popular.[5]

"Politicians are in charge of our welfare," says Weber. "They need to know people will thank them later for a hard decision now. It's like raising teenagers—sometimes thankless in the short term, but rewarding in the long."

RESHAPING SYSTEMS

Soon after Hurricane Sandy devastated large parts of the New York City area, I spoke with Jonathan F. P. Rose, a founder of the green community planning movement, who was writing a book that looks at cities as systems.[6] "We're at an inflection point about the belief that climate change is a serious long-term problem we must deal with," Rose said. "Sandy's worst hit was the Wall Street area. You don't hear any climate warming deniers down there these days. In the Wall Street culture a quarter is a long time away. But Sandy may have gotten them to think about a much longer time horizon.

"If we reduce our production of heat-trapping gases today, it would still take at least three hundred years for the climate to begin to cool, perhaps much longer," Rose added. "We have strong cognitive biases toward our present needs, and are weak thinkers about the long away future. But at least we're starting to recognize the degree to which we have put human and natural systems at risk. What we need now is leadership. Great leaders must have the essential long view that a systems understanding brings."

Take business. Reinventing business for the long future could mean finding shared values supported by all stakeholders, from stock owners to employees and customers to communities where a company operates. Some call it "conscious capitalism," orienting a company's performance around benefiting all such stakeholders, not just aiming for quarterly numbers that please shareholders (and studies show that companies like Whole Foods and Zappos with this broader view actually do better on financials than their purely profit-oriented competitors).[7]

If a leader is to articulate such shared values effectively, he or she must first look within to find a genuinely heartfelt guiding vision. The alternative can be seen in the hollow mission statements espoused by executives but belied by their company's (or their own) actions.

Even leaders of great companies can suffer a blind spot for the long-term consequence if their time frame is too small. To be truly great, leaders need to expand their focus to a further horizon line, even beyond decades, while taking their systems understanding to a much finer focus. And their leadership needs to reshape systems themselves.

That brings to mind Paul Polman, CEO of Unilever, who surprised me when we were both members of a panel at the World Economic Forum in Davos, Switzerland. He took that opportunity to announce that Unilever had adopted the goal of cutting the company's environmental footprint in half by 2020 (this was in 2010, giving it a decade to get there). That was laudable, but a little ho-hum: many socially responsible companies announce global warming goals like that.[8]

But the next thing he said really shocked me: Unilever is committed to sourcing its raw agriculture material from small farms, aiming to link to half a million smallholders globally.[9] The farmers involved mainly grow tea, but the sourcing initiative will also include crops for cocoa, palm oil, vanilla, coconut sugar, and a variety of fruits and vegetables. The farms involved are in areas ranging from Africa to Southeast Asia and Latin America, with some in Indonesia, China, and India.

Unilever hopes not only to link these small farmers into their supply chain, but also to work with groups like Rainforest Alliance to help them upgrade their farming practices and so become reliable sources in global markets.[10]

For Unilever, this diversification of its sourcing lowers risks in a turbulent world, where food security has come on the radar as a future issue. For the farmers, it means more income and a more certain future.

This redrawing of the supply chain, Polman pointed out, would have a range of benefits, from leaving more money in local farm communities to better health and schooling. The World Bank points to supporting smallholder farming as the most effective way to stimulate economic development and reduce poverty in rural areas.[11]

"In emerging markets three out of four low-income people depend directly or indirectly on agriculture for their livelihoods," according to Cherie Tan, who heads this Unilever initiative on sourcing from small farms. Eighty-five percent of all farms worldwide are in this smallholder class, "so there are great opportunities," she adds.

If we see a company as little more than a machine for making money, we ignore its web of connections to the people who work there, the communities it operates in, its customers and clients, and society at large. Leaders with a wider view bring into focus these relationships, too.

While making money matters, of course, leaders with this enlarged aperture pay attention to *how* they make money, and so make choices differently. Their decisions operate by a logic that does not reduce to simple profit/loss calculations—it goes beyond the language of economics. They balance financial return with the public good.[12]

In this view a good decision allows for present needs as well as those of a wider web of people—including future generations. Such leaders inspire: they articulate a larger common purpose that gives meaning and coherence to everyone's work and engage people emotionally through values that make people feel good about their work, that motivate, and that keep people on course.

Focusing on social needs can itself foster innovation, if combined with an expanded field of attention to what people need. Managers at the India division of a global consumer goods company saw village men bloodied by barbers using rusty razors, and so found ways to make new razors cheap enough that those villagers could afford them.[13]

Such projects create organizational climates where work has meaning and engages people's passions. As for teams like the one that developed those cheap razors, their labor can more likely become "good work": where people are engaged, work with excellence, and find meaning in what they do.

BIG-PICTURE LEADERS

Imagine taking to scale what's been happening for years at Ben & Jerry's Ice Cream. One of its popular flavors, Chocolate Fudge Brownie, calls for brownies to be broken up into the ice cream. Ben & Jerry's gets its truckloads of these tasty cakes from the Greyston Bakery, located in a poverty-stricken neighborhood of the Bronx. The bakery trains and employs those who struggle to find work, including once-homeless parents who, with their families, now live in nearby low-cost housing. The bakery's motto: "We don't hire people to bake brownies. We bake brownies to hire people."

Such attitudes represent the kind of fresh thinking intractable dilemmas call for. But there's a hidden ingredient in any true solution: enhancing our attention and understanding—in ourselves, in others, in our communities and societies.

In the sense that leaders influence or guide people toward a shared goal, leadership is widely distributed. Whether within a family, on social media, or in an organization or society as a whole, we are all leaders in one way or another.

The good-enough leader operates within the givens of a system to benefit a single group, executing a mission as directed, taking on the problems of the day. In contrast, a great leader defines a mission, acts on many levels, and tackles the biggest problems. Great leaders do not settle for systems as they are, but see what they could become, and so work to transform them for the better, to benefit the widest circle.

Then there are those rare souls who shift beyond mere competence to wisdom, and so operate on behalf of society itself rather than a specific political group or business. They are free to think far, far ahead. Their aperture encompasses the welfare of humanity at large, not a single group; they see people as We, not as Us and Them. And they leave a legacy for future generations—these are the leaders we remember a century or more later. Think Jefferson and Lincoln, Gandhi and Mandela, Buddha and Jesus.

One of today's wicked messes is the paradox of the Anthropocene: human systems affect the global systems that support life in what seems to be headed for a slow-motion systems crash. Finding solutions requires Anthropocene thinking, understanding points of leverage within these systems dynamics so as to reset a course for a better future. This level of complexity adds to layers of others facing leaders today, as challenges escalate into messes.

For instance, through the health and ecological impacts of our lifestyle, the world's richest people are creating disproportionate pain for the world's poorest. We need to reinvent our economic systems themselves, factoring in human needs, not just economic growth.

Take the growing gap between very richest and most powerful and poorest worldwide. While the rich hold power, as we've seen this very status can blind them to the true conditions of the poor, leaving them indifferent to their suffering. Who, then, can speak truth to power?

"Civilizations should be judged not by how they treat people closest to power, but rather how they treat those furthest from power—whether in race, religion, gender, wealth, or class—as well as in time," says Larry Brilliant. "A great civilization would have compassion and love for them, too."

While the perks and pleasures of a robust economy are alluring, there are also the "diseases of civilization," like diabetes and heart disease, which are worsened by the rigors and stresses of the routines that make those lifestyles possible (plus, of course, by that economic marvel, junk food). This problem intensifies as we fail in much of the world to make medical services equally available to all.

Then there are the perennial problems of inequities in education and access to opportunity; countries and cultures that privilege one elite group while repressing others; nations that are failing and devolving into warring fiefdoms—and on and on.

Problems of such complexity and urgency require an approach to problem-solving that integrates our self-awareness and how we act, and our empathy and compassion, with a nuanced understanding of the systems at play.

To begin to address such messes, we need leaders who focus on several systems: geopolitical, economic, and environmental, to name a few. But sadly for the world, so many leaders are preoccupied with today's immediate problems that they lack bandwidth for the long-term challenges we face as a species.[14]

Peter Senge, who teaches at the MIT Sloan School of Management, developed the "learning organization," which brings a systems understanding into companies.[15] "Essential to understanding systems is your time horizon," Senge told me. "If it's too short, you'll ignore essential feedback loops and come up with short-term fixes that won't work in the long run. But if that horizon is long enough, you'll have a chance of seeing more of the key systems at play."

"The bigger your horizon," adds Senge, "the bigger the system you can see."

But "transforming large-scale systems is hard," said Rebecca Henderson at an MIT meeting on global systems. Henderson teaches on ethics and the environment at Harvard Business School and uses a systems framework to seek solutions. For instance, recycling, she points out, represents "change at the margins," while abandoning fossil fuels altogether would represent a system shift.

Henderson, who teaches a surprisingly popular course at the

business school on "reimagining capitalism," favors transparency that would accurately price say, CO_2 emissions. That would cause markets to favor any means that lowers those emissions.

At the same MIT meeting on global systems where Henderson spoke, the Dalai Lama said, "We need to influence decisión makers to pay attention to the issues that matter for humanity in the long run," like the environmental crisis and the inequity in income distribution—"not just their national interest."

"We have the capacity to think several centuries into the future," the Dalai Lama said, adding, "Start the task even if it will not be fulfilled within your lifetime. This generation has a responsibility to reshape the world. If we make an effort, it may be possible to achieve. Even if it seems hopeless now, never give up. Offer a positive vision, with enthusiasm and joy, and an optimistic outlook."

A triple focus might help us become successful, but toward what end? We must ask ourselves: in the service of what exactly are we using whatever talents we may have? If our focus serves only our personal ends—self-interest, immediate reward, and our own small group—then in the long run all of us, as a species, are doomed.

The largest lens for our focus encompasses global systems; considers the needs of everyone, including the powerless and poor; and peers far ahead in time. No matter what we are doing or what decision we are making, the Dalai Lama suggests these self-queries for checking our motivation:

Is it just for me, or for others?

For the benefit of the few, or the many?

For now, or for the future?

ACKNOWLEDGMENTS

This book weaves together strands from a multitude of sources, many of them people I've spoken with. Their insights enrich my thinking here, and I've named these generous folks throughout. Apart from those mentioned by name in the book, I'm grateful to the following people for leads, tidbits, stories, emails, casual asides, observations, and more:

Steve Arnold, Polaris Venture Partners; Rob Barracano, Champlain College; Bradley Connor, MD, Weill Cornell Medical Center; Toby Cosgrove, Cleveland Clinic; Howard Exton-Smith, Oxford Change Management; Larry Fink, BlackRock; Alan Gerson, AG International Law; Roshi Bernie Glassman, Zen Peacemakers; Bill Gross, Idealab; Nancy Henderson, The Academy at Charlemont; Mark Kriger, BI Norwegian Business School; Janice Maturano, Institute for Mindful Leadership; David Mayberg, Boston University; Charles Melcher, The Future of Storytelling; Walter Robb, Whole Foods Market; Peter Miscovich, Jones Lang LaSalle; John Noseworthy, Mayo Clinic; Miguel Pestana, Unilever; Daniel Siegel, UCLA; Josh Spear, Undercurrent; Jeffrey Walker, MDG Health Alliance; Lauris Woolford, Fifth Third Bank; Jeffrey Young, Cognitive Therapy Center of New York. Special appreciation to Tom Roepke, my kind host at Public School 112, and to Wendy Hasenkamp at Mind and Life Institute for her perceptive feedback. To those inadvertently omitted from this list, my gratitude nonetheless.

I'm grateful to fellow members of the World Economic Forum's Leadership Council and of the Cambridge Mindful Leadership group for an array of thoughtful insights. Another source of key points has been enthusiastic discussions with the Consortium for Research on Emotional Intelligence in Organizations (which I co-direct), a global network of academic researchers and organization-based practitioners.

In addition, I'm harvesting as-yet-unpublished data from studies by my associates at the Hay Group, the global consultancy that partnered with me in developing the Emotional and Social Competence Inventory (ESCI), an assessment for leadership development. Major thanks to Yvonne Sell at Hay Group London for her research with this instrument, and to Ruth Malloy, Hay Group Boston. Also to Garth Havers in South Africa, Scott Speier in Boston, and Georg Veilmetter in Berlin.

As always, I owe a special debt to Richard Davidson, old friend and source of up-to-the-minute neuroscience data, with the patience to explain it all and answer my endless questions. Rowan Foster, my assistant, has been a stalwart in searching out sometimes obscure research articles and keeping this train on its track.

And my wife, Tara Bennett-Goleman, has been an endless source of understanding and insights, inspiration and love.

RESOURCES

DANIEL GOLEMAN

For further information: www.DanielGoleman.info

To contact Daniel Goleman: Contact@danielgoleman.info

Two sets of audio instructions accompany this book: "Cultivating Focus: Techniques for Excellence" and "Focus for Kids: Enhancing Concentration, Caring, and Calmness." See www.MoreThanSound.net.

Organizations

Daniel Goleman codirects the Rutgers University–based Collaborative for Research on Emotional Intelligence in Organizations, which fosters research among academics and organizational practitioners: www.creio.org

Daniel Goleman is a founding board member of the Mind and Life Institute, which began by hosting meetings between the Dalai Lama and scientists and now has a range of initiatives, including fostering research on contemplative methods: www.mindandlife.org

Daniel Goleman was a cofounder of the Collaborative for Academic, Social and Emotional Learning, now at the University of Illinois at Chicago, which has set best practice guidelines for social/emotional learning in schools and fosters evaluation research on the programs: www.casel.org

INFORMATION ON MINDFULNESS

The Center for Mindfulness in Medicine, Health Care, and Society, founded by Jon Kabat-Zinn at the University of Massachusetts Medical Center, has been the driving force in the now widespread use of mindfulness-based stress reduction in health care and medicine, as well as in areas as diverse as the prison system and therapy: www.umassmed.edu/cfm

Mindfulness in Education; Systems and Environment: these are both programs at the Garrison Institute: www.garrisoninstitute.org

Systems and Sustainability has become a program at Peter Senge's Society for Organizational Learning: www.solonline.org

Ecological transparency within a systems perspective, and viewed through the fine-grain lens of lifecycle analysis, has taken several directions at New Earth Foundation, particularly Earthster, a platform for business-to-business ecological transparency in supply chains; Handprinter, a positive way to monitor our environmental impacts; and Social Hotspots, which identifies issues like social injustice or poor worker treatment in supply chains: www.newearth.info

Mindful Leadership is the focus of Chad-Meng Tan's spinoff from his work at Google: Search Inside Yourself Leadership Institute. www.siyli.org

RECOMMENDED BOOKS AND AUDIO

Teresa Amabile and Steven Kramer, *The Progress Principle*. Boston: Harvard Business Review Press, 2011.

Tara Bennett-Goleman, *Emotional Alchemy*. New York, NY: Three Rivers Press, 2002.

Tara Bennett-Goleman, *Mind Whispering: A New Map to Freedom from Self-Defeating Emotional Habits*. San Francisco: HarperOne, 2013.

Mirabhai Bush, *Mindfulness at Work I* (audiotape). Northampton, MA: MoreThanSound Productions, 2013.

Thomas H. Davenport and John C. Beck, *The Attention Economy: Understanding the New Currency of Business*. Boston: Harvard Business Review Press, 2002.

Richard J. Davidson and Sharon Begley, *The Emotional Life of Your Brain: How Its Unique Patterns Affect the Way You Think, Feel, and Live—and How You Can Change Them*. New York: Plume, 2012.

Jean Decety and William Ickes (eds.), *The Social Neuroscience of Empathy*. Cambridge, MA: The MIT Press 2011.

K. Anders Ericsson, ed., *The Road to Excellence: The Acquisition of Expert Performance in the Arts and Sciences, Sports and Games*. Mahwah, NJ: Lawrence Erlbaum Associates, 1996.

Eugene T. Gendlin, *Focusing.* New York: Bantam Books, 1982.

Bill George, *Authentic Leadership: Rediscovering the Secrets to Creating Lasting Value.* Hoboken, NJ: Jossey-Bass, 2004.

Daniel Goleman, *Ecological Intelligence.* New York: Random House, 2009.

Daniel Goleman, *Leadership: The Power of Emotional Intelligence.* Northampton, MA: MoreThanSound Productions, 2012.

Daniel Goleman, *Relax* (audio tape). Northampton, MA: MoreThanSound Productions, 2012.

Daniel Goleman, *Social Intelligence.* New York: Bantam Books, 2006.

Jon Kabat-Zinn, *Wherever You Go, There You Are.* New York: Hyperion, 2005.

Daniel Kahneman, *Thinking, Fast and Slow.* New York: Farrar, Straus and Giroux, 2013.

Linda Lantieri, *Building Emotional Intelligence: Techniques to Cultivate Inner Strength in Children.* Boulder, CO: Sounds True, 2008.

Michael Posner and Mary Rothbart, *Educating the Human Brain.* Washington, DC: American Psychological Association, 2006.

Daniel J. Siegel, *The Mindful Brain: Reflection and Attunement in the Cultivation of Well-Being*. New York: W. W. Norton & Company, 2007.

John D. Sterman, *Business Dynamics: Systems Thinking and Modeling for a Complex World*. New York: McGraw-Hill, 2000.

Chade-Meng Tan, *Search Inside Yourself. The Unexpected Path to Achieving Success, Happiness (and World Peace)*. San Francisco: HarperOne, 2012.

NOTES

CHAPTER 1 : THE SUBTLE FACULTY

1. For instance, the brain stem, just above the spinal cord, houses the neural barometer that senses our relation to the environment, and raises or lowers our energy arousal and attention according to how vigilant we need to be. But each aspect of attention has its own distinct circuitry. For more detail on the basics, see Michael Posner and Steven Petersen, "The Attention System of the Human Brain," *Annual Review of Neuroscience* 13 (1990): 25–42.
2. These systems include, for example, the biological and ecological; economic and social; and chemical and physical—both Newtonian and quantum.
3. M. I. Posner and M. K. Rothbart, "Research on Attention Networks as a Model for the Integration of Psychological Science," *Annual Review of Psychology* 58 (2007): 1–27, at 6.
4. Anne Treisman, "How the Deployment of Attention Determines What We See," *Visual Search and Attention* 14 (2006): 4–8.
5. See Nielsen Wire, December 15, 2011, http://blog.nielsen.com/nielsenwire/online_mobile/new-mobile-obsession-u-s-teens-triple-data-usage.
6. Mark Bauerlein, "Why Gen-Y Johnny Can't Read Nonverbal Cues," *Wall Street Journal*, August 28, 2009.
7. Criteria for being "addicted" do not specify an absolute number of hours for game playing (or bouts of drinking, for that matter), but rather focus on how the habit creates problems in other parts of life—at school, socially, or in the family. A bad gaming habit can create personal havoc on a par with drugs or drinking. Daphne Bavelier et al., "Brains on Video Games," *Nature Reviews Neuroscience* 12 (December 2011): 763–68.
8. Wade Roush, "Social Machines," *Technology Review*, August 2005.
9. Herbert Simon, "Designing Organizations for an Information-Rich

World," in Donald M. Lamberton, ed., *The Economics of Communication and Information* (Cheltenham, UK: Edward Elgar, 1997), quoted in Thomas H. Davenport and John C. Back, *The Attention Economy* (Boston: Harvard Business School Press, 2001), p. 11.

CHAPTER 2: BASICS

1. William James, *Principles of Psychology*, 1890, cited in Jonathan Schooler et al., "Meta-Awareness, Perceptual Decoupling and the Wandering Mind," *Trends in Cognitive Science* 15, no. 7 (July 2011): 319–26.
2. Ronald E. Smith et al., "Measurement and Correlates of Sport-Specific Cognitive and Somatic Trait Anxiety: The Sport Anxiety Scale," *Anxiety, Stress & Coping: An International Journal* 2, no. 4 (1990): 263–80.
3. Trying to focus on one thing and ignore everything else represents a conflict of sorts for the brain. The mediator in such mental conflicts is the anterior cingulate cortex (ACC), which spots these problems and recruits other parts of the brain to solve them. To home in on a focus of attention the ACC taps the prefrontal areas for cognitive control; they squelch the distracting circuits and amplify those for full focus.
4. Each of these essentials reflects aspects of attention that figure in our exploration here. Richard J. Davidson and Sharon Begley, *The Emotional Life of Your Brain* (New York: Hudson Street Press, 2012).
5. Heleen A. Slagter et al., "Theta Phase Synchrony and Conscious Target Perception: Impact of Intensive Mental Training," *Journal of Cognitive Neuroscience* 21, no. 8 (2009): 1536–49.
6. The prefrontal cortex sustains our attention while a nearby region, the parietal cortex, points it toward a particular target. When our concentration blurs, these regions go quiet and our focus becomes rudderless, flitting from one thing to another as each draws our attention.
7. In such studies the brains of people with ADHD exhibit far less activity in the prefrontal area and show less phase-locking synchrony: A. M. Kelly et al., "Recent Advances in Structural and Functional Brain Imaging Studies of Attention-Deficit/Hyperactivity Disorder," *Behavioral and Brain Functions* 4 (2008): 8.
8. Jonathan Smallwood et al., "Counting the Cost of an Absent Mind: Mind Wandering as an Underrecognized Influence on Educational Performance," *Psychonomic Bulletin & Review* 14, no. 12 (2007): 230–36.
9. Nicholas Carr, *The Shallows* (New York: Norton, 2011).
10. Martin Heidegger, *Discourse on Thinking* (New York: Harper & Row,

1966), p. 56. Heidegger is cited in Carr, *The Shallows*, in the latter's warning on "what the internet is doing to our brains"—not much good, in his view.

11. George A. Miller, "The Magical Number Seven, Plus or Minus Two: Some Limits on Our Capacity for Processing Information," *Psychological Review* 63 (1956): 81–97.
12. Steven J. Luck and Edward K. Vogel, "The Capacity for Visual Working Memory for Features and Conjunctions," *Nature* 390 (1997): 279–81.
13. Clara Moskowitz, "Mind's Limit Found: 4 Things at Once," *LiveScience*, April 27, 2008, http://www.livescience.com/2493-mind-limit-4.html.
14. David Garlan et al., "Toward Distraction-Free Pervasive Computing," *Pervasive Computing* 1, no. 2 (2002): 22–31.
15. Clay Shirky, *Here Comes Everybody* (New York: Penguin, 2009).
16. In organizational politics, weak ties can be a hidden strength. In matrixed organizations, instead of working through lines of command, people often have to influence someone over whom they have no direct control. Weak ties amount to social capital, relationships you can draw on for help and advice. Without any natural links to another group you need to influence, chances are slim.
17. See Thomas Malone's interview at Edge.org, http://edge.org/conversation/collective-intelligence.
18. Howard Gardner, William Damon, and Mihalyi Csikszentmihalyi, *Good Work: When Excellence and Ethics Meet* (New York: Basic Books, 2001); Mihaly Csikszentmihalyi, *Good Business* (New York: Viking, 2003).
19. Mihaly Csikszentmihalyi and Reed Larson, *Being Adolescent: Conflict and Growth in the Teenage Years* (New York: Basic Books, 1984).
20. There may even be a moderate level of default network activation while we are in "the zone." Michael Esterman et al., "In the Zone or Zoning Out? Tracking Behavioral and Neural Fluctuations During Sustained Attention," *Cerebral Cortex*, http://cercor.oxfordjournals.org/content/early/2012/08/31/cercor.bhs261.full, August 31, 2012.

CHAPTER 3: ATTENTION TOP AND BOTTOM

1. Henri Poincaré, quoted in Arthur Koestler, *The Act of Creation* (London: Hutchinson, 1964), pp. 115–16.
2. Some cognitive scientists call these systems separate "minds." I've referred to the top-down system as the "high road" and the bottom-up as

the "low road" in my book *Social Intelligence* (New York: Bantam, 2006). Daniel Kahneman, in his book *Thinking Fast and Slow* (New York: Farrar, Straus & Giroux, 2012), uses the terms *system 1* and *system 2*, which he calls "expository fictions." I find these hard to keep straight, like Thing One and Thing Two in *The Cat in the Hat*. That said, the more one delves into the neural wiring, the less satisfying "top" and "bottom" become. But they will do.

3. Kahneman, *Thinking Fast and Slow*, p. 31.
4. The human spine is another of many instances where evolution has come up with a good-enough, but not perfect, design: building upon older systems that single-column stack of bones works adequately—though a flexible tripod of three columns would have been much stronger. Anyone with a slipped disk or cervical arthritis can testify to the imperfections.
5. Lolo Jones in Sean Gregory, "Lolo's No Choke," *Time*, July 30, 2012, pp. 32–38.
6. Sian Beilock et al., "When Paying Attention Becomes Counter-Productive," *Journal of Experimental Psychology* 18, no. 1 (2002): 6–16.
7. Efforts to relax are likely to go wrong, especially in moments when we are straining to perform. See Daniel Wegner, "Ironic Effects of Trying to Relax Under Stress," *Behaviour Research and Therapy* 35, no. 1 (1997): 11–21.
8. Daniel Wegner, "How to Think, Say, or Do Precisely the Worst Thing for Any Occasion," *Science*, July 3, 2009, pp. 48–50.
9. Christian Merz et al., "Stress Impairs Retrieval of Socially Relevant Information," *Behavioral Neuroscience* 124, no. 2 (2010): 288–93.
10. "Unshrinkable," *Harper's Magazine*, December 2009, pp. 26–27.
11. Yuko Hakamata et al., "Attention Bias Modification Treatment," *Biological Psychiatry* 68, no. 11 (2010): 982–90.
12. When psychologists gave the socially anxious folks sessions where their gaze was encouraged to go to neutral or friendly faces in a crowd, rather than fixating on rejecting ones, two thirds had lost their uneasiness. Norman B. Schmidt et al., "Attention Training for Generalized Social Anxiety Disorder," *Journal of Abnormal Psychology* 118, no. 1 (2009): 5–14.
13. Roy Y. J. Chua and Xi Zou (Canny), "The Devil Wears Prada? Effects of Exposure to Luxury Goods on Cognition and Decision Making," Harvard Business School Organizational Behavior Unit Working Paper No. 10-034, November 2, 2009, http://ssrn.com/abstract=1498525 or http://dx.doi.org/10.2139/ssrn.1498525.

14. Gavan J. Fitzsimmons et al., "Non-Conscious Influences on Consumer Choice," *Marketing Letters* 13, no. 3 (2002): 269–79.
15. Patrik Vuilleumier and Yang-Ming Huang, "Emotional Attention: Uncovering the Mechanisms of Affective Biases in Perception," *Current Directions in Psychological Science* 18, no. 3 (2009): 148–52.
16. Arne Ohman et al., "Emotion Drives Attention: Detecting the Snake in the Grass," *Journal of Experimental Psychology: General* 130, no. 3 (2001): 466–78.
17. Elizabeth Blagrove and Derrick Watson, "Visual Marking and Facial Affect: Can an Emotional Face Be Ignored?" *Emotion* 10, no. 2 (2010): 147–68.
18. A. J. Schackman et al., "Reduced Capacity to Sustain Positive Emotion in Major Depression Reflects Diminished Maintenance of Fronto-Striatal Brain Activation," *Proceedings of the National Academy of Sciences* 106 (2009): 22445–50.
19. Ellen Langer, *Mindfulness* (Reading, MA: Addison-Wesley, 1989).

CHAPTER 4: THE VALUE OF A MIND ADRIFT

1. Eric Klinger, "Daydreaming and Fantasizing: Thought Flow and Motivation," in K. D. Markman et al., eds., *Handbook of Imagination and Mental Stimulation* (New York: Psychology Press, 2009), pp. 225–40.
2. Kalina Christoff, "Undirected Thought: Neural Determinants and Correlates," *Brain Research* 1428 (January 2012): 51–59.
3. Ibid., p. 57.
4. Kalina Christoff et al., "Experience Sampling During fMRI Reveals Default Network and Executive System Contributions to Mind Wandering," *Proceedings of the National Academy of Sciences* 106, no. 21 (May 26, 2009): 8719–24. The key executive areas are the anterior cingulate cortex and dorsolateral prefrontal cortex. Default areas are the medial prefrontal cortex and related circuits.
5. J. Wiley and A. F. Jarosz, "Working Memory Capacity, Attentional Focus, and Problem Solving," *Current Directions in Psychological Science* 21 (August 2012): 258–62.
6. Jonathan Schooler et al., "Meta-Awareness, Perceptual Decoupling, and the Wandering Mind," *Trends in Cognitive Science* 15, no. 7 (July 2011): 319–26.
7. Quoted in Steven Johnson, *Where Good Ideas Come From* (New York: Riverhead, 2010).

8. Holly White and Priti Singh, "Creative Style and Achievement in Adults with ADHD," *Personality and Individual Differences* 50, no. 5 (2011): 673–77.
9. Kirsten Weir, "Pay Attention to Me," *Monitor on Psychology*, March 2012, pp. 70–72.
10. Shelley Carson et al., "Decreased Latent Inhibition Is Associated with Increased Creative Achievement in High-Functioning Individuals," *Journal of Personality and Social Psychology* 85, no. 3 (September 2003): 499–506.
11. Siyuan Liu et al., "Neural Correlates of Lyrical Improvisation: An fMRI Study of Freestyle Rap," *Scientific Reports* 2, no. 834 (November 2012).
12. The Einstein quote was cited by Robert L. Oldershaw in a comment posted to *Nature* on May 21, 2012.
13. Jaime Lutz, "Peter Schweitzer, Code Breaker, Photographer; Loved Music; at 80," *Boston Globe*, November 17, 2011, p. B14.
14. More than twelve thousand daily diary entries from the 238 knowledge workers were used. See Teresa Amabile and Steven Kramer, "The Power of Small Wins," *Harvard Business Review*, May 2011, pp. 72–80.

CHAPTER 5: FINDING BALANCE

1. That question has been asked of thousands of people by an iPhone app that rings them at random moments through the day. Almost half the time people's minds had wandered away from the activity they were engaged in. Harvard psychologists Matthew Killingsworth and Daniel Gilbert, who developed the app, analyzed the reports from 2,250 American men and women to see how often their minds were elsewhere, and what their moods were. See Matthew Killingsworth and Daniel Gilbert, "A Wandering Mind Is an Unhappy Mind," *Science*, November 12, 2010, p. 932.
2. Seeing the medial prefrontal cortex as the site of "me" oversimplifies a bit, though many cognitive neuroscientists find this convenient. A more complex version of "me," the self, is seen as an emergent phenomenon based on the activity of many neural circuits, the prefrontal medial among them. See, e.g., J. Smallwood and J. W. Schooler, "The Restless Mind," *Psychological Bulletin* 132 (2006): 946–58.
3. Norman A. S. Farb et al., "Attending to the Present: Mindfulness Meditation Reveals Distinct Neural Modes of Self-Reference," *Social Cognitive and Affective Neuroscience* 2 (2007): 313–22.

4. Or so we humans project onto animals.
5. E. D. Reichle et al., "Eye Movements During Mindless Reading," *Psychological Science* 21 (July 2010): 1300–1310.
6. J. Smallwood et al., "Going AWOL in the Brain—Mind Wandering Reduces Cortical Analysis of the Task Environment," *Journal of Cognitive Neuroscience* 20, no. 3 (March 2008): 458–69; J. W. Y. Kam et al., "Slow Fluctuations in Attentional Control of Sensory Cortex," *Journal of Cognitive Neuroscience* 23 (2011): 460–70.
7. Cedric Galera, "Mind Wandering and Driving: Responsibility Case-Control Study," *British Medical Journal*, published online December 13, 2012, doi: 10.1136/bmj.e8105.
8. Which means that these brain circuits are not always working in opposition.
9. K. D. Gerlach et al., "Solving Future Problems: Default Network and Executive Activity Associated with Goal-Directed Mental Simulations," *Neuroimage* 55 (2011): 1816–24.
10. Conversely, the less we notice our mind has wandered, the stronger the activity in the underlying neural zones, and the greater their disruptive force on the task at hand. At least two prefrontal brain regions involved in that meander are among the very ones that also can notice we have gone off track: the dorsolateral prefrontal cortex and dorsal anterior cingulate.
11. Christoff et al., "Experience Sampling During fMRI Reveals Default Network and Executive System Contributions to Mind Wandering." A technical note: this study used a ten-second window in the probe for mind wandering; ten seconds is a long time in the mind's activity. So the conclusion that both executive and medial circuits are involved is open to objections. Moreover, the authors note, this conclusion is based on reverse inference, the assumption that if a brain region activates during a mental task, it is a neural basis for that task. For higher cognitive abilities this may not hold up, since the same region can be activated by multiple and very different mental processes. If true, this finding challenges the assumption that the executive and default networks always operate in opposition to each other—that is, if one is active the other is quiet. This may, indeed, be the case in very specific mental operations, like intense focus on a task at hand. But in much of mental life it may help to mix heightened focus with a daydreamy openness. It certainly helps pass the time on a long drive. See also M. D. Fox et al., "The Human Brain Is Intrinsically Organized into Dynamic, Anticorrelated Functional Net-

works," *Proceedings of the National Academy of Sciences* 102 (July 5, 2005): 9673–78.

12. Catherine Fassbender, "A Lack of Default Network Suppression Is Linked to Increased Distractibility in ADHD," *Brain Research* 1273 (2009): 114–28.
13. The test for open awareness is called the "attentional blink." See H. A. Slagter et al., "Mental Training Affects Distribution of Limited Brain Resources," *PLoS Biology* 5 (2007): e138.
14. William Falk, writing in the *The Week*, August 10, 2012, p. 3.
15. Stephen Kaplan, "Meditation, Restoration, and the Management of Mental Fatigue," *Environment and Behavior* 33, no. 4 (July 2001): 480–505, http://eab.sagepub.com/content/33/4/480.
16. Marc Berman, Jon Jonides, and Stephen Kaplan, "The Cognitive Benefits of Interacting with Nature," *Psychological Science* 19, no. 12 (2008): 1207–12.
17. Ibid.
18. Gary Felsten, "Where to Take a Study Break on the College Campus: An Attention Restoration Theory Perspective," *Journal of Environmental Psychology* 29, no. 1 (March 2009): 160–67.

CHAPTER 6: THE INNER RUDDER

1. A technique called "focusing" guides people in how to tap into this vast out-of-awareness body-of-life wisdom, by sensing subtle internal shifts in feelings. See Eugene Gendlin, *Focusing* (New York: Bantam, 1981).
2. John Allman, "The von Economo Neurons in the Frontoinsular and Anterior Cingulate Cortex," *Annals of the New York Academy of Sciences* 1225 (2011): 59–71.
3. Lev Grossman and Harry McCracken, "The Inventor of the Future," *Time*, October 17, 2011, p. 44.
4. A. D. Craig, "How Do You Feel? Interoception: The Sense of the Physiological Condition of the Body," *Nature Reviews Neuroscience* 3 (2002): 655–66.
5. Arthur D. Craig, "How Do You Feel—Now? The Anterior Insula and Human Awareness," *Nature Reviews Neuroscience* 10, no. 1 (January 2009): 59–70.
6. G. Bird et al., "Empathic Brain Responses in Insula Are Modulated by Levels of Alexithymia but Not Autism," *Brain* 133 (2010): 1515–25.
7. Somatic markers: this circuitry includes the right somatosensory insular

cortex and the amygdala, among others. Antonio Damasio, *The Feeling of What Happens* (New York: Harcourt, 1999).

8. Farb et al., "Attending to the Present."

CHAPTER 7: SEEING OURSELVES AS OTHERS SEE US

1. See Fabio Sala, "Executive Blindspots: Discrepancies Between Self-Other Ratings," *Journal of Consulting Psychology: Research and Practice* 54, no. 4 (2003): 222–29.
2. Bill George and Doug Baker, *True North Groups* (San Francisco: Berrett-Koehler, 2011), p. 28.
3. Nalini Ambady et al., "Surgeon's Tone of Voice: A Clue to Malpractice History," *Surgery* 132, no. 1 (2002): 5–9.
4. Michael J. Newcombe and Neal M. Ashkanasy, "The Role of Affective Congruence in Perceptions of Leaders: An Experimental Study," *Leadership Quarterly* 13, no. 5 (2002): 601–604.
5. Kahneman, *Thinking Fast and Slow*, p. 216.
6. John U. Ogbu, *Minority Education and Caste: The American System in Cross-Cultural Perspective* (New York: Academic, 1978).

CHAPTER 8: A RECIPE FOR SELF-CONTROL

1. M. K. Rothbart et al., "Self-Regulation and Emotion in Infancy," in Nancy Eisenberg and R. A. Fabes, eds., *Emotion and Its Regulation in Early Development: New Directions for Child Development* No. 55 (San Francisco: Jossey-Bass, 1992), pp. 7–23.
2. Many scientific disciplines see self-control as critical to well-being. Behavioral geneticists look at how much of these abilities is due to our genes, how much to the family environment we grow up in. Developmental psychologists monitor how children master self-control as they mature, getting progressively better at the delay of gratification, managing impulse, emotional self-regulation, planning, and conscientiousness. Health specialists see a link between self-control and life span, while sociologists focus on low self-control as a predictor of joblessness and crime. Psychiatrists look at childhood diagnoses like attention deficits and hyperactivity while people are young, and later in life psychiatric disorders, smoking, unsafe sex, and drunk driving. Finally, economists speculate that self-control might be a key both to financial well-being and to reducing crime.
3. Posner and Rothbart, "Research on Attention Networks as a Model for

the Integration of Psychological Science." The network for the alerting system weaves together the thalamus and the right frontal and parietal cortex and is modulated by acetylcholine. Orienting weaves together structures in the superior parietal, temporal parietal junction, frontal eye fields, and superior colliculus, and is modulated by norepinephrine. Executive attention involves the anterior cingulate, lateral ventral prefrontal, and basal ganglia areas, and is modulated by dopamine.

4. Selective attention seems to have some heritability, though there is little to none for alerting, where we maintain a state of readiness for whatever comes next. See J. Fan et al., "Assessing the Heritability of Attentional Networks," *BMC Neuroscience* 2 (2001): 14.
5. Lawrence J. Schweinhart et al., *Lifetime Effects: The High/Scope Perry Preschool Study Through Age 40* (Ypsilanti, MI: High/Scope Press, 2005).
6. J. J. Heckman, "Skill Formation and the Economics of Investing in Disadvantaged Children," *Science* 312 (2006): 1900–1902.
7. Terrie E. Moffitt et al., "A Gradient of Childhood Self-Control Predicts Health, Wealth and Public Safety," *Proceedings of the National Academy of Sciences* 108, no. 7 (February 15, 2011): 2693–98, http://www.pnas.org/cgi/doi/10.1073/pnas.1010076108.
8. They were assessed variously by their teachers, their parents, trained observers, and themselves, at ages 3, 5, 7, 9, and 11.
9. June Tangney et al., "High Self-Control Predicts Good Adjustment, Less Pathology, Better Grades, and Interpersonal Success," *Journal of Personality* 72, no. 2 (2004): 271–323.
10. Tom Hertz, "Understanding Mobility in America," Center for American Progress, 2006.
11. Thanks to Sam Anderson, whose article "In Defense of Distraction" gave me this idea. *New York*, May 17, 2009, http:/nymag.com/news/features/56793/index7.html.
12. Jeanne Nakamura, "Optimal Experience and the Uses of Talent," in Mihalyi and Isabella Csikszentmihalyi, eds., *Optimal Experience* (New York: Cambridge University Press, 1988).
13. Davidson and Begley, *The Emotional Life of Your Brain.*
14. Adele Diamond et al., "Preschool Program Improves Cognitive Control," *Science* 318 (2007): 1387–88.
15. Angela Duckworth and Martin E. P. Seligman, "Self-Discipline Outdoes IQ in Predicting Academic Performance of Adolescents," *Psychological Science* 16, no. 12 (2005): 939–44.

16. B. J. Casey et al., "Behavioral and Neural Correlates of Delay of Gratification 40 Years Later," *Proceedings of the National Academy of Sciences* 108, no. 36 (September 6, 2011): 14998–15003, http://www.pnas.org/cgi/doi/10.1073/pnas.1108561108.
17. Jeanne McCaffery et al., "Less Activation in the Left Dorsolateral Prefrontal Cortex in the Reanalysis of the Response to a Meal in Obese Than in Lean Women and Its Association with Successful Weight Loss," *American Journal of Clinical Nutrition* 90, no. 4 (October 2009): 928–34.
18. Walter Mischel, quoted in Jonah Lehrer, "Don't!" *New Yorker*, May 18, 2009.
19. The tale is told in Buddhaghosa, *The Path to Purification*, trans. Bhikku Nanomoli (Boulder, CO: Shambhala, 1979), I, p. 55.

CHAPTER 9: THE WOMAN WHO KNEW TOO MUCH

1. Justine Cassell et al., "Speech-Gesture Mismatches: Evidence for One Underlying Representation of Linguistic and Nonlinguistic Information," *Pragmatics & Cognition* 7, no. 1 (1999): 1–34.
2. Facial expressions during marital conflict that have been coded using the Specific Affect Coding System (SPAFF) accurately predict the number of months of marital separation within the next four years. In particular, the fleeting facial expression of contempt seems to be highly predictive. John Gottman et al., "Facial Expressions During Marital Conflict," *Journal of Family Conflict* 1, no. 1 (2001): 37–57.
3. F. Ramseyer and W. Tschacher, "Nonverbal Synchrony in Psychotherapy: Relationship Quality and Outcome Are Reflected by Coordinated Body-Movement." *Journal of Consulting and Clinical Psychology* 79 (2011): 284–95.
4. Justine Cassell et al., "BEAT: The Behavior Expression Animation Toolkit," *Proceedings of SIGGRAPH '01*, August 12–17, 2001, Los Angeles, pp. 477–86.

CHAPTER 10: THE EMPATHY TRIAD

1. Each of the three kinds of empathy has its own neural building blocks and course of development. Empathy in all its faces draws on a huge array of brain structures. For one analysis see Jean Decety, "The Neurodevelopment of Empathy," *Developmental Neuroscience* 32 (2010): 257–67.

2. For details of the circuitry for each kind of empathy, see Ezequiel Gleichgerrcht and Jean Decety, "The Costs of Empathy Among Health Professionals," in Jean Decety, ed., *Empathy: From Bench to Bedside* (Cambridge, MA: MIT Press, 2012).
3. Alan Mulally, CEO Ford Motor Company, quoted in Adam Bryant, *The Corner Office* (New York: Times Books, 2011), p. 14.
4. John Seabrook, "Suffering Souls," *New Yorker*, November 10, 2008.
5. "Empathic cruelty" occurs when one person's brain mirrors the distress of another but also takes pleasure in the suffering. D. de Quervain et al., "The Neural Basis of Altruistic Punishment," *Science* 305 (2004): 1254–58.
6. Cleckley quoted in Seabrook, "Suffering Souls."
7. On the dissociation between emotional and cognitive processing in sociopaths, see, e.g., Kent Kiehl et al., "Limbic Abnormalities in Affective Processing by Criminal Psychopaths as Revealed by Functional Magnetic Resonance Imaging," *Biological Psychiatry* 50 (2001): 677–84; Niels Bribaumer et al., "Deficient Fear Conditioning in Psychopathy," *Archives of General Psychiatry* 62 (2005): 799–805.
8. Joseph Newman et al., "Delay of Gratification in Psychopathic and Nonpsychopathic Offenders," *Journal of Abnormal Psychology* 101, no. 4 (1992): 630–36.
9. See, e.g., Loren Dyck, "Resonance and Dissonance in Professional Helping Relationships at the Dyadic Level" (Ph.D. diss., Department of Organizational Behavior, Case Western Reserve University, May 2010).
10. Emotional empathy neural wiring includes the amygdala, hypothalamus, hippocampus, and orbitofrontal cortex. See Decety, "The Neurodevelopment of Empathy," for neural details on this and other forms of empathy.
11. Greg J. Stephens et al., "Speaker-Listener Neural Coupling Underlies Successful Communication," *Proceedings of the National Academy of Sciences* 107, no. 32 (2010): 14425–30.
12. Circuits in the social brain read the other person's emotions, intentions, and actions and simultaneously activate in our own brain those same brain regions, giving us an inner sense of what's going on in the other person. Along with mirror neurons, circuitry like the ventromedial prefrontal cortex is key. See Jean Decety, "To What Extent Is the Experience of Empathy Mediated by Shared Neural Circuits?" *Emotion Review* 2, no. 3 (2010): 204–207. In studies of hundreds of people watching clips of those in pain, Decety finds no gender difference in how their brains respond—but a big

difference in their social response: women rate themselves as more empathic than do men.

13. P. L. Jackson et al., "To What Extent Do We Share the Pain of Others? Insight from the Neural Bases of Pain Empathy," *Pain* 125 (2006): 5–9.
14. Singer finds that the insula records pain, suffering, and negative affect, while another circuit in the orbitofrontal cortex responds to pleasant sensations, like a soft touch from someone. Tania Singer et al., "A Common Role of Insula in Feelings, Empathy and Uncertainty," *Trends in Cognitive Sciences* 13, no. 8 (2009): 334–40; C. Lamm and T. Singer, "The Role of Anterior Insular Cortex in Social Emotions," *Brain Structure & Function* 241, nos. 5–6 (2010): 579–91.
15. C. J. Limb et al., "Neural Substrates of Spontaneous Musical Performance: An fMRI Study of Jazz Improvisation," *PLoS ONE* 3, no. 2 (2008).
16. Jean Decety and Claus Lamm, "The Role of the Right Temporoparietal Junction in Social Interaction: How Low-Level Computational Processes Contribute to Meta-Cognition," *Neuroscientist* 13, no. 6 (2007): 580–93.
17. Jean Decety, presentation to the Consortium for Research on Emotional Intelligence in Organizations, Cambridge, MA: May 6, 2011.
18. Sharee Light and Carolyn Zahn-Waxler, "The Nature and Forms of Empathy in the First Years of Life," in Decety, ed., *Empathy: From Bench to Bedside.*
19. See, e.g., Carr, *The Shallows.*
20. C. Daniel Batson et al., "An Additional Antecedent to Empathic Concern: Valuing the Welfare of the Person in Need," *Journal of Personality and Social Psychology* 93, no. 1 (2007): 65–74. Also, Grit Hein et al., "Neural Responses to Ingroup and Outgroup Members' Suffering Predict Individual Differences in Costly Helping," *Neuron* 68, no. 1 (2010): 149–60.
21. Subjects witnessing either people who have previously behaved unfairly in economic games or outgroup members suffering pain did not show the habitual empathic response in the anterior insula cortex and anterior cingulate cortex but instead showed increased activation in the nucleus accumbens, an area associated with reward processing. Tania Singer et al., "Empathic Neural Responses Are Modulated by the Perceived Fairness of Others," *Nature* 439 (2006): 466–69.
22. Chiara Sambo et al., "Knowing You Care: Effects of Perceived Empathy and Attachment Style on Pain Perception," *Pain* 151, no. 3 (2010): 687–93.

23. John Couhelan et al., "'Let Me See If I Have This Right . . .': Words That Build Empathy," *Annals of Internal Medicine* 135, no. 3 (2001): 221–27.
24. See, e.g., W. Levinson et al., "Physician-Patient Communication: The Relationship with Malpractice Claims Among Primary Care Physicians and Surgeons," *Journal of the American Medical Association* 277 (1997): 553–69.
25. Jean Decety et al., "Physicians Down-Regulate Their Pain-Empathy Response: An ERP Study," *Neuroimage* 50, no. 4 (2010): 1676–82.
26. William Osler quoted in Decety, ed., *Empathy: From Bench to Bedside*, p. 230.
27. Jodi Halpern, "Clinical Empathy in Medical Care," ibid.
28. M. Hojat et al., "The Devil Is in the Third Year: A Longitudinal Study of Erosion of Empathy in Medical School," *Academic Medicine* 84, no. 9 (2009): 1182–91.
29. Helen Riess et al., "Empathy Training for Resident Physicians: A Randomized Controlled Trial of a Neuroscience-Informed Curriculum," *Journal of General Internal Medicine* 27, no. 10 (2012): 1280–86.
30. Helen Riess, "Empathy in Medicine: A Neurobiological Perspective," *Journal of the American Medical Association* 304, no. 14 (2010): 1604–1605.

CHAPTER 11: SOCIAL SENSITIVITY

1. Prince Philip quoted in Ferdinand Mount, "The Long Road to Windsor," *Wall Street Journal*, November 14, 2011, p. A15.
2. Kim Dalton et al., "Gaze Fixation and the Neural Circuitry of Face Processing in Autism," *NatureNeuroscience* 8 (2005): 519–26. Richard Davidson has proposed that for those with autism, failure to understand what is appropriate in a social situation stems from a deficit in acquiring social intuition.
3. This is still under debate, with some studies showing this effect, others not.
4. See, e.g., Michael W. Kraus et al., "Social Class Rank, Threat Vigilance, and Hostile Reactivity," *Personality and Social Psychology Bulletin* 37, no. 10 (2011): 1376–88.
5. Michael Kraus and Dacher Keltner, "Signs of Socioeconomic Status," *Psychological Science* 20, no. 1 (2009): 99–106.
6. Gerben A. van Kleef et al., "Power, Distress, and Compassion," *Psychological Science* 19, no. 12 (2008): 1315–22.

7. Michael Kraus, Stephane Cote, and Dacher Keltner, "Social Class, Contextualism, and Empathic Accuracy," *Psychological Science* 21, no. 11 (2010): 1716–23.
8. Ryan Rowe et al., "Automated Social Hierarchy Detection Through Email Network Analysis," Proceedings of the 9th WebKDD and 1st SNA-KDD 2007 Workshop on Web Mining and Social Network Analysis, 2007, 109–117.

CHAPTER 12: PATTERNS, SYSTEMS, AND MESSES

1. K. Levin et al., "Playing It Forward: Path Dependency, Progressive Incrementalism, and the 'Super Wicked' Problem of Global Climate Change," *IOP Conference Series: Earth and Environmental Science* 50, no. 6 (2009).
2. Russell Ackoff, "The Art and Science of Mess Management," *Interfaces*, February 1981, pp. 20–26.
3. Jeremy Ginsberg et al., "Detecting Influenza Epidemics Using Search Engine Query Data," *Nature* 457 (2009): 1012–14.
4. So I was told by Thomas Davenport, Harvard Business School.
5. But bringing people into the information equation can also complicate things: there's jealousy over who controls data, infighting, and organizational politics that can prevent information sharing or lead to hoarding and to simply ignoring data.
6. Thomas Davenport's book in progress, tentatively called "Keeping Up with the Quants," was reported in Steve Lohr, "Sure, Big Data Is Great: but So Is Intuition," *New York Times*, December 30, 2012, Business, p. 3.
7. As reported by Lohr, "Sure, Big Data Is Great."

CHAPTER 13: SYSTEM BLINDNESS

1. Of course, the "system" that got into the room was just a partial slice of larger, interlocking systems, such as the information dispersal system, which is in the midst of shifting from print to digital formats.
2. John D. Sterman, *Business Dynamics: Systems Thinking and Modeling for a Complex World* (New York: McGraw-Hill, 2000).
3. See my book *Ecological Intelligence* (New York: Broadway, 2009) for more details on supply chains, emissions, and the true environmental cost of things man-made. Or see Annie Leonard's twenty-minute video, "The Story of Stuff," http://www.storyofstuff.org.

4. Originally proposed by Yale psychologist Frank Keil's group, the illusion has been extended from purely mechanical or natural systems to social, economic, and political ones. See, e.g., Adam L. Alter et al., "Missing the Trees for the Forest: A Construal Level Account of the Illusion of Explanatory Depth," *Journal of Personality and Social Psychology* 99, no. 3 (2010): 436–51. That illusion may be at play in this book, when it has to do with the broad strokes with which I paint a wide variety of cognitive, emotional, social, and neural systems. This risk is inherent in science journalism. That's why this book has lots of endnotes, for those who want to pursue these threads of understanding. Congratulations for reading this one.
5. See, e.g., Elke Weber, "Experience-Based and Description-Based Perceptions of Longterm Risk: Why Global Warming Does Not Scare Us (Yet)," *Climatic Change* 77 (2006): 103–20.

CHAPTER 14: DISTANT THREATS

1. Nassim Nicholas Taleb, *The Black Swan: The Impact of the Highly Improbable* (New York: Random House, 2010).
2. Johan Rockstrom et al., "A Safe Operating Space for Humanity," *Nature* 461 (2009): 472–75.
3. Will Steffen et al., "The Anthropocene: Are Humans Now Overwhelming the Great Forces of Nature?" *Ambio: A Journal of the Human Environment* 36, no. 8 (2007): 614–21.
4. China's carbon economy, based on World Bank figures, as reported in Fred Pearce, "Over the Top," *New Scientist*, June 16, 2012, pp. 38–43. On the other hand, see "China Plans Asia's Biggest Coal-Fired Power Plant," at http://phys.org/news/2011-12-china-asia-biggest-coal-fired-power.html.
5. When a global consumer goods company used LCA to analyze its CO_2 footprint, it turned out the biggest factor was when customers heated water to use warm-water detergents (conveniently displacing responsibility to the consumer—you wonder what the second through tenth factors were).
6. The German social theorist Niklas Luhmann argues that every major human system organizes around a single principle. For the economy, it's money; for politics, power; for the social world, love. And so the most elegant decisions in these realms become manageably binary: money/no money; power/no power; love/no love. Perhaps it is no co-

incidence that our brain applies a primal either/or decision rule in every moment of perception; the micro-instant we notice something, the emotional centers summate our relevant experience and tag it "like" or "don't like." Niklas Luhmann's work in the original German on sociological systems theory has not yet been translated into English, though it has been highly influential throughout Eastern Europe. I have read only secondhand accounts and been briefed on the key points by Georg Vielmetter, whose dissertation was based in part on Luhmann's theories.

7. Streamlined versions of life cycle analysis software are being designed that can do this.
8. Jack D. Shepard et al., "Chronically Elevated Corticosterone in the Amygdala Increases Corticotropin Releasing Factor mRNA in the Dorsolateral Bed Nucleus of Stria Terminalis Following Duress," *Behavioral Brain Research* 17, no. 1 (2006): 193–96.
9. That was the premise of my book *Ecological Intelligence: The Hidden Impacts of What We Buy* (New York: Random House, 2009).
10. U.S. Department of Energy data shows that water heating accounts for 18–20 percent of residential energy use nationally. In New England, annual water heating costs for a family of four range from $500 to well above $800, depending on the fuel used. Data from the Residential Energy Consumption Survey also shows that only 12 percent of U.S. homes have an insulating blanket installed on their water heater tank, despite the fact that such a blanket, which costs only about $20, can save $70 per year in energy consumption and will last for the life of your water heater (which is thirteen years, on average). The simple act of installing water heater blankets and adjusting temperatures to 120 degrees Fahrenheit could cut total U.S. household energy consumption by approximately 2 percent, along with providing major benefits for the climate, biodiversity, and human health—and the economy.
11. The children in the school will give the blankets away to households throughout the community, and make a deal: houses that get the blankets will give the first nine months of savings back to the school, then just keep the money after that. In all, that should raise around $15,000. The school will keep $5,000 to help do things like make needed playground improvements. It will use the remaining $10,000 to buy water blankets to give away to two other schools to do the same.
12. The specifics differ for each of the many polluting emissions—for some the payback point is in months; for others, years. For instance, there

are two major classes of particulate emissions, both of which penetrate deeply into our lungs. Their reduction rates vary, but handprints roll the total consequence for health and biodiversity loss of all types of pollution in a single score.

13. Will Wright, quoted in Chris Baker, "The Creator," *Wired*, August 2012, p. 68.
14. Celia Pearce, "Sims, Battlebots, Cellular Automota, God and Go," *Game Studies*, July 2002, p. 1.
15. Outdoor air pollution contributed to 1.2 million premature deaths in China; the global total was 3.2 million. See "Global Burden of Disease Study 2010," *The Lancet*, December 13, 2013.
16. My book *Ecoliterate*, cowritten with Lisa Bennett and Zenobia Barlow of the Center for Ecoliteracy, makes the argument for engaging students' emotions in environmental education, though it does not include the kind of curriculum described here.
17. Paul Hawken, "Reflection," *Garrison Institute Newsletter*, Spring 2012, p. 9.

CHAPTER 15: THE MYTH OF 10,000 HOURS

1. The biggest boost to the fame of the 10,000-hour rule was from Malcolm Gladwell's nearly perpetual best seller, *Outliers*. I, too, had a small hand in its popularity: in 1994 I wrote in the *New York Times* about the research this comes from—the work of Anders Ericsson, a cognitive scientist at Florida State University. His research found, for example, that top violinists in the best music academies had already practiced their instruments for 10,000 hours, while those who had done just 7,500 hours tended to be, literally, second fiddles. Daniel Goleman, "Peak Performance: Why Records Fall," *New York Times*, October 11, 1994, p. C1.
2. I interviewed Anders Ericsson for that 1994 *New York Times* article.
3. Anders Ericsson et al., "The Role of Deliberate Practice in the Acquisition of Expert Performance," *Psychological Review* 47 (1993): 273–305. Take Itzhak Perlman, who came to the Juilliard School—that hyperselective performing arts conservancy—as a prodigy at thirteen, and studied for eight years with Dorothy DeLay, his violin instructor there. She expected great discipline; her students practiced five hours a day, and DeLay gave them constant feedback and encouragement. For Perlman, that amounted to at least 12,000 hours of smart practice by the time he

left the school. But once you are launched, is that level of practice enough to let you coast on your own? Lifetime coaches are commonplace among professional performers: singers routinely rely on voice coaches, just as elite athletes do on their coaches. No one reaches world-class levels without a master teacher. Even Perlman still has a coach: his wife, Toby, herself a concert-level violinist, whom he met while at Juilliard. For more than forty years Perlman has valued her tough critiques as an "extra ear."

4. And, remember, once a routine becomes automatic, trying to think about how you are executing it can interfere with that execution: top-down takes over from bottom-up, but not effectively.
5. K. Anders Ericsson, "Development of Elite Performance and Deliberate Practice," in J. L. Starkes and K. Anders Ericcson, eds., *Expert Performance in Sports: Advances in Research on Sport Expertise* (Champaign, IL: Human Kinetics, 2003).
6. Although he studied and taught at Cambridge University, Thupten Jinpa tells me his accent actually comes from having learned spoken English in his youth by listening to the BBC World radio broadcasts to India.
7. I interviewed Herbert Simon for the *New York Times*. See Goleman, "Peak Performance: Why Records Fall."
8. Wendy Hasenkamp et al., "Mind Wandering and Attention During Focused Attention," *NeuroImage* 59, no. 1 (2012): 750–60.
9. Resting state connectivity in experienced meditators was increased between the medial region and parietal regions that are involved in disengaging of attention. This suggests that the regions that control disengagement have more access to the mPFC regions that may underlie self-related mind-wandering, suggesting a neuroplastic effect as practice made this connectivity stronger. Wendy Hasenkamp and Lawrence Barsalou, "Effects of Meditation Experience on Functional Connectivity of Distributed Brain Networks," *Frontiers in Human Neuroscience* 6, no. 38 (2012): 1–14.
10. Larry David's reactions to the Yankee Stadium crowd were reported in "The Neurotic Zen of Larry David," *Rolling Stone*, August 4, 2011, p. 81.
11. Taylor Schmitz et al., "Opposing Influence of Affective State Valence on Visual Cortical Decoding," *Journal of Neuroscience* 29, no. 22 (2009): 7199–7207.
12. Barbara Fredrickson, *Love 2.0* (New York: Hudson Street Press, 2013).
13. Davidson and Begley, *The Emotional Life of Your Brain*.
14. Anthony Jack et al., "Visioning in the Brain: An fMRI Study of Inspirational Coaching and Mentoring," submitted for publication, 2013.
15. M. Losada and E. Heaphy, "The Role of Positivity and Connectivity in

the Performance of Business Teams: A Nonlinear Dynamics Model," *American Behavioral Scientist* 47, no. 6 (2004): 740–65.

16. B. L. Fredrickson and M. Losada, "Positive Affect and the Complex Dynamics of Human Flourishing," *American Psychologist* 60, no. 7 (2005): 678–86.

CHAPTER 16: BRAINS ON GAMES

1. The tale of Daniel Cates was told by Jay Kaspian Kang in "The Gambler," *New York Times Magazine*, March 27, 2011, pp. 48–51.
2. Poker, of course, is not just a skill; a run of bad hands can put even the best player at a disadvantage. But a slight advantage in skill, if pursued over thousands of games, pays off. One trait of online poker winners is, understandably, a kind of fearless abandon about risk-taking, an essential attitude when you can lose hundreds of thousands of dollars in the blink of an eye.
3. Marc Smith was quoted in the *Boston Globe*, July 28, 2012, p. A6.
4. Daphne Bavelier et al., "Brains on Video Games," *Nature Reviews Neuroscience* 12 (December 2011): 763–68.
5. Gentile, quoted ibid.
6. Ibid.
7. Enhanced aggression was the finding from the most comprehensive meta-analysis to date, based on 136 separate studies of a total of 30,296 gamers or controls. Craig A. Anderson, "An Update on the Effects of Playing Violent Video Games," *Journal of Adolescence* 27 (2004): 113–22. But see also John L. Sherry, "Violent Video Games and Aggression: Why Can't We Find Effects?" in Raymond Preiss et al., eds., *Mass Media Effects Research: Advances Through Meta-Analysis* (Mahwah, NJ: Lawrence Erlbaum, 2007), pp. 245–62.
8. The key part: the anterior cingulate gyrus. See M. R. Rueda et al., "Training, Maturation, and Genetic Influences on the Development of Executive Attention," *Proceedings of the National Academy of Sciences* 102, no. 41 (2005): 1029–40.
9. There's another brain correlate of ADD: underactivity in the prefrontal areas that manage attention, executive functioning, and self-control. M. K. Rothbart and M. I. Posner, "Temperament, Attention, and Developmental Psychopathology," in D. Cicchetti and D. J. Cohen, eds., *Handbook of Developmental Psychopathology* (New York: Wiley, 2006), pp. 167–88.

10. O. Tucha et al., "Training of Attention Functions in Children with Attention Deficit Hyperactivity Disorder," *Attention Deficit and Hyperactivity Disorders*, May 20, 2011.
11. Merzenich in Bavelier et al., "Brains on Video Games."
12. Gus Tai, quoted in Jessica C. Kraft, "Digital Overload? There's an App for That," *New York Times*, Sunday, July 22, 2012, Education Supplement, p. 12.

CHAPTER 17: BREATHING BUDDIES

1. The voice they listen to is my own, on a CD I narrated for Linda Lantieri, *Building Emotional Intelligence* (Boulder, CO: Sounds True, 2008). The script I read was written by Linda, based on her work with children in the New York public schools and elsewhere.
2. Linda Lantieri et al., "Building Inner Resilience in Students and Teachers," in Gretchen Reevy and Erica Frydenberg, eds., *Personality, Stress and Coping: Implications for Education* (Charlotte, NC: Information Age, 2011), pp. 267–92.
3. So Richard Davidson told me, referring to a study still in progress at the Center for Investigating Healthy Minds.
4. Joseph A. Durlak et al., "The Impact of Enhancing Students' Social/Emotional Learning: A Meta-Analysis of School-Based Universal Interventions," *Child Development* 82, no. 1 (2011): 405–32.
5. Nathaniel R. Riggs et al., "The Mediational Role of Neurocognition in the Behavioral Outcomes of a Social-Emotional Prevention Program in Elementary School Students: Effects of the PATHS Curriculum," *Prevention Science* 7, no. 1 (March 2006): 91–102.
6. Of course for some kids willpower comes naturally with ordinary practice, whether it's via studying for next week's test or saving up to buy an iPod.
7. Philip David Zelazo and Stephanie M. Carlson, "Hot and Cool Executive Function in Childhood and Adolescence: Development and Plasticity," *Child Development Perspectives* 6, no. 4 (2012): 354–60.
8. Rueda et al., "Training, Maturation, and Genetic Influences on the Development of Executive Attention."
9. Unless that imp of the perverse, impulse priming, enticed you to read this endnote.
10. Mark Greenberg, in an email.
11. As of this writing there is little direct research on the effects of

mindfulness on children's attention skills, although several studies are in the pipeline. For instance, in one pilot study with thirty preschoolers who got mindfulness plus "kindness training," Richard Davidson's group found improvements in attention and in kindness itself. At this writing, the study is being replicated with a sample of two hundred preschoolers; see http://www.investigatinghealthyminds.org/cihmProjects.html#prek.

12. Smallwood et al., "Counting the Cost of an Absent Mind."
13. Stephen W. Porges, *The Polyvagal Theory* (New York: Norton, 2011).
14. I first heard this data presented by Barbara Fredrickson at a conference for the inauguration of the Center for Healthy Minds at the University of Wisconsin, on May 16, 2010. She reported the results in her book *Love 2.0*, cited above.
15. Judson Brewer et al., "Meditation Experience Is Associated with Differences in Default Mode Network Activity and Connectivity," *Proceedings of the National Academy of Sciences* 108, no. 50 (2011): 20254–59. The default mode decreases in activity when we engage in any focused task; the fact that it was less active during meditation is to be expected. The finding that experienced meditators are better at this mental task than naive controls suggests a training effect.
16. For another analogue of a nonorganic approach with unintended consequences, consider the Green Revolution in agriculture. In the 1960s the introduction of cheap chemical fertilizers in places like India disproved the dire predictions at the time that the world would soon run out of food. But this technological fix for famine prevention had an unanticipated downside: rivers, lakes, and huge patches of ocean where fertilizer concentrated began to "die." The nitrogen-boosted plant growth had a fatal impact in the world's waters.
17. Richard J. Davidson et al., "Alterations in Brain and Immune Function Produced by Mindfulness Meditation," *Psychosomatic Medicine* 65 (2003): 564–70.
18. Mindfulness (which takes short, regular sessions to learn, not hours and hours daily) avoids a danger inherent in gaming, which can deprive young people of huge hunks of time when they could be with other people—talking, playing, goofing off. Those are life's learning labs, where the social and emotional circuitry grows.
19. Daniel Siegel, *The Mindful Brain* (New York: Norton, 2007).
20. On the other hand, mindfulness does not remedy every need. Those of us who are tuned out of our own feelings—or who do not register pain

and distress in others—might also benefit from learning to pay attention in a different way. Here purposely focusing on our own distress and the pain of others might mean working at getting more deeply into our emotions and sustaining those feelings in our awareness. An approach like gestalt therapy, combined with mindfulness of our own sensations, might strengthen the circuitry that resonates with the insula.

21. See http://www.siyli.org.
22. I've paraphrased these questions, from Gill Crossland-Thackray, "Mindfulness at Work: What Are the Benefits?" *Guardian Careers*, December 21, 2012, http://careers.guardian.co.uk/careers-blog/mindfulness-at-work-benefits.
23. Typically this me-focused mode of mind comes and goes all day long (and all night, too—sleep studies find that if you wake people at any time of night and ask what they were just thinking, they always have a fresh thought to report).
24. Norman Farb et al., "Attending to the Present: Mindfulness Meditation Reveals Distinct Neural Modes of Self-Reference," *Social Cognitive Affective Neuroscience* 2, no. 4 (2007): 313–22. See also Aviva Berkovich-Ohana et al., "Mindfulness-Induced Changes in Gamma Band Activity," *Clinical Neurophysiology* 123, no. 4 (April 2012): 700–10.
25. Here's the technical language from Farb et al., "Attending to the Present": "In trained participants, EF resulted in more marked and pervasive reductions in the mPFC, and increased engagement of a right lateralised network, comprising the lateral PFC and viscerosomatic areas such as the insula, secondary somatosensory cortex and inferior parietal lobule. Functional connectivity analyses further demonstrated a strong coupling between the right insula and the mPFC in novices that was uncoupled in the mindfulness group."
26. Feidel Zeidan et al., "Mindfulness Meditation Improves Cognition: Evidence of Brief Mental Training," *Consciousness and Cognition* 19, no. 2 (June 2010) 597–605.
27. David M. Levy et al., "Initial Results from a Study of the Effects of Meditation on Multitasking Performance," *Proceedings of CHI '11 Extended Abstracts on Human Factors in Computing Systems*, 2011, pp. 2011–16.
28. See Tim Ryan, *A Mindful Nation* (Carlsbad, CA: Hay House, 2012), and Jeffrey Sachs, *The Price of Civilization* (New York: Random House, 2011).

CHAPTER 18: HOW LEADERS DIRECT ATTENTION

1. Adam Bryant interviewed Steve Balmer in "Meetings, Version 2.0, at Microsoft," *New York Times*, May 16, 2009.
2. Davenport and Back, *The Attention Economy.*
3. See, e.g., the summit on the Future of Story-Telling: http://futureofstorytelling.org.
4. See Howard Gardner with Emma Laskin, *Leading Minds: An Anatomy of Leadership* (New York: Basic Books, 1995).
5. Davenport and Back, *The Attention Economy*, cite data from a small company showing a very high (though less strong) correlation between what leaders focused on and the focus of employees. For a multinational, there was still a high (though less strong) correlation between the two.
6. William Ocasio of the Kellogg School of Management, who argues for viewing corporations in terms of the flow of attention, defines business strategy as organizing patterns of attention in a distinct focus of time and effort by the company on a particular set of issues, problems, opportunities, and threats. William Ocasio, "Towards an Attention-Based View of the Firm," *Strategic Management Journal* 18, S1 (1997): 188.
7. Steve Jobs quoted in Walter Isaacson, "The Real Leadership Lessons of Steve Jobs," *Harvard Business Review*, April 2012, pp. 93–102. As Jobs was dying of liver cancer he was visited by Larry Page, the Google cofounder who was about to take the reins as CEO there. Jobs's advice to Page: instead of being all over the map, focus on a handful of products.
8. Michael Porter, "What Is Strategy?" *Harvard Business Review*, November–December, 1996, pp. 61–78.
9. Ian Marlow, "Lunch with RIM CEO Thorsten Heins: Time for a Bite, and Little Else," *Globe and Mail*, August 24, 2012.
10. James Surowiecki, "BlackBerry Season," *New Yorker*, February 13 and 20, 2012, p. 36.
11. Apple's first iPod was released in 2001, the Zune in 2006. Microsoft killed the Zune in 2012, folding the software into its Xbox.
12. Clay Shirky, "Napster, Udacity, and the Academy," November 12, 2012, www.shirky.com/weblog.
13. Charles O'Reilly III and Michael Tushman, "The Ambidextrous Organization," *Harvard Business Review*, April 2004, pp. 74–81.
14. James March, "Exploitation and Exploration in Organizational Learning," *Organizational Science* 2, no. 1 (1991): 71–87.
15. Daniella Laureiro-Martinez et al., "An Ambidextrous Mind," working

paper, Center for Research in Organization and Management, Milan, Italy, February 2012. Exploitation strategies are associated with activity in the brain's dopamine networks and the ventromedial prefrontal areas; exploration with areas for executive function and attention control.

CHAPTER 19: THE LEADER'S TRIPLE FOCUS

1. Rainer Greifeneder et al., "When Do People Rely on Affective and Cognitive Feelings in Judgment? A Review," *Personality and Social Psychology Review* 15, no. 2 (2011): 107–41.
2. Gird Gigerenzer et al., *Simple Heuristics That Make Us Smart* (New York: Oxford University Press, 1999).
3. David A. Waldman, "Leadership and Neuroscience: Can We Revolutionize the Way That Inspirational Leaders Are Identified and Developed?" *Academy of Management Perspectives* 25, no. 1 (2011): 60–74.
4. Among brain areas crucial for emotional intelligence that also play key roles in varieties of attention: the anterior cingulate gyrus, the temporoparietal junction, the orbitofrontal cortex, and the ventromedial area. For brain areas in common for attention and emotional intelligence, see, e.g., Posner and Rothbart, "Research on Attention Networks as a Model for the Integration of Psychological Science"; R. Bar-On et al., "Exploring the Neurological Substrate of Emotional and Social Intelligence," *Brain* 126 (2003): 1790–1800. The story will no doubt become more complex, and the attention-emotional intelligence links even stronger, as more such research is done using a wider variety of EI measures and neuroscience methods.
5. Steve Balmer, CEO of Microsoft, in Bryant, "Meetings, Version 2.0."
6. Scott W. Spreier, Mary H. Fontaine, and Ruth L. Malloy, "Leadership Run Amok: The Destructive Potential of Overachievers," *Harvard Business Review*, June 2006, pp. 72–82.
7. McClelland was quoted ibid.
8. George Kohlrieser et al., *Care to Dare* (San Francisco: Jossey-Bass, 2012).
9. Estimates put the liabilities to BP from the Deepwater Horizon spill at close to $40 billion; four BP executives face criminal charges for negligence.
10. Elizabeth Shogren, "BP: A Textbook Example of How Not to Handle PR," NPR, April 21, 2011.
11. Lyle Spencer and Signe Spencer, *Competence at Work* (New York: Wiley,

1993). Signe Spencer is global practice leader for Capability Assessment at Hay Group.

CHAPTER 20: WHAT MAKES A LEADER?

1. Another reason the debate continues: competence models are typically proprietary information, commissioned by an organization to gain competitive advantage, and so are not typically shared publicly, let alone published in peer-reviewed journals—and so many academic psychologists dismiss the evidence (though many models have been published in peer-reviewed journals, too). Meanwhile other psychologists—mostly industrial/organizational specialists—continue creating competence models, which are used extensively throughout the organizational world. This bespeaks a wider rift between academics and practitioners, one that goes far beyond this particular debate.
2. Gerald Mount, "The Role of Emotional Intelligence in Developing International Business Capability: EI Provides Traction," in Vanessa Druskat et al., eds., *Linking Emotional Intelligence and Performance at Work* (Mahwah, NJ: Lawrence Erlbaum, 2005). There are very few published studies like this analyzing competence models, in part because the models are often proprietary.
3. This was based on a sample of 404 leaders who had data on EI competencies, leadership styles, and organizational climate, analyzed by Yvonne Sell, Hay Group, London.
4. Tellingly, these leaders overly relied on a narrow range of leadership styles—typically pacesetting and command-and-control. Leadership styles display underlying EI leadership competencies; styles drive climate, and climate accounts for about 30 percent of business performance, according to data analyzed at Hay Group.
5. Alastair Robertson and Cathy Wail, "The Leader Within," *Outlook* 2 (1999): 19–23.
6. So I'm told by Cary Cherniss of the Rutgers Consortium for Research on Emotional Intelligence in Organizations, who has surveyed many competence models.
7. Vanessa Druskat and Steven Wolff, with their colleague Dr. Joan Manuel Batista-Foguet of the ESADE Business School in Barcelona, used this method. Vanessa Druskat, Joan M. Batista-Foguet, and Steven Wolff, "The Influence of Team Leader Competencies on the Emergence of Emotionally Competent Team Norms," paper presented at the An-

nual Academy of Management Conference, San Antonio, TX, August 2011.

8. The metric: a leader's styles accounts for 50–70 percent of the climate. And climate, in turn, drives about 30 percent of business results due to that leader. The more strengths leaders have in the underlying emotional intelligence competencies, the more styles in their repertoire. (The problem: fewer than 10 percent of leaders are this effective. Most leaders have only one dominant style. Exhibiting three or more is high—and rare.) For those leaders high in self-awareness, followers rated the climate positive 92 percent of the time, while for those low the rating was positive just 22 percent of the time.
9. Jeffrey Sanchez-Burks and Quy Nguyen Huy, "Emotional Aperture and Strategic Change: The Accurate Recognition of Collective Emotions," *Organization Science* 20, no. 1 (2009): pp. 22–34.
10. T. Masuda et al., "Placing the Face in Context: Cultural Differences in the Perception of Facial Emotion," *Journal of Personality and Social Psychology* 94 (2008): 365–81.
11. Partnership for Public Service, "Critical Skills and Mission Critical Occupations, Leadership, Innovation," research report, 2011, http://ourpublicservice.org/OPS/publications/viewcontentdetails.php?id=158.
12. Simon Baron-Cohen, *The Essential Difference: Men, Women, and the Extreme Male Brain* (London: Allen Lane, 2003).
13. See Vanessa Urch Druskat and Steven B. Wolff, "Building the Emotional Intelligence of Groups," *Harvard Business Review*, March 2001, pp. 80–90.

CHAPTER 21: LEADING FOR THE LONG FUTURE

1. Alvin Weinberg favored thorium-based reactors, because they are immune to Fukushima-type accidents; the spent fuel has a far shorter half-life than uranium and, unlike uranium, cannot become used in nuclear weapons. There is a movement to resurrect thorium reactors and replace uranium-based ones. See http://www.the-weinberg-foundation.org/.
2. I don't know if Alvin ever took that view as a public stand. As for me, I'd rather see our energy needs met by nonnuclear, noncoal, and non-petroleum-based systems one day.
3. Alvin Weinberg, "Social Institutions and Nuclear Energy," *Science*, July 7, 1972, p. 33.
4. National Intelligence Council, "Global Trends 2025: A Transformed World," November 2008.

5. Both these could be case studies (but are not) out of Ronald Heifetz and Marty Linksy, *Leadership on the Line* (Boston: Harvard Business Review Press, 2002). Heifetz's theory of adaptive leadership urges leaders to take unpopular stances like these when they are for the public good—and suggests savvy ways to handle the inevitable resistance.
6. Jonathan Rose, *The Well-Tempered City*, should be published in 2014.
7. Jim Collins makes a similar argument in his classic work *Good to Great* (New York: HarperBusiness, 2001). What Collins calls "Level Five" leaders take the long view, creating sustainable change. They seek prosperity over decades, not just for the quarterly return; they involve many stakeholders—not just stockholders—and create pride and loyalty in employees. They inspire commitment with a compelling vision and the corporate equivalent of immense focus and willpower, while remaining humble themselves. These are the leaders, Collins argues, of companies that are not just good, but great.
8. An Accenture survey of 750 global CEOs found that more than 90 percent endorse sustainability as a company goal. See http://www.accenture.com/us-en/Pages/insight-un-global-compact-reports.aspx.
9. Unilever does not buy directly from the farmers, but rather buys through suppliers, and will expand its web of suppliers to include those with strong networks of small farms.
10. While this will mean better profits, exactly what these might be will vary from crop to crop and season to season.
11. World Bank, "The Future of Small Farms: Synthesis Report," World Development Report 2008, http://wdronline.worldbank.org/worldbank/a/nonwdrdetail/87.
12. John Mackey, co-CEO of Whole Foods Market, has been the front-and-center spokesman for this view, which he sees as part of "conscious capitalism." Mackey, for example, gets a salary only 14 times greater than that of the lowest-paid Whole Foods workers; the fish sold there are carefully chosen so they do not deplete ocean biodiversity—among a long list of other tenets. See John Mackey and Raj Sisodia, *Conscious Capitalism* (Boston: Harvard Business Review Press, 2013). The view has caught the zeitgeist. See, e.g., Rosabeth Moss Kanter, "How Great Companies Think Differently," *Harvard Business Review*, November 2011, pp. 66–78.
13. The five-rupee blade isn't the least expensive in India, but it's at a level most can afford. Ellen Byron, "Gillette's Latest Innovation in Razors: The 11-Cent Blade," *Wall Street Journal*, October 1, 2010.

14. Job levels seem to link roughly to time horizons, the late consultant Elliott Jacques argued. Jobs like salesclerk or police officer, he proposed, encourage thinking in a time horizon of one day to three months; foremen and small-business owners tend to think in terms of three months to a year. The CEOs of smaller companies and division heads of larger ones might think as far as ten years ahead. And CEOs of global companies should think decades ahead. See Art Kleiner, "Elliott Jacques Levels with You," *Strategy + Business*, First Quarter, 2001.
15. Peter Senge's best-known book is *The Fifth Discipline: The Art and Practice of the Learning Organization* (New York: Doubleday Business, 1990).

INDEX

Index

Index

Index

Index

Index

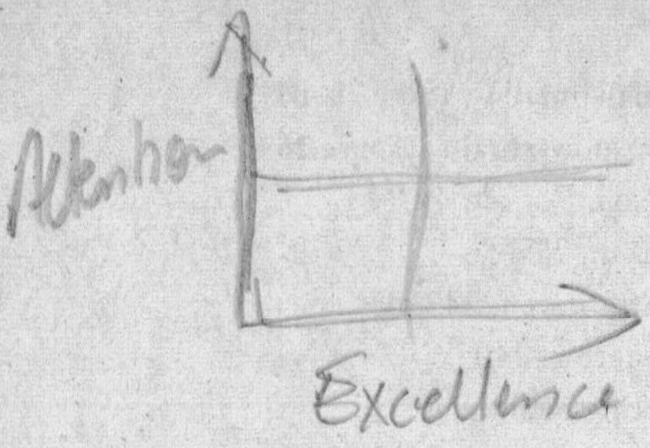
Attention
Excellence